Religious Symbols and the Intervention of the Law

In contemporary pluralist states, where faith communities live together, different religious symbols and practices have to coexist. This may lead to conflicts between certain minority practices and the dominant majority, particularly around the manifestation of belief in the public domain which may be seen both by the religious and secular majorities as a threat to their cultural heritage or against the secular values of the host country. The law has to mitigate those tensions in order to protect the public from harm and preserve order but in doing so, it may where necessary have to limit citizens' ability to freely manifest their religion. It is those limitations that have been disputed in the courts on grounds of freedom of religion and belief. Religious symbols are often at the heart of legal battles, with courts called upon to consider the lawfulness of banning or restricting certain symbols or practices.

This book analyses the relationship between the state, individuals and religious symbols, considering the three main forms of religious expression, symbols that believers wear on their body, symbols in the public space such as religious edifices and rituals that believers perform as a manifestation of their faith. The book looks comparatively at legal responses in the U.K., the U.S.A. and France comparing different approaches to the issues of symbols in the public sphere and their interaction with the law. The book considers religious manifestation as a social phenomenon taking a multidisciplinary approach to the question mixing elements of the anthropology, history and sociology of religion in order to provide some context and examine how this could help inform the law.

Sylvie Bacquet is Senior Lecturer in Law at the University of Westminster, UK.

Law and Religion

The practice of religion by individuals and groups, the rise of religious diversity, and the fear of religious extremism, raise profound questions for the interaction between law and religion in society. The regulatory systems involved, the religion laws of secular government (national and international) and the religious laws of faith communities, are valuable tools for our understanding of the dynamics of mutual accommodation and the analysis and resolution of issues in such areas as: religious freedom; discrimination; the autonomy of religious organisations; doctrine, worship and religious symbols; the property and finances of religion; religion, education and public institutions; and religion, marriage and children. In this series, scholars at the forefront of law and religion contribute to the debates in this area. The books in the series are analytical with a key target audience of scholars and practitioners, including lawyers, religious leaders, and others with an interest in this rapidly developing discipline.

Series Editor: Professor Norman Doe, Director of the Centre for Law and Religion, Cardiff University, UK

Series Board:
Carmen Asiaín, Professor, University of Montevideo
Paul Babie, Professor and Associate Dean (International), Adelaide Law School
Pieter Coertzen, Chairperson, Unit for the Study of Law and Religion, University of Stellenbosch
Alison Mawhinney, Reader, Bangor University
Michael John Perry, Senior Fellow, Center for the Study of Law and Religion, Emory University

Titles in this series include:

The Genealogy of Terror
How to Distinguish between Islam, Islamism and Islamist Extremism
Matthew L. N Wilkinson

State and Religion
The Australian Story
Renae Barker

Ecclesiastical Law, Clergy and Laity
A History of Legal Discipline and the Anglican Church
Revd Neil Patterson

For more information about this series, please visit:
www.routledge.com/Law-and-Religion/book-series/LAWRELIG

Religious Symbols and the Intervention of the Law

Symbolic Functionality in Pluralist States

Sylvie Bacquet

Routledge
Taylor & Francis Group

LONDON AND NEW YORK

First published 2020
by Routledge
2 Park Square, Milton Park, Abingdon, Oxon OX14 4RN

and by Routledge
52 Vanderbilt Avenue, New York, NY 10017

Routledge is an imprint of the Taylor & Francis Group, an informa business

© 2020 Sylvie Bacquet

British Library Cataloguing in Publication Data
A catalogue record for this book is available from the British Library

Library of Congress Cataloging-in-Publication Data
Names: Bacquet, Sylvie, author.
Title: Religious symbols and the intervention of the law : symbolic functionality in pluralist states / Sylvie Bacquet.
Description: Abingdon, Oxon ; New York, NY : Routledge, 2019. |
Series: Law and religion
Identifiers: LCCN 2019003365| ISBN 9781138953833 (hb) |
ISBN 9781315667171 (eb)
Subjects: LCSH: Christian art and symbolism--Law and legislation. | Christian art and symbolism--Law and legislation--England. | Christian art and symbolism--Law and legislation--France. | Christian art and symbolism--Law and legislation--United States. | Religious minorities--Legal status, laws, etc. | Religious minorities--Legal status, laws, etc.--England. | Religious minorities--Legal status, laws, etc.--France. | Religious minorities--Legal status, laws, etc.--United States.
Classification: LCC K3258.5 .B33 2019 | DDC 342.08/52137--dc23
LC record available at https://lccn.loc.gov/2019003365

ISBN: 978-1-138-95383-3 (hbk)
ISBN: 978-1-315-66717-1 (ebk)

Typeset in Galliard
by Taylor & Francis Books

To Noa and Tamar for their patience and understanding over the years.
In loving memory of Noa Chaya Popovsky and Elisenda Vila

Contents

PART III
The Future of Religious Symbols and the Law in 21st Century
Pluralist States   133

Figures

Table of cases

England and Wales

Acknowledgments

This book is the culmination of a long research journey, a quest for identity and constant challenging of my own assumptions on the interaction between the state and religion. I became interested in this area when navigating the exigencies of two jurisdictions with opposite attitudes towards religion namely France and England, while at the same time debating the nature of my own identity: a fusion of Jewish ethnicity, Middle Eastern culture, Catholic influences and secular inclinations. I am therefore particularly thankful to my parents for leaving me the choice to become who I am.

The research has demonstrated that with the right amount of knowledge, understanding and openness it is possible to challenge one's assumptions about religion and how it is catered for by the state. This book has developed many arguments and ideas which were originally formed through previous publications but also from teaching on the undergraduate and postgraduate Law and Religion modules at the University of Westminster as well as supervising a number of dissertations in the area. I am grateful to my students and colleagues at the Westminster Law School for the thought-provoking debates over the years and in particular to my colleague and friend, Stephen Bunbury, for giving me the drive to go away on writing retreats.

I am particularly grateful to the late Professor Kevin Boyle for inspiring me to use my own experience to pursue my research interest in this field. I am forever thankful to my colleague now friend Professor Lisa Webley for believing in me and for her years of valuable mentoring in research and teaching. I am also particularly indebted to colleagues and friends at Cardiff Law School and the Centre for Law and Religion for allowing me to share ideas during LARSN conferences. Particular thanks are due to Professor Norman Doe for supporting me with this book project. I am also particularly thankful to Professor Russell Sandberg, Dr Helen Hall, Dr Javier Garcia Oliva, Professor Peter Cumper, Dr Tom Lewis and Dr Harriet Samuels for their advice on several parts of the manuscript and to everyone at Routledge Publishing for being so helpful and understanding throughout the process.

This project would not have come to term without the support of friends and family. This book is dedicated to them for their support and encouragement over the years.

Foreword

It is widely agreed that religious and cultural pluralism is one of the defining characteristics of a liberal democratic society. It is conceived of as the peaceful coexistence in the public sphere of a diversity of approaches towards political, cultural, religious and philosophical matters. The benefits which pluralism brings to societies as a whole are undeniable, it does not simply operate for the protection of minorities. Amongst other positive attributes, it provides new perspectives and sources of inspiration when dealing with current social challenges, and enriches the range and appropriateness of responses, by taking into account different sensibilities when resolving conflict.

Although in the contemporary world religious pluralism can be easily perceived in the public arena, it remains the case that managing the practical ramifications of the coexistence of contrasting beliefs and ideologies is a work in progress. This is inevitable, given that integrating a diverse range of practices frequently requires a delicate balance to be struck between private and public interests, and achieving the optimal solution is a challenge. When it comes to this crucial endeavour, the law is called upon to play a decisive role in furthering societal ends. By establishing an abstract framework of principles, it provides the mechanism whereby conflicts may be resolved, according to recognised, known and agreed norms.

When analysing disputes relating to the manifestation of religious symbols from a juridical perspective, a distinction is commonly drawn between tensions caused by religious dress, and those revolving around the presence of religious symbols in the public arena. This distinction is based on the consensus that issues relating to religious dress should be seen through the prism of individual religious freedom, whereas the latter are better analysed from the perspective of the state's obligation to accord all faiths and views equal respect. However, as the in-depth analysis of the most relevant jurisprudence contained in this book demonstrates, these pathways are not mutually exclusive, and frequently run in tandem. Both sets of considerations may be applied in resolving the same dispute. For instance, this can be observed when courts have ruled on the presence of religious symbols in public educational institutions, where insights from both the religious neutrality perspective and the freedom of religion approach are applied.

As the systemic treatment of religion differs even amongst liberal democratic paradigms, Bacquet adopts a comparative perspective when analysing the response to conflicts under different models of church–state relations. This makes it possible to emphasise the contrasts between England, the United States and France. For instance, the strict religious neutrality which defines the French *laïcité* has led to the ban of ostentatious religious symbols in educational institutions, in order to protect this overarching principle. In sharp contrast, the positive conception of religion within the North American model of separation meant that such a stark prohibition could not be justified in that context. The Establishment Clause of the American Constitution is mainly conceived as a guarantee of the free exercise of religion by individuals and groups, not as an end in itself. Furthermore, using guarantees of free exercise as a means of stifling religious expression would be inherently self-defeating.

Bacquet makes a very thought-provoking point when discussing the conflicts derived from the use of personal religious symbols in liberal democracies: namely, that it is necessary to consider religion as an element of personal identity and not merely as something circumstantial and of a purely cultural or social origin. This insight contrasts with the common tendency to conceptualise religion as an elective characteristic of individuals, which may be linked to their culture and traditions, but is ultimately a matter of choice. The consequence of such analysis is to downgrade religion in relation to other protected characteristics which are deemed inherent (sex, age, disability, etc.) and therefore worthy of robust protection because they are inseparable from individual identity. Evidence of this kind of reasoning can be easily discerned when analysing European Union legislation and jurisprudence on equality and discrimination in the workplace, where protected characteristics other than religion are granted stronger protection.

Undoubtedly, recognising religion as a characteristic that is fundamental to the person serves to promote the recognition of the right to accommodation of religious practices in different contexts, particularly in the workplace. On the contrary, if religion is a matter of choice then the individual has to accept the consequences of its exercise when it collides with general dispositions of secular nature.

It is interesting to note that the Report of the European Network of Legal Experts on Non-Discrimination (2013) – promoted by the European Commission – presented a number of arguments against the extension of the 'duty to accommodate' to religion. According to its authors, this kind of accommodation would be problematic, as by its very nature it places religious and secular values in democratic societies in tension and privileges the former. In effect, it challenges the contention that religious values deserve preferential treatment over non-religious ones. The issue raised is illustrated well by the following dilemma: a worker would be able to demand accommodation in order to enjoy weekly rest on a certain day of the week prescribed by his or her faith, whilst workers requesting the same treatment on secular grounds (a desire to spend time with their family, or to participate in sporting or cultural activities, etc.) would not have access to the same leverage. In addressing this, I fully agree with Bacquet in her conclusion that 'it is possible to accommodate religious manifestation without putting religion on a pedestal and giving it special protection but that such a theory requires a modification of the current judicial approach which places less emphasis on religion itself and more focus on the individual.'

Considering religion as a fundamental aspect of the identity of individuals does not preclude any acknowledgement of the social dimension of religion. On the contrary, this collective feature of religion can be seen in the public sphere in many ways, in particular through certain traditions of religious significance, and the presence of religious symbols in public buildings or other public places. Given that the US is one of the Western countries where these traditions are part of the cultural fabric, it is highly positive that the book discusses the US constitutional soundness of a wide range of practices and symbols which are fully integrated into the American public life. The impression is not given however, that this phenomenon is exclusive to the United States, and a variety of comparable traditions are identified across Europe. For instance, Nativity scenes are displayed on public properties over the Christmas period, public authorities get involved in religious processions taking place during Holy Week (the period immediately prior to the Christian festival of Easter) and the crucifix is placed in educational settings.

Bacquet analyses the legal profiles of the so-called 'American ceremonial deism', which according to Justice Brennan is understood as a set of references that, on the one hand, have lost their religious significance through their constant repetition and, on the other, serve entirely secular purposes such as solemnising public events, or inspiring citizen commitment to certain national challenges. Those practices through which the government has recognised religion since ancient times are probably necessary, Brennan asserts, to attend to certain secular functions. This need, springing from the secular function, combined with a long history, endows these displays with an essentially secular meaning.

There is a persuasive case that in embracing 'ceremonial deism', public authorities do not intend to send a message fostering religion in general, or any of its forms, but rather to recognise a common heritage of values, which are widely shared by the American society. Accordingly, US courts have not seen any incompatibility between these traditions and the state's religious neutrality.

According to Bacquet, similar traditions of religious significance can be identified as well in Europe, and have been considered constitutional, as long as they do not affect the free exercise of religion. In this respect, the Grand Chamber of the ECHR held in *Lautsi v. Italy* (2014) that hanging a crucifix on the wall of public schools constitutes a social tradition that the Italian government is entitled to keep, as such a symbol is not capable of violating any fundamental rights of the members of the educational community.

From my perspective, Bacquet has been successful is showing that religious neutrality does *not* require that all religious manifestations should be removed from the public sphere. Such absolutism would be contrary to the social traditions of most Western societies, and rather than promoting equity of treatment between differing worldviews, would in fact promote non-religious over religious perspectives, generating the very kind of social conflict and injustice which religious state neutrality is designed to avoid.

It is also true that the appropriateness of these traditions must be also viewed through the lens of religious freedom. This is particularly important when the performance of a given practice involves individuals with secular views. In Western democracies it is commonly agreed that these traditions are acceptable from a religious freedom perspective, provided that no one is forced to participate directly or indirectly.

In this context, and for the sake of clarity, it is helpful to refer to the Spanish Constitutional Court Judgment 177/1996, resolving an appeal (*recurso de amparo*) put forward by a member of the army who was disciplined for refusing to take part in a parade in honour of the Holy Virgin. The Court affirmed that although the participation of the Armed Forces in acts of religious significance was not *per se* incompatible with the State's duty of religious neutrality, the Army do form part of the State administration, and consequently must recognise the right of individuals to decline to join in with a religious expression. Therefore, no one can legitimately be punished for declining to take part or assist.

Similarly, the Constitutional Court in its Judgment 53/2011 affirmed that the appointment of the Immaculate Conception as the patron saint of the Seville Bar Association – a public law Corporation – was compatible with the religious State neutrality. The court took into consideration, on one hand, that the policy was not intended to foster religion but to recognise a social tradition and, on the other, that the holistic approach taken was respectful towards members' religious freedom, given that no one would have been made to feel any obligation to embrace Catholicism or Christianity.

There is no doubt that conflicts caused by religious symbols are growing in liberal democracies under the weight of social change, and that they demand the adoption of more balanced solutions than those applied in previous generations. There is now widespread consensus that it is essential for all of the relevant competing interests to be duly taken into account. There can be no doubt that this book constitutes a crucial contribution to this endeavour. It sets out with impeccable clarity and an easy to follow structure, the main points of friction caused by religious symbols in Western liberal democracies. It also insightfully explores the impact of the systemic position adopted by the state in relation to religious faith, when it comes to assessing the solutions adopted in different contexts. Furthermore, it provides an in-depth reflection on the anthropological, social and juridical dimension of religion, which is essential for a profound discussion of one of the most challenging areas for debate within law and religion in a western democratic context.

Santiago Canamares,
Complutense University (Spain)

Part I

Religious Symbols in a Socio-Historical Context

1 Introduction

1.1 Context and background of the study

In contemporary pluralist states, where faith communities are prone to living together, different religious symbols and practices are forced to coexist; this is an inevitable consequence of international migrations and globalisation. In Europe for instance, where Christianity was once the norm, most states remain predominantly Christian,[1] even though migration flows have over the decades transformed the demographic landscape, giving rise to a more heterogeneous society with a number of significant minority groups. This new demographic landscape however may lead to conflicts between certain minority practices and the dominant majority. The type of conflict that is likely to arise mostly relates to manifestation of belief in the public domain which may be seen both by the religious and secular majorities as a threat to their cultural heritage or against the secular values of the host country. Examples of such controversial practices include: the display of faith via religious clothing in the public sphere as well as religious rituals such as, for instance, funeral pyres, circumcision or religious slaughter of animals. The law has to mitigate those tensions in order to protect the public from harm and preserve order but in doing so, it may where necessary have to limit citizens' ability to freely manifest their religion. It is those limitations that have come to be disputed in the courts on grounds of freedom of religion and belief. Religious symbols are often at the heart of legal battles, with courts called upon to consider the lawfulness of banning or restricting certain symbols or practices. Achieving the right balance between the right of individuals and groups to manifest their belief and the right of others to be protected from religion and not to be discriminated against is a sensitive exercise riddled with controversies, as demonstrated by the existing body of case law in the UK and elsewhere.[2]

This book seeks to contribute to the on-going debate on the interface between the law and manifestation of religion. The debate revolves around the extent to which the state and the law should intervene with the individual's freedom to manifest his/her religion. While some states like the UK mostly value the display of religious symbols in the public sphere as an element of public recognition of religious diversity,[3] others such as France argue that religious freedom can only be attained by removing religious symbols from the public sphere in order to achieve state neutrality and equality.[4] Amongst legal academics the debate on religious manifestation has tended to focus on issues of integration, extremism, national identity, discrimination, human rights and security.[5] There has been less attention given to understanding the role of manifestation of belief in 21st century modern pluralist states[6] which is what this book seeks to do. Traditionally, lawyers[7] have relied on political philosophy rather than social theory to inform legal critiques; this book takes a different approach in an attempt to deepen our understanding of religious manifestation as a social phenomenon. This requires an interdisciplinary approach to the question which mixes elements of the anthropology and sociology of religion and symbols. The book draws from some of the author's previous empirical research exploring the relationship between the state, individuals and religious symbols[8] and uses other disciplines which have studied religion and its manifestation to seek a wider understanding of the issue and how it affects individuals. Those disciplines have the ability to enhance our understanding of the role of religion and symbols in the 21st century and therefore inform the legal approach. If for instance we consider Geertz' view of religion as a cultural system of symbols and his proposition that '[m]an depends upon symbols and symbol systems with a dependence so great as to be decisive for his creatural viability …',[9] it may change one's 'secular vision'[10] of symbols and lead to a better appreciation of the importance and significance of symbols for individuals, which in turn may inform law and policy makers. The benefits of multidisciplinary studies have been documented despite their scarcity within the field of law and religion;[11] so far, anthropologists, sociologists and legal academics have studied religion but each under their separate banner. As Sandberg argues, much can be gained in the field of law and religion from a multidisciplinary study which mixes sociology and law.[12] Sandberg uses case studies from law to test sociological propositions about religion, but he does not explore symbols per se. Elements of his thesis in relation to seeing religious freedom as part of subjective identity and fusing sociological and legal approaches will be used in this book.

At the outset, it is submitted that the law tends to make a number of assumptions on manifestation of belief and religion more generally. *Religious Symbols and the Intervention of the Law* argues that these assumptions derive from the dominant Christian majority which, as discussed above, is still very influential in Europe and the United States (US). A common assumption is that religious symbols are mostly imposed on individuals. For instance, many believe that the hijab is imposed on Muslim females and is therefore a symbol of oppression,[13] that manifestation of belief should be reserved to the private sphere or that symbols are mere artefacts of decoration which people can easily part with.[14]

Models of state–religion relations on which the law is based also derive from these assumptions. French *laïcité* which is a form of secularism, albeit militant,[15] seeks to confine manifestation of religion to the private sphere in order to achieve liberal universalism, while Britain's liberal pluralism aims to reinforce religious differences via the public recognition of cultural diversity.[16] The US, like France and in contrast to England, upholds the constitutional separation of church and state but, unlike in France, religion still has a role to play in public life.[17] The nuances of those three legal systems and their respective models of church–state relations will be explored in detail in Part II of the book and will form the basis for a critique of judicial approaches to religious manifestation.

This is not to say that some of the above assumptions are unfounded; some countries like France have a long history of power struggle between the state and religion and this permeates the legal framework in relation to religion. Throughout the 19th century the Catholic Church and what was to become the French Republic conflicted over who would hold ultimate authority. This is evident for instance in the Law of 1905 separating church and state which relegated religion to the private sphere and set the tone for France's *laïcité*. [18] Religious institutions may at times use coercive powers to attract followers – cross burning for instance has long been associated with the Ku Klux Klan movement in the US,[19] while certain religious symbols can be seen as oppressive or dictating gender norms and expectations – this has been the case for instance with representations of the Virgin Mary which have led to women being valued for being a mother.[20] However, religious symbols may also serve to confer legitimacy on a particular group and can represent power and authority. This will be discussed further in Chapter 3's historical analysis. Assumptions also differ depending on whether an individual is seen as an autonomous egoistic being making choices or a more constructed or communitarian being gaining recognition through culture and religion. This comes through the empirical data presented in Chapter 4.

The book, therefore, focuses on the following research questions: What is the functionality of symbols and rituals in modern pluralist states? What is the relationship between symbols and individuals? How can a multidisciplinary study of symbols (using history, anthropology and sociology) inform our understanding of the role of symbols in contemporary pluralist states and form the basis for a critique of the existing legal approach? To what extent is religious expression in the 21st century still a public affair and what can the current legal framework gain from a social investigation of manifestation of belief?

In answering these questions, the book concentrates on the social function of manifestation of belief in an age where the place of religion in society is subject to much debate and controversy. Even if it is now generally accepted that modernisation has not led to the death of religion originally predicted by sociologists in the second half of the 20th century, Europe remains mostly secular. Recent research surveys consistently show a rise in 'non-religion' across Europe and the US.[21] According to the Pew Research Institute, censuses and surveys show that in 2015 there were 1.17 billion people declaring themselves as either atheist, agnostic or of no religion and that number is expected to rise to 1.20 billion by 2060 even if their global share of the population is expected to decrease due to the parallel growth of the global population including other religious groups.[22] Yet, we cannot talk about a demise of religion altogether as we witness in parallel an increase in religion's visibility which some call a 'resurgence of religion'[23] or an 'augmented prominence' of religion.[24] The place of religion in pluralist societies is complex and we cannot talk about a decline or a resurgence as such but more of a religious transformation.[25] As explored in Chapter 4, there are different patterns within this transformation including a rise in non-religious movements and minority faith such as Islam and a decline in Christianity and church attendance. As a result of this transformation, religion has become more visible and new forms of religion have started to emerge. The book makes a case for those new forms of religion being afforded the same level of protection as more traditional ones when there is evidence that such practices go to the core of individual and collective identity.

1.2 Method, theoretical framework and preliminary considerations

The book looks at the question of religious symbols and their interaction with the law by using an interdisciplinary approach to the issue that combines history, anthropology and sociology with law. A purely legal approach to the question of symbols and the interference of the law would only provide a narrow view, as each discipline individually tends to look at the world through their own lens. Using other disciplines adds depth and nuance. As pointed by Ferrari, Law and Religion as a discipline has crossed the boundaries of the law and human sciences scholars such as sociologists, political scientists and anthropologists have made an important contribution to the field and have approached the subject from new angles.[26] As will be explored in the next chapter, other disciplines have been critical of the definition of religion adopted by lawyers. The French philosopher and political scientist Olivier Roy for instance accuses the law of contributing to what he calls the 'standardization' of religion whereby only the religions recognised by mainstream culture are defined as such. The law therefore creates 'a legal status' for religion. As a result of this classification, a community may be deemed 'religious' through its fiscal status; religion rather than being recognised by its content comes to be at the mercy of its legal position. In France for instance Jehovah Witnesses and the Church of Scientology are both considered as cults[27] despite being both recognised religions in the UK[28] and the US.[29] Roy claims that 'normative practices force diasporic religions to submit to the prevailing religious model of the West.'[30] He argues that it is legislation that creates religion in the US and secular France. Religion therefore is at the mercy of the legal definition and this has a direct impact on religious manifestation. Religion as defined by law also builds categories and separates the sacred from the profane, the religious from the secular, and the pure from the polluted. Bowie argues that classifications always derive from a particular view of the world and preconceptions of the categories. Whether something is classed as sacred or profane, secular or religious can have a serious impact on people's lives.[31] The law therefore arguably defines religion to fit its own categories and this can be detrimental for individuals. The book aims to provide a better understanding of the social context surrounding religious manifestation in order for lawyers to become more aware of those problems and adapt the way they approach manifestation of belief.

The law and religion relationship is complex and bears the mark of a historical power struggle. Law and religion hold in common many features including that of holding society together. As the importance of religion in society diminished, the law took over that function and inevitably therefore the law and religion relationship is tainted with power and politics. As Turner and Kirsch put it, 'the relationship between law and religion has always been a political issue: relevant to a given polity, and involving authority and power.'[32] Turner and Kirsch are critical of the law and religion categories which separate the law from religion and find lawyers' definitions too abstract. Religion is defined by the legal definition, thereby suggesting the unequal bargaining position of the law in the law and religion relationship. The law, by imposing its definition on religion, places itself above religion. This book argues that it is the individual not religion itself which must be at the centre of any legal dispute arising in relation to manifestation of belief.

Given the nature of the relationship between law and religion, it is difficult to detach the legal approach from politics and power. It has been argued that other disciplines within the social sciences may be better placed for looking at the complexities of law and religion.[33] Anthropology is particularly useful when dealing with religious symbols because it uses symbols as a theoretical thinking tool. As argued by anthropologist Bowie, 'an anthropological approach to religion involves seeing how symbols, myths, rituals, ethics, and experience of "the sacred" operate within, and are produced by society.'[34] Similarly, in relation to sociology it has been argued that there is a gap between how the law works as opposed to how society functions and sociology is better placed to contextualise religion and symbols within the public sphere[35] just as the history of religion is essential to understanding the authentic structures and functions of symbols.[36]

While lawyers seek practical solutions to problems and are in search for normative solutions, anthropologists and sociologists alike (as well as more generally social theorists) tend to adopt a more theoretical and descriptive approach allowing for a more systematic exploration of cultural meanings and human behaviours. Riis and Woodhead highlight that anthropological studies provide more cues by analysing the emotional significance of symbols for individuals and groups.[37] The research therefore is based on the premise that an interdisciplinary approach to religious symbols is crucial to understanding the role of symbols in 21st century pluralist states. As will be discussed in subsequent chapters, this understanding arguably is what has often escaped the attention of lawyers and courts as they have embarked on religious investigations which often fall beyond their remits.

Throughout the book, I will argue that the current legal approach to religious manifestation is 'discriminatory' to groups which the law does not classify as 'religious'. This could be because those groups do not fit in the Western legal categories as in the case of orthopraxy faith or because they fall outside the traditional conception of 'religion' as in the case of groups with distinctive identities such as Goth or new religious movements. I argue that a more suitable approach would not use the definition of religion itself but look at other indicators of a particular practice such as identity, culture, function rather than trying to fit things into predetermined categories which is what the law does. I will argue that by removing 'religion' from the equation more adequate protection can be offered to those beliefs and practices which go to the core of individual and collective identity but may not fit neatly into the legal categories.

The geographical focus of the study will be England,[38] France and the US. While England and France lie at opposite ends of the spectrum in relation to their model of religion/state relations, the US has features of both countries. The English establishment model discussed in Chapter 6 will be contrasted to the French secularism (*laïcité*) discussed in Chapter 5 and both models will be compared to the US tolerant neutrality in Chapter 7. Three main forms of religious expression will be explored in this book; namely, symbols that believers wear on their body, symbols in the public space such as religious edifices and rituals that believers perform as a manifestation of their faith.

1.3 Outline structure

The book is divided into three parts. Part I (Chapters 1–4) looks at manifestation of belief from a social and historical perspective, Part II (Chapters 5–7) takes a comparative legal approach to religious symbols and Part III (Chapters 8 and 9) focuses on the future of religious symbols and the law in 21st century modern pluralist states and attempts to offer some recommendations.

Chapter 2 attempts to define religion and religious manifestation by taking a multidisciplinary approach which combines law with anthropology and sociology; Chapter 3 provides a historical account of religious symbols in order to understand the social significance of religious manifestation and the extent to which it is worthy of protection by the law. Chapter 4 looks at the locus of religious symbols in contemporary pluralist states and examines the contribution of symbols and rituals to the building of contemporary religious identities.

Chapter 5 looks at manifestation of belief in France and explores the legal framework for religious freedom including *laïcité*; Chapter 6 focuses on the English model of church–state relations and the legal mechanism in place for protecting religious freedom, while Chapter 7 is dedicated to the US model of church–state relations and how it affects religious manifestation.

Chapter 8 draws from the legal approach and attempts to examine the extent to which the legal mechanism can be informed by a multidisciplinary approach to the question of religious manifestation. Taking identity rather than religion as a justification for legal protection, it suggests a modified legal test which aims to be more inclusive and sensitive to the relationship between individuals and manifestation of belief in general.

Chapter 9 reaches conclusions as to the future of religious symbols and the law in 21st century pluralist states.

Notes

1 This is true of *inter alia* France, Italy, Spain, Germany and the UK who follow a Christian calendar and where the influence of the church is evident in architecture, celebration of public holidays and even Government. The UK for instance has an established church with no legal separation between church and state, UK Parliament sessions still open with prayers and there are 26 Bishops sitting in the upper house of the Westminster Parliament. This is discussed further in Chapter 6. On the historical influence of Christianity in Europe see further Blei 2002.

2 See for example in the UK *Surayanda v The Welsh Ministers* [2007] EWCA Civ 893 (23 July 2007); R *(Playfoot) v Governing Body of Millais School* [2007] EWHC 1698 (Admin), [2007] ELR 484; R *(Begum (by her Litigation Friend, Rahman)) v Head-teacher and Governors of Denbigh High School* [2006] UKHL 15; Singh Juss 2013. For case law in France and in the United States see further Chapters 5 and 7 respectively.

3 This approach is commonly known as multiculturalism. See further Modood 2013.

4 On the French model of state–religion relations see further Bacquet 2012.

5 See for instance Addison 2007; Cooper and Lodge 2008; Knights 2007.

6 But see for example Moeschberger and Phillips DeZalia 2014; Van Ooijen 2012; Ellens 1981.

7 The term lawyers here is used loosely to refer to legal scholars, practitioners and judges, in contrast to other categories of social scientists such as sociologists and anthropologists.

8 See Bacquet 2015.

9 Geertz 1966. 13.

10 By 'secular vision' I refer to the assumptions that are often made of symbols discussed in the next paragraph.

11 See Sandberg 2014. 10–30.

12 Sandberg 2014 ibid.

13 See for example French Republican Laïcistes, liberal perfectionists and French republican feminists discussed in Laborde 2006. See also militant secularists' arguments in countries like France and Turkey.

14 See further Cane, Evans and Robinson 2008. Ch. 4.

15 Secularism is normally defined by the separation of religion from the state but there is a spectrum of secularism and some states are more extreme and militant in their secular practice than others – see further Ahdar and Leigh 2013.

16 See further Laborde 2001.

17 While England has an established church, there is quasi-separation between the Church and the state. This is explained further in Chapter 6.

18 See further Bacquet 2012. French *laïcité* will be discussed in detail in Chapter 5.

19 See further ADL – KKK symbols.

20 See further Engelhardt Herringer 2008.

21 On the UK see Woodhead 2016. On the rest of the world see Pew Research Center 2015.

22 Lipka and McClendon 2017.

23 See for example Huntington 1996.

24 Turner and Kirsch 2009.

25 On the debate surrounding the secularisation thesis see further Sandberg 2014.

26 Ferrari 2015.

27 French Parliamentary report No. 2468 of 1995. 'Les sectes en France'.

28 See R *(on the application of Hodkin and another) v Registrar-General of Births, Deaths and Marriages* [2013] UKSC 77. In the *Hodkin* case it was held that Scientology could be recognised as a religion for the purpose of the Worship Registration Act 1855 and therefore it is possible to perform a marriage ceremony in a Scientology Church. However, in the UK Scientology does not have charitable status as in the US.

29 Despite growing opposition due to ongoing controversy, the Church of Scientology in the United States has enjoyed tax exempt status since 1993. See further Frantz 1997.

30 Roy 2013. 26.

31 Bowie 2006. 35.

32 Turner and Kirsch 2009. 99.

33 See for instance Ferrari, 2015, op. cit. Bowie 2006, op. cit. and Benda-Beckmann 2009. 227.

34 Bowie, 2006, op. cit. 35.

35 Fokas 2015. 59.

36 Eliade 1991. 37.
37 Riis and Woodhead 2010. 8.
38 Given that the UK is a union of four countries, namely, England, Scotland, Wales and
    Northern Ireland, and that there are three distinct legal jurisdictions in the UK: England and
    Wales, Northern Ireland and Scotland, the book only focuses on England and Wales as a legal
    jurisdiction. References to England should be read as meaning England and Wales for legal
    purposes. However, while the Church of England is an established church in England, it was
    largely disestablished in Wales from 1920 and the Church of Wales is now self-governing.

References

Books

Addison, N., 2007. *Religious Discrimination and Hatred Law*. London: Routledge.
Ahdar, R. and Leigh, I., 2013. *Religious Freedom in the Liberal State*. 2nd ed., Oxford: Oxford University Press.
Blei, K., 2002. *Freedom of Religion and Belief: Europe's Story*. Assen, The Netherlands: Van Gorcum.
Bowie, F., 2006. *The Anthropology of Religion: An Introduction*. 2nd ed., Oxford: Blackwell Publishing.
Cane, P., Evans, C. and Robinson, Z., 2008. *Law and Religion in Theoretical and Historical Context*. Cambridge: Cambridge University Press.
Cooper, Z. and Lodge, G., 2008. *Faith in the Nation: Religion, Identity and the Public Realm in Britain Today*. London: The Institute for Public Policy Research.
Eliade, M., 1991. *Images and Symbols*. Princeton: Princeton University Press.
Engelhardt Herringer, C., 2008. *Victorians and the Virgin Mary: Religion and Gender in England*. Manchester: Manchester University Press.
Ferrari, S. ed., 2015. *Routledge Handbook of Law and Religion*. Abingdon, Oxon: Routledge.
Huntington, S. P., 1996. *The Clash of Civilisations and the Remaking of World Order*. New York: Simon & Schuster.
Knights, S., 2007. *Freedom of Religion, Minorities and the Law*. Oxford: Oxford University Press.
Modood, T., 2013. *Multiculturalism*. 2nd ed., Cambridge: Polity Press.
Moeschberger, S. L. and Phillips DeZalia, R. eds., 2014. *Symbols that Bind, Symbols that Divide: The Semiotics of Peace and Conflict*. London: Springer.
Riis, O. and Woodhead, L., 2010. *A Sociology of Religious Emotion*. Oxford: Oxford University Press.
Roy, O., 2013. *Holy Ignorance: When Religion and Culture Diverge*. Oxford: Oxford University Press.
Sandberg, R., 2014. *Religion, Law and Society*. Cambridge: Cambridge University Press.
Turner, T.G. and Kirsch, B. eds., 2009. *Permutations of Order: Religion and Law as Contested Sovereignties*. Abingdon, Oxon: Routledge.
Van Ooijen, H., 2012. *Religious Symbols in Public Functions: Unveiling State Neutrality*. Cambridge: Intersentia.

Articles, book chapters and conference papers

Bacquet, S., 2015. 'Religious Symbols and the Making of Contemporary Religious Identities' in Sandberg R. ed. *Religion and Legal Pluralism*. Farnham: Ashgate. 113–130.

Bacquet, S., 2012. 'Religious Freedom in a Secular Society: an Analysis of the French Approach to Manifestation of Belief in the Public Sphere' in Cumper P. and Lewis T. eds. *Religion, Rights and Secular Society*. Cheltenham: Edward Elgar. 147–168.

Benda-Beckmann, F., 2009. 'Beyond the Law-Religion Divide: Law and Religion in West Sumatra' in Turner T.G. and Kirsch B. eds. *Permutations of Order: Religion and Law as Contested Sovereignties*. Abingdon, Oxon: Routledge. 227–246.

Ellens, G., 1981. 'Religious Symbols and their Functions', *Journal of the Royal Asiatic Society*, 113: 88.

Fokas, E., 2015. 'Sociology at the Intersection between Law and Religion' in FerrariS. ed. *Routledge Handbook of Law and Religion*. Abingdon, Oxon: Routledge. 59–74.

Geertz, C., 1966. 'Religion as a Cultural System' in Banton, M. ed. *Anthropological Approaches to the Study of Religion*. London: Tavistock. 1–46.

Laborde, C., 2001. 'The Culture(s) of the Republic. Nationalism and Multiculturalism in French Republican Thought'. *Political Theory*, 29(5): 716–735.

Laborde, C., 2006. 'Female Autonomy, Education and the Hijab'. *Critical Review of International Social and Political Philosophy*, 9(3): 351–377.

Singh Juss, S., 2013. 'Kirpans, Law and Religious Symbols in Schools'. *Journal of Church and State*, 55(4): 758–795.

Woodhead, L., 2016. 'The Rise of "No Religion" in Britain: The Emergence of a New Cultural Majority'. *Journal of the British Academy*, 4: 245–261.

Websites

Attributed author

Frantz, D., 1997. 'Scientology's Puzzling Journey from Tax Rebel to Tax Exempt'. *The New York Times*, http://www.nytimes.com/1997/03/09/us/scientology-s-puzzling-journey-from-tax-rebel-to-tax-exempt.html [Accessed 30 August 2018]

Lipka, M. and McClendon, D., April 2017. 'Why People with No Religion Are Projected to Decline as a Share of the World's Population'. http://www.pewresearch.org/fact-tank/2017/04/07/why-people-with-no-religion-are-projected-to-decline-as-a-share-of-the-worlds-population/ [Accessed 30 August 2018]

No attributed author

ADL. KKK symbols. https://www.adl.org/education/references/hate-symbols/burning-cross [Accessed 30th August 2018]

French Parliamentary report No. 2468 of 1995, 'Les sectes en France'. https://www.gemppi.org/politique-de-confidentialite?view=article&id=77 [Accessed 30 August 2018]

Pew Research Center. April 2015. 'The Future of World Religions: Population Growth Projections, 2010–2050'. http://www.pewforum.org/2015/04/02/religious-projections-2010-2050/ [Accessed 30 August 2018]

2 A multidisciplinary approach to the definition of religious manifestation

2.1 Introduction

We live in a world of signs and symbols and virtually every human being would have come across symbols throughout the course of their lives. From the time they are born, human beings are surrounded with colours, images, objects or sounds which have been given a symbolic meaning.[1] Cars stop at red lights, pedestrians cross at zebra crossings, red means hot, blue means cold, married women in the West are usually identified by the ring they wear on their ring finger, police officers wear a specific uniform, poppies are a symbol of remembrance days, a pink ribbon is almost universally recognised as support for breast cancer while a red one signifies support for AIDS sufferers. These are only a few examples of how objects can be given a specific function in human life and therefore acquire a symbolic character. Symbols and signs therefore are a tool human beings use to create meanings. This chapter explores how symbols are used by individuals to manifest deeply held religious or cultural beliefs. It then looks at the way the law interacts with those symbols and manifestations of religious belief more generally. This requires an examination of how the law defines religion itself, as the legal definition of religion has a direct impact on religious symbols. Indeed, whether something is defined as a religion for the purpose of the law is a determinant of whether a particular symbol or ritual may be worthy of legal protection. The legal approach to religion and religious manifestation is then contrasted to the anthropological and sociological approaches in order to gauge what can be gained from an interdisciplinary approach to the question of religious manifestation and its interaction with the law.

2.2 Manifestation of religious belief and symbols

Religious belief can be manifested in a number of ways, including body ornaments or clothing, building of religious monuments, which serve as places of worship to the believers or rituals that are performed by individuals within the religious communities.

2.2.1 Religious symbols and the body

The human body is the one thing that all human beings have in common;[2] it is universal in the sense that we are all born with a biologically inherited body which is our own blank canvas to express our individuality. It is common therefore for the human body to be clothed with religious or cultural symbols such as clothing or body ornament. For the anthropologist F. Bowie, the body is a mediator between the self and society.[3] Symbols are often found on the body itself; this is the case with tattoos, body piercing and jewellery, or they can be placed over the body as seen with head coverings, religious/cultural dress, and face veils. It is common for the law to be called upon to make decisions as to whether a particular symbol constitutes manifestation of religion or belief and as such deserves legal protection.

2.2.2 Religious symbols in space: architecture

The space in which we live is riddled with symbols. Religious symbols in space take the shape of religious edifices such as churches, temples, or mosques, but also include the display of religious or cultural signs such as crucifixes, Nativity scenes or the Ten Commandments. The religious space is a very important tool for religious, cultural and ethnic minorities who seek to negotiate the recognition of their collective identity through space.[4] When a religious minority obtains a planning permission to build a place of worship they are given a share of the public space and this is significant of their acceptance by the majority. On the other hand, when a community faces multiple refusals, it will experience a sense of rejection which may also impinge on the community's freedom of worship. As such, courts have been called upon to negotiate disputes relating to the building of places of religious worship such as when planning permission has been refused. Disputes have also arisen when a 'secular' state has displayed religious symbols such as crucifixes in public buildings like schools or Government departments.[5]

2.2.3 Religious symbols in action: rituals

It is common for religious expression to become ritualised. Belief is then manifested through a particular course of action such as following a particular diet, fasting, eating or performing a particular rite of passage such as initiation rites or rites associated with marking life events like birth, marriage and death.[6] Bell identifies six categories of rituals: rites of passage, calendrical and commemorative rites, rites of exchange and communication, rites of affliction, rites of feasting, fasting and festivals and political rituals.[7] Just as with the two preceding categories of religious expression, the law has been called upon to intervene in relation to symbols in action especially when a particular religious practice is contested as unsafe or unethical. This may be the case for funeral pyres, circumcision or animal slaughtering. In such cases, the role of the law is to strike a delicate balance between the freedom of religion of a given religious community or individual and maintaining public order, health and safety and the rights and freedoms of others. If a certain religious practice is harmful for the wider community then the role of the law is to protect the citizens from harm without compromising religious freedom. The law therefore is only concerned with the action associated with the symbol not the symbol itself or the intention behind it, as this is a matter for the internal laws of religion. It is not for the law of the land for instance to question the Muslim or Jewish way of animal slaughtering per se but the law may have to consider the impact of such ritual on animal welfare in order to decide whether an exemption may be granted.

2.2.4 Discussion

The anthropologist Bowie rightly reminds us that symbols fall under various categories. They can be personal or collective, optional or obligatory, ritualised or conventional, passively received or actively performed, arbitrary or contingent.[8] The symbols that people wear on their body are usually classed as personal symbols whereas architectural symbols and rituals are generally a form of collective expression. When a symbol is optional, the need to wear it arises from a psychological need of the individual rather than a religious or cultural obligation.[9] This is the case for body piercing or tattoos in Western societies while religious head coverings such as the Islamic head scarf, the Jewish yarmulke or the Hindu turban tend to be perceived by their wearer as obligatory.[10] Other symbols are personal but recognised by a person's culture as normal and meaningful, for example a Jew wearing a Star of David or a Christian wearing a cross. These may not necessarily be seen as obligatory but they serve to identify the wearer with a particular group. In that sense, they are both individual and collective. These are different from ritualised or conventional symbols such as a bride wearing white or people wearing black at a funeral which are more remote emotionally from the wearer than personal symbols since they originate from certain cultural practices and conventions rather than being strictly personal to the wearer. Finally, while some symbols are perceived as arbitrary or random as they derive from a personal choice rather than being dictated by religious or conventional practice, others derive from biological (male and female body, hair, skin colour)[11] and psychological factors (reassurance, protection, superstition). There are inevitable overlaps between those categories though and, in reality, it is difficult to separate them. Cultural symbols for instance play an important role in the maintenance of cultural identity and as such they have been found to contribute to psychological security.[12] This implies that an individual may turn to symbols for both cultural and psychological reasons, not just religious ones.

While placing symbols in various categories therefore is useful to gaining a clearer understanding of the range and diversity of manifestation of belief as well as how they impact an individual, one must be careful not to use those categories to infer that one is more important than the other. It would be a grave mistake for anyone to assume that collective symbols are more important than personal ones, for instance, or that those symbols that are perceived as obligatory are worthier of legal protection, because it would negate the subjectivity of religion and follow a narrow interpretation of religion and religious manifestation which would be exclusive and patronising. English courts as will be discussed in Chapter 6 have come close to doing this when they held that something needed to be a requirement of a particular faith to attract the protection of article 9 of the European Convention on Human Rights (ECHR).[13] The role that symbols play in individuals' lives is subject to personal interpretation, hence the different meanings given to symbols by individuals. Holding that one meaning deserves more protection than another is violating the freedom of conscience.

Even if it is possible to categorise symbols, it would be impossible to provide a single explanation for what symbols mean because there is no universally accepted meaning for symbols since the same symbol can be given different meanings by different individuals. The Eucharistic bread and wine, for instance, which stands for the body and blood of Christ, is spiritual food for Christians but has a cannibalistic resonance for Hindus.[14] Symbols therefore are culturally relative; the meaning of symbols is mostly acquired by individuals throughout their upbringing, it is neither fixed in time nor space.[15] A Westerner for instance may be brought up to see a cow as a farming product designed to enter the food chain but later in life embrace the Hindu faith, become a vegetarian and view the cow as sacred. Given the absence of universal meanings, the significance of symbols is assigned by individuals and groups and therefore is highly subjective. It follows therefore that the understanding of symbols presupposes the understanding of the cultural context in which a particular symbol has evolved. This is why the adjudication of disputes relating to manifestation of religious belief through symbols is a particularly controversial area.

Although manifestation of religion and belief is a human right, the law provides that it can be subject to certain limitations, in particular, when it becomes necessary for the protection of others. In the next section, we examine the nature of the interaction between religious symbols and the law.

2.3 The interaction between religious symbols and the law

The law in relation to religion intervenes in a number of areas. These are mainly, the charity sector: the law grants certain religious groups charity status resulting in tax exemptions;[16] discrimination is another area where law and religion come together, with the law seeking to protect individuals from religious discrimination – see for instance the Equality Act 2010 in the UK; the Civil Rights Act 1964 in the United States and Law No 2008–469 in France which prohibits discrimination on the grounds of ethnicity, race or religion. The law also intervenes in family cases when there is a dispute as to religious upbringing of children.[17] Finally, the law concerns itself with religion when human rights are at stake to ensure that the state is in a position to preserve its citizens' religious freedom. While none of the statutory provisions provide a clear definition of religion and religious manifestation, we can at least identify some common themes. These will be discussed in the next section.

When the law meets symbols, it is mainly to deal with the display of faith in the public sphere or if it is brought to the attention of the courts that a specific religious or cultural practice has a negative impact on individuals. As mentioned above, this could be through religious clothing, rituals or architectural display. The relationship between religious symbols and the law is mostly driven by the search for freedom of religion and belief, the protection from discrimination and protection of individuals in general. The law is called upon to intervene when one's religious freedom is allegedly restricted by the state or by a private entity or when one's religious freedom allegedly interferes with someone else's freedom, such as freedom from discrimination on the basis of sexual orientation.[18]

Consider the following scenarios: a court is called upon to decide whether a sacred bull tested positive for tuberculosis should be put down,[19] the French Parliament drafts legislation that seeks to ban religious symbols in the classroom,[20] animal rights activists protest against religious slaughtering of animals[21] and the drafters of the ECHR agree that manifestation of belief can be separated from freedom of religion resulting in the current article 9 distinguishing between the absolute freedom of thought, conscience and religion and the manifestation of such freedom being subject to limitations.[22] These are only a few examples of symbols' encounter with the law. However, when symbols or rituals meet the law it is often in the 'abstract' rather than in context. Ferrari argues that courts pay less attention to the cultural meaning of rules[23] as they use a more objective approach rather than considering subjectively what a particular religious symbol means to an individual. This is not because the law is insensitive to religious symbols and what they mean for individuals but more because legal personnel tend to focus on concrete issues which require practical solutions[24] and also because judges do not want to get involved with the internal matters of religion itself as it is beyond their remit. When a court is required to decide whether a claimant's freedom to manifest his or her belief has been infringed, it requires a clear and definite answer. As argued by Ferrari, lawyers approach issues from a practical and normative perspective and as a result the cultural meaning of religious manifestation remains in the background,[25] but one could argue that when judges attempt to delve too much into religious and cultural matters they run the risk of becoming arbiters of faith.[26] This will be discussed in Part II in the context of the case law.

2.3.1 The need for a legal definition of religion and religious manifestation

The law exists to impose boundaries and as such it requires technical definitions of terms;[27] religion is not exempt from this requirement despite obvious difficulties in providing such a definition due to the elusiveness of religion as a concept. Without a clear definition, the law is unable to offer protection to both individuals and groups. This includes protecting society from religion itself and ensuring that religious organisations do not become too powerful. This is because in order to be interpretable, the law needs to be precisely defined.[28] However, due to the sensitive and subjective nature of religion, any legal definition can be seen as imposed upon religion itself – thus inevitably impacting negatively on some followers whose said 'religion' or 'belief' falls outside the scope of the legal definition. As discussed further below, Scientology provides a good illustration of this dilemma.[29] The search for a legal definition has been widely documented by law and religion academics[30] but what stands out from these discussions is the difficulty in formulating such a definition. As Sandberg points out, any legal definition has the potential of being either inclusive or exclusive.[31] If we define religion too narrowly, certain groups which deem themselves religious may end up being excluded from the protection afforded by the law. On the other hand, if we define it too widely we run the risk of undermining religion altogether and opening the floodgates for vexatious claims. Yet, judicial decisions about what constitutes religion can have a very strong impact on the lives of individuals.[32] The purpose of a legal definition therefore is primarily to enable the law to offer protection to individuals as well as deciding whether or not a group is entitled to claim the privileges and exemptions that being legally recognised as a religion confers but if the definition is culturally 'biased' it could create some inequalities with some religions being labelled as 'real' and others 'non-real'.

Some commentators have even questioned the need for a definition of religion altogether. Gunn for instance highlights the inefficiencies of legal definitions of 'religion' in instances where those definitions are based on particular assumptions. They either incorporate certain political and cultural attitudes towards preferred religions or fail to account for social and cultural attitudes against less favoured ones.[33] As a result of those assumptions some religions are classed as 'acceptable' or 'not acceptable' which introduces a bias in legal analysis since, as discussed above in Chapter 1, it is the law that has the power to dictate what is or is not religion and what is or is not religious manifestation. In France for instance there is a distinction between 'religions' and 'sects' where the former are deemed lawful but the latter are considered as dangerous.[34] Religions therefore are being categorised by legal systems. Gunn argues that defining religion is not helpful to adjudicators because if someone is subject to discrimination or any kind of abuse, it should be irrelevant whether they are a member of something defined as a religion or a cult.[35]

2.3.2 The absence of a clear statutory definition

While the right to freedom of thought, conscience and religion is guaranteed by international, regional and national legal instruments, none of the statutory provisions provide a clear definition of either 'religion' or 'manifestation of religion'. The Universal Declaration of Human Right (UDHR) 1948 provides that:

> 'Everyone has the right to freedom of thought, conscience and religion; this right includes freedom to change his religion or belief, and freedom, either alone or in community with others and in public or private, to manifest his religion or belief in teaching, practice, worship and observance.'[36]

Both article 18 of the International Covenant on Civil and Political Rights (ICCPR) and article 9 of the ECHR are based on the same wording as article 18 of the UDHR and therefore also do not provide as such a definition of religion or manifestation. We have to look at General Comment (GC) 22 of the Human Rights Committee (HRC)[37] in order to find an attempt at a definition. GC 22 on article 18 of the ICCPR defines religion as including theistic, non-theistic and atheistic beliefs as well as the right to not have a religion. Religion and belief therefore are interpreted broadly. 'Religion' includes traditional and non-traditional religions and the HRC is in favour of extending protection to newly established religions or those that may be subject to hostility from the majority.[38] As will be discussed below, this approach is not always followed by the courts.

The HRC defines manifestation of belief as 'worship including ritual and ceremonial acts giving direct expression to belief'; it includes the observance of dietary requirements; the wearing of distinctive clothing as well as the practice of rituals associated with stages of life and the building of places of worship.[39]

In common to all of the international provisions mentioned above is the distinction between on the one hand the freedom to believe (*forum internum*) and on the other hand the freedom to manifest such belief (*forum externum*). Some commentators have argued that this view of freedom of religion and belief derives from a Western and Christian conception of religion as separate from law, science and politics[40] and that this separation is alien to religions such as Islam for instance. As argued by Assad, the right to freedom of religion and belief is a product of Western culture and as such is more functional to the needs of that culture than others.[41] The aforementioned distinction between the absolute freedom to believe and the more controlled manifestation of belief/religion is a common feature of most Western international and national instruments therefore providing the sovereign states with some margin of appreciation in relation to manifestation of belief. The HRC recalls however that any limitations placed on article 18 must be strictly proportionate to the aims pursued.[42]

The issue becomes then whether something is a belief or religion for the purposes of the law rather than in absolute. Manifestation therefore is highly dependent on how the religion or belief driving this manifestation is considered and therefore the extent to which protection is afforded is highly dependent on classification of something as religious or non-religious. An individual could be wearing a symbol or performing a ritual, which they view as a manifestation of their belief but if this belief/religion is not acknowledged as such by the law, then the legal protection would not be afforded. This highlights the divide between orthodoxy and orthopraxy faith, with the latter being more vulnerable to legal interpretations due to its emphasis on practice. This is discussed throughout the book.

In addition to the international framework for the protection of religion and its manifestation, each of the countries studied (England, France and the US) has domestic legal provisions to protect citizens against religious discriminations by public and private actors but none of those provisions provide a clear definition of either religion or manifestation thereof. In France, religion and manifestation are protected via Article 1 of the Constitution of 1958 as well as article 9 of the ECHR. In the UK, freedom of religion is afforded protection via the HRA 1998 which incorporates article 9 of the ECHR into UK law and makes public authorities liable under the HRA, while in the US, freedom of religion is guaranteed by the 1st amendment of the Constitution.[43]

The absence of a concrete statutory definition of religion and religious manifestation allows for religion and belief to be interpreted broadly but also results in some states adopting a narrower interpretation or restricting manifestation altogether on one of the justifiable grounds as per article 18(3) of the ICCPR or 9(2) of the ECHR. The absence of a clear definition also means that judges are left with the task of adopting a case by case approach. The next section looks at how judges deal with religious symbols.

2.4 Judicial interpretation of symbols

Given the nature of symbols, there is a consensus amongst legal academics that any attempt by the courts to delve into interpreting religious symbols is problematic.[44] Scharffs has gone as far as describing it 'an unnecessarily destructive act of judicial violence.'[45] This is because judicial methods of interpretation run contrary to the very nature of symbols. Judges have a tendency to search for an actual meaning of symbols which implies that there is such thing as a single 'true' meaning of symbol. This, as argued by Scharffs, inevitably brings judicial bias[46] and is potentially damaging to those who feel excluded from what they see as 'the truth'.

The legal scholar Robert Cover argues that the law's claim to apply equally and impartially to all is false. He recognises that the law does not accommodate a pluralist society where different people live together but have their own beliefs.[47] Cover highlights two aspects of the law which he calls 'jurisgenerative' and 'jurispathic'; while the first function promotes the recognition of pluralism, the second is destroying. When using their 'jurispathic' function, judges have the power to decide amongst multiple meanings. It is this process which may lead to what Cover calls 'an act of violence'. Judges as authoritative figures, speak with a certain level of authority and the finality of their decisions may resonate as truth which, when it comes to religious symbols, is problematic. Cover recognises however that this process is nonetheless necessary to enable the community to live in peace rather than fight about what a particular text or symbol means. When dealing with religious symbols however, Scharffs argues that judges should avoid the unnecessary exercise of their 'jurispathic' function.[48]

Sandberg, along the same line, also argues that judges have the capacity to 'kill' freedom of religion.[49] It is not so much the outcome of the case law that Sandberg criticises but instead the process of judicial decision. Judges in the UK have had a tendency to rely on whether the freedom to manifest religion has been interfered with and sometimes this is answered negatively, which excludes the practice in question from legal protection.[50] Sandberg argues that instead judges ought to acknowledge that the freedom to manifest religion has been interfered with and move on to the second test which is whether such interference was justified. Justification as argued by Sandberg is a much better approach which has the merits of acknowledging that manifestation of belief is subject to individual interpretation.[51] In the English case of *Playfoot* for instance it was held that wearing a purity ring cannot constitute a manifestation of the Christian faith since it is not a religious requirement.[52] I have also argued elsewhere that judges are becoming arbiters of faith by attempting to make decisions as to whether something is or is not a religious symbol.[53] Fokas similarly discusses the *Lautsi* case[54] from a socio-logical perspective and questions the extent to which the courtroom is an appro-priate place for determining the meaning of the cross or crucifix.[55]

While law and religion scholars and professionals have been the main actors called upon by governments to engage in the regulation of religious belief and manifestation, the extent to which they are capable of understanding the com-plexities of the law and religion relationship has been questioned.[56] Donovan argues that law lacks the tools to set out 'objective and reliable' indicators to reflect the object of beliefs and the effect of those beliefs on individuals and that anthropology is better placed to do this.[57]

Trying to impose a single meaning on symbols is counter-intuitive to their very nature, which is better captured by looking at other disciplines such as anthro-pology and sociology. Anthropology is particularly relevant to the understanding of religious symbols because of the emphasis many anthropologists have placed on religious and cultural practice. For anthropologists, religion must be studied in its social and cultural context. It cannot be separated from other aspects of society such as politics, agriculture, magic or medicine. Generally, there is a consensus amongst anthropologists that one must start from the people themselves rather than the texts – this avoids importing any Christian or Western bias.[58] The merits of cooperation between the two disciplines have been explored in the context of asylum cases[59] but actual cooperation remains the exception rather than the norm, although the benefits of cooperation between lawyers and anthropologists have been acknowledged.[60]

2.4.1 Anthropological definition of religion and religious manifestation

Law and anthropology literature share in common an attempt to define religion but the two disciplines differ in their methods. While law relies on normative standards, anthropology is a cross-cultural discipline which relies mainly on parti-cipant observation for the generation of its data.[61] Issues raised by religion have been at the centre of anthropological debates since its origin in the 19th century to the present day. Tylor,[62] Durkheim,[63] and Geertz[64] have all engaged with defin-ing religion. An anthropological approach to religion is holistic – anthropologists, contrary to lawyers, see religious facts as part of a cultural whole – they do not base their analysis on a demarcation between the 'religious' and the 'non-religious' sphere[65] as lawyers tend to do. This is evident from the current legal approach to symbols where protection or toleration of a particular symbol is determined by its belonging to a particular category – be it secular or religious. The crucifix for instance can be tolerated in Italian secular classrooms if it is interpreted in histor-ical and cultural terms rather than religious ones.[66] Hijabs and yarmulke are excluded from French classrooms because they are deemed religious, but secular forms of head covering are tolerated.

Another important feature of anthropology is that it does not separate Western societies from smaller societies and in that sense, it is universal whereas the law tends to be more culturally relative. A recurrent theme within the anthropology of religion over the centuries has been to attempt to understand the nature of religious practices in both Western and non-Western societies.[67] This understanding is useful to inform judicial approaches to religious symbols. Anthropology has attempted to contribute to society being less ethnocentric by teaching about other people's cultures and practices through ethnographies. Those ethnographies have closed the gap between Western and non-Western civilisations by providing the West with a better understanding of civilisations which were otherwise known as 'primitive' or 'savage'.[68]

Defining religion in anthropology is no less complex than in law and there have been many attempts to do so over the years. Most contemporary anthropological analyses are informed by Tylor, Durkheim and Geertz. There is no single definition of religion within anthropology but broadly speaking anthropologists and sociologists agree that religion is part of symbolic systems and as such part of culture.[69] Definitions can be classified into two broad categories: inclusivists and exclusivists, with the point of discord being whether a belief in a supreme being is a necessary aspect of the definition of religion.

The English anthropologist Tylor, in the 19th century defined religion as the 'belief in Spiritual Beings'.[70] This is referred to as a rationalist or intellectualist definition of religion as it is dependent on the assumption of a rational thinker.[71] Tylor sees religion as an attempt by human beings to make sense of the world they live in; the purpose of religion as such is to explain human life. While Tylor's definition has stood the test of time, it is arguably a narrow and incomplete definition which requires the belief in a spiritual being and therefore might exclude certain groups from the definition. Buddhism for instance would be excluded from Tylor's definition as it does not focus on a personal god.

The influence of this definition in the legal sphere can be seen in the recent English case of *Hodkin v Registrar General of Births, Deaths and Marriages* [72] where the UK Supreme Court had to decide whether the Church of Scientology could be recorded as a 'place of meeting for religious worship' so that a valid marriage ceremony could be performed. The Defendant had initially rejected the application based on the older case of *R v Registrar General, ex parte Segerdal* [73] where the Court of Appeal had held that scientology did not involve as such 'religious worship' since it did not involve 'reverence or veneration of God or of a Supreme Being.' The UK SC however reversed that decision.

In *Hodkin*, Lord Toulson at [57] defined religion as:

> … a spiritual or non-secular belief system, held by a group of adherents, which claims to explain mankind's place in the universe and relationship with the infinite, and to teach its adherents how they are to live their lives in conformity with the spiritual understanding associated with the belief system. By spiritual or non-secular I mean a belief system which goes beyond that which can be perceived by the senses or ascertained by the application of science. I

prefer not to use the word 'supernatural' to express this element, because it is a loaded word which can carry a variety of connotations. Such a belief system may or may not involve belief in a supreme being, but it does involve a belief that there is more to be understood about mankind's nature and relationship to the universe than can be gained from the senses or from science. I emphasise that this is intended to be a description and not a definitive formula.

Hodkin's 're-definition' marks an important departure from previous judicial attempts to define religion and provides a more inclusive definition.

Theism has also played an important part in the judicial definition of religion by US courts although the definition of religion by the courts has evolved over the years. While the US Supreme Court has never provided a standardised definition of religion, there have been many attempts at a definition over the years and the courts have gradually become more liberal in their approach to religion.[74] This will be discussed fully in Chapter 7.

Within the anthropological debate, Tylor's definition was criticised by Durkheim, who adopted a more functionalist definition of religion. Durkheim's definition departs from Tylor and rests on a system of classification as opposed to a specific belief. For Durkheim religion is a natural expression of society and it provides a form of social cohesion. As opposed to Tylor, Durkheim's position recognises the symbolic quality of religion.[75] He argues that religious ideas and rituals express and regenerate society. Durkheim's focus therefore is primarily on religious and cultural practices which provides us with a useful basis for exploring religious symbols and their social function. Durkheim's definition has the merit of being more inclusive and without specific reference to a supreme being. It assists us in understanding the subjectivity of symbolic meaning. Durkheim's definition, which provides that 'there are no religions which are false',[76] is inclusive as every religion fulfils a specific function of human existence whether mainstream or primitive. Durkheim's definition also has the merit of giving equal importance to both beliefs and practices, whereas earlier definitions such as Tylor's were based on the Christian assumption that belief is central to religion. Durkheim relies on a classification which divides the world between 'sacred' (ideals by which society seeks to live) and 'profane' (everyday activities).[77] Anything according to Durkheim has the capacity to be sacred and the category of sacred objects cannot be fixed; it varies from religion to religion. Sacred things are normally superior to profane things. This approach supports the thesis that the Western, intellectual conception of religion is too narrow and leaves some gaps in protection.

Durkheim's more functionalist approach to religion is supported by Malinowski who argued that customs and practices should be understood in their full context and explained in terms of their function.[78] The function of religion for Malinowski was to provide psychological support in the face of death – he agreed with Durkheim that religion serves to bind people together.[79] As discussed in Chapter 4, this function still bears much relevance today despite the secularisation of society.

The importance of symbols is also highlighted by cultural anthropologists. Geertz for instance sees symbols as a primary human product and human tool. They are the building blocks of religion, language, culture, society and practice. For Geertz, religion is

> a system of symbols which acts to establish powerful, pervasive, and long-lasting moods and motivations in men by formulating conceptions of a general order of existence and clothing these conceptions with such an aura of faculty that the moods and motivations seem uniquely realistic.[80]

Symbols according to Geertz are extrinsic sources of information, unlike genes which are inherent to humans. This however does not make them less vital than genes. Geertz argues that:

> Man depends upon symbols and symbol systems with a dependence so great as to be decisive for his creatural viability and, as a result, his sensitivity to even the remotest indication that they may prove unable to cope with one or another aspect of experience raises within him the gravest sort of anxiety ...[81]

If religion is a system of symbols, then religion cannot exist without symbols and therefore religion cannot be detached from symbols. In a pluralist society therefore, the freedom of religion would include the freedom to display symbols of some religion. The attempt by some states to interfere with symbols therefore is a direct interference with one's freedom of religion.

2.5 Concluding remarks: what do we learn from juxtaposing legal and social definitions of manifestation of belief?

Religion and religious manifestation have been major preoccupations for lawyers, anthropologists and sociologists alike. As mentioned above, collaborations have so far been limited, although anthropologists have in the past been called as expert witness in UK courts,[82] but much more is needed. As we have seen in this chapter, while lawyers tend to categorise the world into Western and non-Western, secular and religious, elaborate and primitive, anthropologists have a different style of categorisation. As observed by Geertz, while anthropologists are prompted by what they observe through taking into account the context, lawyers, instead of reading the facts of legal phenomena, create those facts to reflect their categories and render them justiciable.[83]

As a result, anthropological studies for the most part break down the Christian and Western conception that belief is central to religion. Both law and anthropology as disciplines have different approaches to religion; while the law provides religion with special protection and as such it could be argued that the law puts religion on a pedestal, anthropology views religion as part of society. By looking at religion in its social context rather than in semi-isolation, anthropology is more attuned to the social function of religion and symbolic manifestation. Both disciplines have attempted to define religion and religious manifestation but it is clear that the law has a tendency to be less concerned with manifestation of belief than with belief itself, arguably because the latter is easier to categorise and define. This tendency is reflected in the international legal human rights framework for the protection of religion which clearly divides belief from manifestation and allows state parties to place restrictions on manifestation of belief. An anthropological perspective on symbols is useful in understanding the interaction between symbols and society in both Western and non-Western societies. It highlights the importance of symbols and religion for society and that symbols have multiple meanings. The legal approach is, as we have seen, problematic, as judges have a tendency to ignore the meaning of symbols in order to focus instead on whether a symbolic object or action can be taken as a manifestation of belief or religion as this is what determines whether the claimant is in a position to attract the protection of the law. The meaning and importance of symbolic manifestation to the individual therefore is not as such addressed since the focus is placed on religion and whether a particular object, practice or ritual can fit into the legal categories. This is what has led judges to consider religious symbols as secular[84] or to exclude others from the religious category.[85]

With this in mind, the next chapter looks at the history of symbols in an attempt to gain a better understanding of the function of symbols and the pathway to gaining recognition in law. This is key to understanding manifestation of belief in modern pluralist states as it will provide context which is lacking in judicial interpretations of symbols.

Notes

1 See further, Rasmussen 1974.
2 Bowie 2006. 35.
3 Ibid.
4 See further, Gale 2004.
5 See for instance Italy (Case of *Lautsi and Others v. Italy*, Application no. 30814/06) and Germany (*Bayerischer Verwaltungsgerichtshof [BayVGH]* [Bavarian Higher Administrative Court] 3 June 1991, *122 Bayerische Verwaltungsblatter* [BayVBI] 751 (751–54) (F.R.G.)); those cases are discussed in Mancini 2010.
6 See Bell 1997. 138 onwards.
7 Ibid.
8 Bowie 2006, op. cit., 54–57.
9 Bowie 2006, op. cit., 54.
10 See further Bacquet 2015.
11 See further Obeyesekere 1984.
12 See for example Obeyesekere 1990.
13 See for instance *R (on the application of Playfoot) v Millais School Governing Body* [2007] EWHC 1698 (Admin).
14 See Neville 1995. 98.
15 See further Bacquet 2015, op. cit.
16 In the UK, see for instance The Charities Act 2011 s. 3(1)(c).
17 See for example the recent case of *J v. B* (Ultra-Orthodox Judaism: Transgender) [2017] EWFC 4.

18 See for instance in the UK the *Ladele v London Borough of Islington* [2009] EWCA Civ 1357 which is discussed further in Chapter 6.

19 See for instance *Surayanda v The Welsh Ministers* [2007] EWCA Civ 893 (23 July 2007).

20 Loi n° 2004–228 du 15 mars 2004 encadrant, en application du principe de laïcité, le port de signes ou de tenues manifestant une appartenance religieuse dans les écoles, collèges et lycées publics (Law of 2004 on religious symbols in primary and secondary state schools).

21 *Cha'are Shalom Ve Tsedek v. France* (Application no. 27417/95).

22 Article 9 ECHR *1. Everyone has the right to freedom of thought, conscience and religion; this right includes freedom to change his religion or belief and freedom, either alone or in community with others and in public or private, to manifest his religion or belief, in worship, teaching, practice and observance. 2. Freedom to manifest one's religion or beliefs shall be subject only to such limitations as are prescribed by law and are necessary in a democratic society in the interests of public safety, for the protection of public order, health or morals, or for the protection of the rights and freedoms of others.*

23 Ferrari 2015. 4.

24 Ibid.

25 Ibid.

26 See further Bacquet 2008.

27 Sandberg 2014. 28.

28 Donovan 1995.

29 See *R v Registrar General, ex parte Segerdal* [1970] 2 QB 697 and *R (on the application of Hodkin and another) v Registrar General of Births, Deaths and Marriages* [2013] UKSC 77; both cases are discussed further below.

30 See for instance Sandberg 2014 op. cit. and Gunn 2003. 191.

31 Sandberg 2014, op. cit. 39.

32 Gunn 2003, op. cit. 191.

33 Gunn 2003, op. cit. 195.

34 See Circulaire du Premier ministre du 27 mai 2005 relative à la lutte contre les dérives sectaires. JORF n°126 du 1 juin 2005 page 9751. While cults (sects) are not legally defined due to the principle of *laïcité*, a list of criteria has been established by various Parliamentary groups in order to identify sectarian practices. These include: mental destabilisation, indoctrination of children, high financial exigencies, public disorder.

35 Gunn 2003, op. cit. 199.

36 Article 18 UDHR 1948.

37 Note that General Comments are not legally binding as such but have a persuasive influence.

38 UN Human Rights Committee (HRC), CCPR General Comment No. 22: Article 18 (Freedom of Thought, Conscience or Religion), 30 July 1993, CCPR/C/21/Rev.1/Add.4.

39 Ibid. Para 4.

40 Assad 1993. 28.

41 Assad 2003.

42 GC 22 op. cit. Para 8.

43 Full details of the constitutional set up of each country are provided in Part II.

44 See for example Scharffs 2012. 35–58. See also Bacquet 2008, op. cit.; Mancini 2009; Cover 1986.

45 Scharffs 2012, op. cit. 37.

46 Idem.

47 Beckett 2011.

48 Scharffs, 2012, op. cit. 50.

49 See Sandberg 2014, op. cit. Chapter 1.

50 See *Playfoot* 2007, op. cit. The case is discussed in Chapter 6.

51 See Sandberg 2014, op. cit. Chapter 10.
52 *Playfoot* case 2007, op. cit.
53 Bacquet 2008, op. cit.
54 *Lautsi* case 2011, op. cit.
55 Fokas 2015, op. cit. 59.
56 Ferrari 2015, op. cit. 2, 3.
57 Donovan 1995, op. cit. 98.
58 Gellner 1999. 38.
59 See Good 2007.
60 Ferrari 2015, op. cit. 3, 4, Donovan 1995, op. cit. 71.
61 Donovan 1995, op. cit. 71.
62 Tylor 1971.
63 Durkheim 1915.
64 Geertz 1966.
65 Lambek 2008. 2, 3.
66 *Lautsi* case 2011, op. cit.
67 See for example the work of anthropologist and ethnologist Claude Levi-Strauss, 1908–2009.
68 This can be seen for instance in B. Malinowski's account of the Trobriand Islands. See Young 1979.
69 Roy 2013. 26.
70 Tylor 1871.
71 Lambek, 2008. 9.
72 [2013] UKSC 77.
73 [1970] 2 QB 697.
74 See for example: *Davies v Beason* 133 US 333 (1890); *Torcaso v Watkins* 367 US 488 (1961); *US v. Seeger*, 380 US 163 (1965); *Welsh v. US* (No. 76) 398 US 333 (1970); *Wisconsin v. Jonas Yoder*, 406 US 205 (1972).
75 Durkheim 1915.
76 Ibid. 3.
77 Ibid. 36.
78 See further Malinowski 1948. 19 onwards.
79 Idem.
80 Geertz 1973. 90.
81 Ibid. 99.
82 See for example Good 2006.
83 Geertz 1973, op. cit. 167.
84 *Lautsi* case 2011, op. cit.
85 *Eweida v British Airways Plc* [2010] EWCA Civ 80.

References

Books

Assad, T., 1993. *Genealogies of Religion: Discipline and Reasons of Power in Christianity and Islam*. Baltimore: Johns Hopkins University Press.
Assad, T., 2003. *Formations of the Secular: Christianity, Islam, Modernity*. Stanford, CA: Stanford University Press.
Bell, C., 1997. *Ritual Perspectives and Dimensions*. Oxford: Oxford University Press.
Bowie, F., 2006. *The Anthropology of Religion*, 2nd ed. Oxford: Blackwell Publishing.
Durkheim, E., 1915. *The Elementary Forms of the Religious Life*. London: George Allen and Unwin.

Ferrari, S. ed., 2015. *Routledge Handbook of Law and Religion.* Abingdon, Oxon: Routledge.

Geertz, C., 1973. *The Interpretation of Cultures.* New York: Basic Books.

Good, A., 2006. *Anthropology and Expertise in the Asylum Courts.* London: Routledge-Cavendish.

Lambek, M., ed., 2008. *A Reader in the Anthropology of Religion,* 2nd ed. Oxford: Blackwell Publishing.

Malinowski, B., 1948. *Magic, Science and Religion.* Boston, MA: Beacon Press.

Neville, R.C., 1995. *The Truth of Broken Symbols.* Albany: State University of New York Press.

Obeyesekere, G., 1984. *Medusa's Hair.* Chicago: Chicago University Press.

Obeyesekere, G., 1990. *The Work of Culture: Symbolic Transformation in Psychoanalysis and Anthropology.* Chicago: Chicago University Press.

Rasmussen, D., 1974. *Symbol and Interpretation.* The Hague: Martinus Nijhoff.

Roy, O., 2013. *Holy Ignorance: When Religion and Culture Part Ways.* Oxford: Oxford University Press.

Sandberg, R., 2014. *Religion, Law and Society.* Cambridge: Cambridge University Press.

Tylor, E. B., 1971. *Primitive Culture.* London: John Murray.

Young, M. W., ed., 1979. *Ethnography of Malinowski: Trobriand Islands, 1915–18.* Abingdon, Oxon: Routledge.

Articles, book chapters, conference papers, government reports, NGO-reports

Bacquet, S., 2008. 'School Uniforms, Religious Symbols and the Human Rights Act 1998: The "Purity Ring" Case'. *Education Law Journal* 9(1): 13–22.

Bacquet, S., 2015. 'Religious Symbols and the Making of Contemporary Religious Identities', in SandbergR. ed., *Religion and Legal Pluralism.* London: Ashgate. 113–130.

Cover, R., 1986. 'Violence and the Word', *Yale Law Journal* 95(8): 1601–1629.

Donovan, J., 1995. 'God is as God Does: Law, Anthropology, and the Definition of "Religion."'6*Seton Hall Const. L.J.* 23(96): 25.

Fokas, E., 2015. 'Sociology at the Intersection between Law and Religion' in FerrariS. ed., *Routledge Handbook of Law and Religion.* Abingdon, Oxon: Routledge. 59–74.

Gale, R., 2004. 'The Multicultural City and the Politics of Religious Architecture: Urban Planning, Mosques and Meaning-making in Birmingham, UK', *Built Environment,* 30(1): 18–32.

Geertz, C., 1966, 'Religion as a Cultural System', in GeertzC., 1973. *The Interpretation of Cultures: Selected Essays.* London: Fontana Press. 87–125.

Gellner, D. N., 1999. 'Anthropological Approaches', in ConnollyP. ed., *Approaches to the Study of Religion.* London: Continuum. 10–41.

Gunn, J., 2003. 'The Complexity of Religion and the Definition of "Religion" in International Law'. 16*Harv. Hum. Rts. J.,* 189.

Mancini, S., 2010. 'The Crucifix Rage: Supranational Constitutionalism'. *European Constitutional Law Review,* 6: 6–27.

Mancini, S., 2009. 'The Power of Symbols and Symbols as Power: Secularism and Religion as Guarantors of Cultural Convergence', *Cardozo Law Review,* 30(6): 2629–2668.

Scharffs, B. G., 2012. 'The Role of Judges in Determining the Meaning of Religious Symbols', in TempermanJ., ed. *The Lautsi Papers: Multidisciplinary Reflections on Religious Symbols in the Public Classroom.* Leiden: Martinus Nijhoff. 35–58.

Tylor, E. B., 1871. 'Religion in Primitive Culture. Researches into the Development of Mythology', *Philosophy, Religion, Art, and Custom*, Volume 1. London: John Murray.

Websites

No attributed author

Beckett, J. A., May 2011. 'The violence of wording: Robert Cover on legal interpretation'. NoFo 8, http://www.helsinki.fi/nofo/NoFo8Beckett.pdf [Accessed 16 August 2018]

Circulaire du Premier ministre of 27 May 2005 relative à la lutte contre les dérives sectaires. JORF n°126 du 1 juin 2005 p. 9751, https://www.legifrance.gouv.fr/affichTexte.do?cidTexte=JORFTEXT000000809117&fastPos=1&fastReqId=1732374811&categorieLien=id&oldAction=rechTexte [Accessed 15 August 2018]

UN Human Rights Committee (HRC), CCPR General Comment No. 22: Article 18 (Freedom of Thought, Conscience or Religion), 30 July 1993, CCPR/C/21/Rev.1/Add.4, http://www.refworld.org/docid/453883fb22.html [Accessed 15 August 2018]

3 Historical origin and significance of religious symbols

3.1 Introduction

'We are symbols and inhabit symbols.'[1]

By their very nature, symbols are mysterious; those outside of the 'defined' group tend to be suspicious, fascinated or simply intrigued and curious.[2] The fairly recent 'preoccupation' with symbols however should not distract us from the historical reality of symbols and rituals;[3] they have always existed and formed an integral part of human life. While it is impossible to date the beginning of religion and its symbols, archaeological evidence which has survived in the shape of graves, sanctuaries, temples, cult objects, sculptures or engravings gives us some clues as to how religion began before sacred texts were written.[4] We have to rely therefore on the interpretation of historians, archaeologists and anthropologists to understand how religion began and developed over the years. What we observe when examining the history of religion is that it developed alongside humanity and dates back from prehistoric times. It originally stemmed from humans' desire to establish beneficial relations with natural surroundings which were then unexplainable and therefore mysterious. This chapter will trace the historical origin of symbols, rituals and religious architecture by exploring how those forms of expression have shaped social norms throughout the years. This is done via an examination of the role of symbols in primitive religion and ancient civilisations as well as looking at the internal laws of more modern religions. This historical overview will enhance our understanding of how religious manifestation via symbols and rituals has acquired a special status worthy of legal protection.

3.2 Definitions

A symbol can be a mark or character used to represent something else such as the letters used to represent a chemical element (O for oxygen), it can be a shape or a sign to represent a particular faith or an organisation such as the red cross symbol to represent the Red Cross organisation, it can be something that stands for something else by association such as a nice house or a nice car being interpreted as a sign of wealth.[5] Religious symbols are artistic forms and gestures used to convey religious concepts and the representation of religious ideas and events. A religious symbol, whether it is an object, a sign, a picture, words spoken, or gestures, has a revealing and esoteric function in the sense that it requires a certain amount of cooperation from its interpreter to understand its meaning. It is usually based on the convention of a group which agrees its meaning.[6] Religious symbols are used to convey concepts related to humanity's relationship with the divine, they are primarily intended for those who are initiated and have acknowledged the experience it expresses.[7] In that sense, symbols contribute to the construction of group identity.

Like symbols, rituals serve both the individual and the group, they are used to channel or express emotions. This is evident in rituals performed around major life events such as birth, marriage or death. Rituals allow for a culture's most deeply held values to be transmitted through generations. Anthropologist Tambiah defines ritual as 'a culturally constructed system of symbolic communication. It is constituted of patterned and ordered sequences of words and acts, often expressed in multiple media.'[8] A ritual therefore is a performative act which is carried out by a community through various actions including singing, praying, chanting and dancing. The ritual performed as such makes sense only to those inside the said community and often derives from religious law or oral customs. The ultimate objective of a religious ritual can be a covenant with God as in Christian baptism or Jewish circumcision. To the outsider it may appear irrational, meaningless or even suspicious but to those inside the group it brings comfort and a sense of belonging. Both rituals and symbols therefore provide a bridge between the outside world and the community.

By their very nature therefore symbols are akin to a code and do not reveal their meaning at first sight. As such, they do not lend themselves to a literal interpretation, which is the common method of legal interpretation, because the meaning of symbols is dependent upon layers of culture. This partly explains the reluctance of judges to engage with symbolic interpretation. Lord Nicholls of Birkenhead at the House of Lords (now UK Supreme Court) highlighted the subjective nature of religious beliefs in the case of R. *v. Secretary of State for Education and Employment*[9] para. 22:

> ... it is not for the court to embark on an inquiry into the asserted belief and judge its 'validity' by some objective standard such as the source material upon which the claimant founds his belief or the orthodox teaching of the religion in question or the extent to which the claimant's belief conforms to or differs from the views of others professing the same religion. Freedom of religion protects the subjective belief of an individual.

However, as will be discussed in Part II, this subjective nature is not always accommodated by the courts and the legal framework.

The meaning of symbols and rituals is not only dependent on culture but also on the context in which a symbol operates. Symbols are dependent on what legal scholar Stanley Fish calls 'Interpretative communities' which suggests that it is the interpreter who lends symbols their social meaning.[10] Fish's concept of 'Interpretative communities' is an extension of Pierce's theory of signs or semiotics, holding that a symbol is given meaning by its interpreter and therefore is dependent for meaning on its interpreter.[11] Scharffs suggests that this approach is an oversimplification and that the first layer of symbolic interpretation should involve looking at the creator of the symbol while the various interpretations of a community constitute added layers of meaning.[12] Adopting a single conception of a given symbol therefore is not a satis-factory approach, yet courts have often taken views on contested symbols and their meaning; whether it is French judges on Islamic headscarves which they tend to see as necessarily coercive, English courts on crosses and purity rings which have been held to constitute non-obligatory religious symbols or US judges taking a view on the Crucifix.[13] This is discussed further in Part II.

3.3 Early forms of religious beliefs, symbols and rituals

The earliest traces of religious belief and practice as recorded by archaeologists date back to prehistoric religion,[14] before the arrival of Homo sapiens and centre around death and burials.[15] The archaeological evidence points to Palaeolithic burial rituals such as the cult of the skulls[16] which shows evidence of funeral feasts where brains would be extracted and eaten probably to absorb their religious qualities and bodies disposed of in caves which were used for ritual purposes as sacred ossuary.[17] The evidence also points to Neolithic burials such as the ones discovered in Egypt across the Nile valley evidencing the cult of the dead, which as discussed below occupied a central place in the history of Ancient Egypt. Disposal of the dead remained an important aspect of early religious beliefs and practices and the evidence available from archaeologists suggests that rituals associated with death evolved over time. In the Bronze Age, there is evidence of cremations in Europe[18] as well as urn burials and mummification in ancient Egypt.[19]

It is not surprising that the earliest forms of religious belief centre on death rituals because death appears to be the most mysterious, disturbing and devastating event which humanity has been confronted with and it continues to be so in most cultures. Mortuary rituals could be interpreted as liberation of the deceased from its human existence and preparation for its new existence in the spirit world.[20] This is testimony of how the first symbols acted as a coping mechanism for our ancestors.

3.3.1 Symbols as a coping mechanism

Symbolic representations allowed our ancestors to make sense of the world around them.[21] Natural forces and events which were overwhelming for early humans were interpreted as supernatural powers and associated with particular species of animals and physical phenomena such as mountains, rivers, the sun, the wind or the moon.[22] The archaeological data reveals that prehistoric religion centred on and developed around critical and perplexing situations which early forms of human beings were confronted with in everyday experience, namely birth, death and daily survival. The daily struggle for survival combined with the external world experiences which were outside their control and comprehension caused an emotional strain which needed to be overcome. Life depended on hunting, seasons and such unpredictable events and situations. This led to ritual techniques being devised in order to relieve the strains of daily life and give expression to urgent needs associated with stressful and conflicted situations such as the need to kill animals to eat which necessarily interfered with man's sense of kinship.[23] It also led to the visualisation of divine forces and to symbolic representation in order to control phenomena which are now explained by science. This was a way of redirecting energy into activities and to gain strength in order to overcome life crises. Symbols therefore are a testimony to the timeless effort of human beings to explain and contain the unknown forces of the universe.[24]

3.3.2 Symbols as an early form of expression

Symbols throughout history have been used to convey meaning[25] and as such they operate in the realm of consciousness rather than being external to the self. Cultural anthropology defines symbols as the building blocks of language, culture and social practice and as such they have shaped our understanding of the world throughout history.[26] At the dawn of civilisation, the world was interpreted symbolically, human beings used images and symbols to make sense of their surroundings and to attempt to explain what then seemed inexplicable as well as to predict the unpredictable.[27] In that sense, the use of symbols satisfied the human desire to control earthly forces which seemed alien to humans and as such induced fear. Early forms of symbols therefore emerged as a means of expression and communication and as such preceded language.[28] With the emergence of language, symbols continued to be used to express deeply spiritual concepts which could not be translated into words[29] and to a certain extent cultural and religious symbols continue to perform that function today. Lighting candles for instance is a long-standing practice common to many religions and can be used for prayer, as a way to remember the deceased, as a source of hope or to bring divine light into one's life. The light of a candle has a reassuring and soothing effect but the exact significance of the ritual is deeply spiritual and cannot fully be articulated or described. As such, symbols can be seen as codification of metaphors which provide an insight into centuries of 'profound thinking'.[30] Over time, images and signs developed into sacred symbols or symbols of identity.[31] In world religions, those symbols came to be considered as a bridge to the sacred. In contemporary forms of religions, those symbols continue to provide a bridge between the world of humans and the world of God. The function of symbols therefore is to allow access to invisible realities[32] such as coming into being, passing away, light and darkness, good and evil and to direct the individual away from the superficial concerns of life towards the centre of existence. Lurker points out that the true symbol is 'a signpost to another world';[33] it allows individuals to see below the surface of material things to access the spiritual. This is still true of those symbols that have survived in the modern world such as for instance the worship of idols in certain religions or incantations and rituals around light which serve a spiritual as opposed to purely material function.

3.3.3 Symbols as a source of power

Throughout history symbols have been used to convey power, might and status. The first symbols were linked to power, humans derived powers from the sacred in order to gain protection from those forces of the universe which they were trying to contain. In order to understand how symbols, rituals and sacred spaces developed it is useful to use Eliade's understanding of symbolism called 'symbolism of the centre'.

In his seminal work *Images and Symbols*, the historian of religion, Eliade, describes symbols and images as a metaphor for lost paradise. He explains how throughout history man had a propensity to living at the 'Centre', which he describes as a sacred space as opposed to profane. The Centre according to Eliade is akin to a search for 'lost paradise'.[34] He argues that archaic[35] and traditional societies construed their surroundings as 'microcosm' and that anything beyond this closed world was seen as the dangerous unknown, place of the dead, the enemies and general chaos.[36] The centre of this microcosm however is considered as 'the sacred space', provider of reassurance, protection and justification. Enemies threatening the microcosm were imagined as the incarnation of hostile and destructive power.[37] The first symbols therefore were intended as magical defences to destructive powers and evil spirits. Eliade posits that ditches, labyrinths and ramparts found in many cities such as Carcassonne in France or Bath in England could have been used as defence against evil spirits,[38] although archaeologists normally attribute them to physical defences.[39] The 'Centre' therefore was considered by archaic and traditional society as the only safe place to evolve. This safe centre is what Eliade calls 'the sacred', it represents the only reality man is sure of and as such the centre is a place of power and represents reality.[40] This centre or sacred space is the 'cosmos' and beyond the cosmos there is 'chaos'.[41] The most primitive forms of lives therefore drew power and force from the sacred.[42] Eliade argues that symbols and rituals developed from these primary experiences of sacred space. Temples for instance were seen as 'imago mundi' or an image of the world, a miniature replica of the cosmos. Symbols at the centre can take different forms and expression, such as for instance the Cosmic Mountain, the World Tree or the central Pillar which we find in primitive religions. For example, Chief Mountain in Montana remains a sacred place to the Blackfoot Americans who continue to consider it as part of their identity and as a spiritual place emanating from the creator. This has given rise to a number of legal disputes concerning interference with the land by the Federal state.[43] Similarly, according to Mayan mythology, the Ceiba tree was considered sacred by the ancient Maya who saw it as a symbol of the universe with roots going into the underworld, the trunk representing the middle world and the branches reaching to the Over world considered as the heavens.[44] Symbols at the centre may be an object such as the cross in Christianity, for instance, or can be a sacred space such as Mecca for Muslims,[45] or Jerusalem for Jews. Access to these sacred centres for Eliade deepens religious commitment[46] and as such it empowers individuals with energy and confidence by providing a sanctuary for people to energise. This will be discussed further below in relation to ancient civilisations.

3.3.4 Symbols as the building blocks of collective identity

Symbols allow people to lay claim to a distinct identity. Symbolisation, which is the use of symbols to convey meanings, was used throughout history to communicate aspects of social identity. Membership of a family, clan, tribe or country has been asserted symbolically. This can be seen for instance with African scarification marks which may symbolise initiation or tribal identity,[47] country flags which are the defining symbol of national identity and summary of a country's history, culture and idiosyncrasies.[48] Similarly, in North America, sculptures carved into large trees called totem poles were used by indigenous people from the Pacific North-West Coast as an emblem of a clan or tribe. The poles were painted and carved with figures of totemic creatures such as animals or plants believed to have symbolic significance. A totem pole (see Figure 3.1) tells the story of a particular tribe or clan and as such is unique to the tribe or clan it represents. The word 'totem' is derived from the Odjibwe (indigenous language) word '*odoodem*' which means 'his kinship group'.[49]

Symbols, as an early form of expression also had a unifying function. To appreciate the value of a symbol one needs to be part of the group to which it relates as the symbol only makes sense to the group it is intended for and as such requires all parties to know its meaning. As noted by Lurker, a symbol is meant to direct the initiate to something higher and to reveal it to him while at the same time concealing it from the ignorant.[50] A good example is the *ichthys* or 'sign of the fish' in Christianity (see Figure 3.2) which was used by early Christians (1st century AD) as a secret symbol when they had to hide their belief in Jesus Christ to avoid persecutions by the Romans.[51] The Fish symbol which is made up of two arcs pointing in different directions to form a fish was used by Christians to mark meeting places, tombs or in order to distinguish friends from foes.[52]

Figure 3.1 Totem pole

Figure 3.2 Ichthys

Similarly, in contemporary Judaism spinning top games called 'dreidels'[53] are a symbol of the Festival of Light (*Hanukkah*) and they serve to recall a time when according to the story, Jews under Greek rule were forbidden to study the Bible (*Torah*). The story relates that children used to meet secretly to study Torah and when the Greeks questioned them they pretended to play with a dreidel. The story of *Hanukkah* dates back to the second century BC – unlike most of the Jewish holidays it is not mentioned in the Bible but recorded in Macabees I and II which are two books not considered part of the Jewish canon.[54]

Symbols throughout history therefore have contributed to the construction of collective identity by rallying believers, forming group allegiance and keeping the community in good connection. Symbols were a way of gathering a community via a visible sign.[55] This will now be discussed in relation to ancient civilisations and more modern religions.

3.4 Symbols in ancient civilisations: The Egyptians and the Americans

Egyptian art in the form of wall paintings, statues and architecture is a testimony to the importance that symbols had in ancient Egypt.[56] The Egyptians used symbols to evoke basic concepts of human life such as health, prosperity or eternity[57] and the whole environment around them was depicted symbolically as a means to express fears and doubts about the nature of life.[58] The Egyptians therefore lived in a world of images. All Egyptian culture was of religious origin and laws were religious commandments given by the Creator and enforced by the Pharaoh.[59] There is no codified record of Egyptian laws but the evidence available shows the existence of a legal system based on Maat,[60] a goddess who was the representation of truth, justice and order.[61] Symbols therefore primarily derived from a need to understand the forces of the universe and to create a bridge between the macrocosm (the universe) and the microcosm (the self) in order to connect with the Divine. Egyptian symbols could be found in architecture,[62] rituals[63] and body ornaments.[64] Many symbols could be worn on the person and were also buried with the dead in the hope that they would bring rebirth. Many of the Egyptian symbols were linked to the success of the Pharaoh's kingdom and as such embodied power and conferred a status to the individual. This is a common function of symbols in ancient civilisations. There are ample representations of the Pharaoh in Egyptian Art and he can be seen wearing the *Nemes* headdress (Figure 3.3), a wig-covering usually made of striped material which goes

Figure 3.3 Nemes

across the forehead and is tied at the back with two flaps hanging down the side. The *Nemes* was usually worn over a crown and can also be found on funeral masks like the blue and gold mask of Tutankhamun.[65]

The Egyptians saw divine forces in earthly elements such as water, air and fire, which were all personified in mythical figures.[66] As a result, there are countless symbols associated with Ancient Egypt and here is not the place to provide an exhaustive list but it suffices to evoke a few of them to understand the place symbols played in our ancestors' history. The original significance of Egyptian symbols is not known but studies by archaeologists, historians and Egyptologists have resulted in a number of plausible interpretations for symbols. In addition, the Egyptians were literate and had a writing system called hieroglyphs where symbols or drawings were used to represent sounds and words. Ancient Egypt is usually associated with the ankh (Figure 3.4), the eye of Horus (Figure 3.5) and the *was* sceptre (Figure 3.6). The ankh is a hieroglyphic ideograph which means life and is believed to have been a symbol of eternal life associated with the gods of ancient Egypt. It appears frequently in Egyptian tomb paintings and art and is often seen in the hands of a god or goddess being offered to the kings as a sign of eternal life.[67] The Eye of Horus is a symbol of protection – it was regarded as the symbol of the moon and was believed to protect against evils and was found on jewellery or on the side of coffins.[68] The *was* sceptre is a long straight instrument with an angled top terminating with an animal head and a forked bottom which was often depicted in the hands of the gods and goddesses or carried by pharaohs as a symbol of well-being and happiness. In Egyptian hieroglyphs, the *was* sceptre character means power.[69]

Similar themes can be observed with symbols amongst native Americans whose belief system was based on animism, a belief that everything including objects and nature is alive. While different Native American tribes had different myths,

Figure 3.4 Ankh

Figure 3.5 Eye of Horus

Figure 3.6 Sceptre

animism was a shared belief amongst Native Americans and rituals and symbols served as a way of venerating the sources of nature as well as attempting to control what were sometimes seen as angry spirits.[70] Native Americans used rituals and symbols as a means of communication with nature as well as a way of acquiring personal dignity and power by clothing their body with artefacts made from natural resources which would give the wearer the qualities of the material they were made of.[71] Feather headdresses (Figure 3.7) for instance were worn to gain power and calm the spirits of the universe. In the same way, feather capes worn by the Cherokee were intended to give the wearer the attributes of the bird which was seen as extremely powerful and as such conferred status on the wearer.[72]

Rituals and symbols also had an important community building function amongst Native Americans. Villages had a designated space where rituals and dances would take place. This is where totem poles (discussed above) were erected. The dances were aimed at celebrating and thanking the forces of nature. The Sun dances for example alluded to the generation and regeneration of the world and were a way of thanking the sun for a flourishing harvest.[73] These dances were often accompanied by body 'sacrifices' representing an act of bravery and suffering as a way of acknowledging the beneficence of nature. During the Sun dance for instance young men were harpooned by skewers through the skin and muscles and hoisted above the ground as a sign of sacrifice on behalf of the community in order to ask for healing and purification. Evidence of the Sun Dance can be found in paintings.[74] In ancient civilisations therefore symbols and rituals formed an integral part of human life and assisted our ancestors in making sense of the world around them. In the next section, we explore how rituals and symbols have evolved in modern religions.

Figure 3.7 Feather headdress

3.5 Symbols in modern religions

In this section, we examine the role of symbols in the three major mono-theistic religions namely, Judaism, Christianity and Islam. There are various movements both within Judaism and Christianity and beliefs, practices and orthodoxy vary greatly between them. Symbols are also present in polytheistic and non-religious movements. Hinduism and Buddhism for instance use the Aum symbol (Figure 3.8), the lotus flower (Figure 3.9) as well as the swastika (Figure 3.10), while Humanists use the Happy Human Symbol (Figure 3.11). It is not possible within the constraints of this section to provide a full account of all of these religions or to address the complexities of religious laws, but the aim here is at least to provide the reader with an overview of the place of symbols in modern religions.

Figure 3.8 Aum

Figure 3.9 Lotus

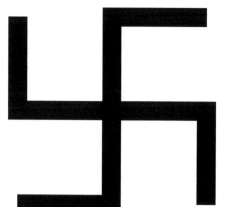

Figure 3.10 Swastika

Figure 3.11 Happy Human

3.5.1 Religions of the book: Judaism and Christianity

Judaism

While there is a proscription in the Jewish Bible of the depiction of living creatures: 'You shall not make for yourself an image in the form of anything in heaven above or on the earth beneath or in the waters below',[75] there are ample representations of mystical concepts in Judaism. The star of David, a 6-pointed star made up of two interlocking triangles pointing in opposite directions is the primary symbol of Jewish identity (Figure 3.12) and appears on the flag of Israel although it is not per se a religious symbol as it is not mentioned in the Jewish Bible (*Torah*) or Talmud (the collection of commentaries on the Jewish Bible). There are a number of explanations for the significance of the Magen David

Figure 3.12 Maguen David (Star of David)

(Hebrew for 'shield of David') including the star being the shape of King David's[76] shield, hence its name. In addition to the Israeli flag the symbol can be found on Israeli ambulances, at the entrance of synagogues and on Jewish sacred items such as *mezuzot* (small boxes containing a parchment scroll with verses from the Torah written on it and placed on the doorposts of Jewish homes to fulfil a mitzvah (biblical commandment)). Other Jewish symbols include the Menorah, a seven branched candelabra, and the *shofar*, a hollowed-out ram's horn used as a ritual trumpet.[77]

Jewish Law called *Halakhah* is a combination of the divine commandments which are believed to come from God found in the Torah and the rabbinic laws and traditions which are the laws which derive from the rabbinical decrees, interpretations and customs. Jewish law governs not just religious practice per se but every aspect of Jewish life, including food, clothing, family life, running one's household, conducting business, etc.[78]

Clothing the body forms an important part of Judaism and many rituals and observances are performed through clothing. The Torah provides a set of laws for both men's and women's clothing mainly based on the concept of modesty (*Tzniut*). Deuteronomy (*D'varim*) 22:5 notably prohibits dressing in clothes of the opposite sex for both men and women which is why Orthodox Jewish women do not wear trousers and adhere to certain rules concerning modesty. More liberal denominations such as Conservative or Reform Jews are generally less observant and do not follow these rules strictly. Observant Jewish men for instance can sometimes be seen with fringes hanging from their shirt, these are called *tzitzit* and originate from the Jewish Bible. *Torah* 15:38–39 refers to *tzitzit* as four knotted tassels which must hang from each corner of a two panel undergarment. There are two forms of *tzitzit*, one is a form of undergarment which is worn every day while the other one is a prayer shawl called *tallit* traditionally worn to attend morning and Saturday (*Shabbat*) prayers at synagogue. The *tallit* is also part of burial rites as men are wrapped in their *tallit* for burial. The *tzitzit* or fringes are worn as a reminder to perform all the other commandments contained in the Jewish Bible (15:38–39). The fringes are a symbol for the 613 commandments (*mitzvot*) of the Bible which are believed to be God's law and are a form of contract between God and the Jewish people. Each Hebrew letter has a numerical value and the letters of the Hebrew word *tzitzit* added up together make 600, if we add the eight strings and five knots of each tassel, the total is 613 like the 613 *mitzvot* of the Bible.[79]

In addition, Jewish men also wear a skullcap (*kippah*) as a symbol of submission to God, but this is not as such an obligation stemming from the *Torah* but rather a custom that evolved from Talmudic times. There is some level of disagreement amongst rabbinical authorities as to whether wearing a *kippah* is or is not a halachic requirement. While some classify it as a measure of piety,[80] others maintain that it should now be recognised as a religious requirement.[81] Some say that covering one's head in Judaism also came as a reaction to the Christian custom to pray bareheaded and therefore arose from a desire of Jews to be different and assert their identities.[82] It remains that the *kippah* has become a strong symbol of Jewish identity. Jewish Orthodox married women also cover their hair to achieve modesty and privacy.[83]

The Torah also provides for circumcision of male infants (Leviticus 12:3). If a woman gives birth to a baby boy, on the eighth day he is to be circumcised. The *Brit Milah* or ritual circumcision is a symbol of partnership with God. The Hebrew word '*brit*' means covenant and as such the ceremony which consists of removing the foreskin from a baby boy's penis symbolises his entrance into a Covenant with God. The practice of circumcision which also takes place amongst Muslims is a controversial practice which has come under criticism mainly for health and ethical reasons. The health benefits of the practice have been highly questioned by professionals and there seems to be no agreement as to whether the practice brings health benefits.[84] Some have argued that the practice is akin to male genital mutilation[85] and that it infringes a child's autonomy as the child is unable to agree the practice which affects his own body integrity. The practice has given rise to court cases and especially in situations when parents do not agree as to whether a child should be circumcised.[86]

This brief overview of Judaism therefore demonstrates that Judaism as a religion is a way of life, imbued with practice as every aspect of life is government by religious commandments. Symbols and rituals play a very important part in the Jewish faith as they relate to the core of group identity. In addition, manifestation of belief plays a very important part in making the faith visible. We will see that this is similar in Islam but less so in Christianity.

Christianity

The Christian Bible consists of the Old and the New Testament. Christianity is regulated by canon law, the religious law of the Church. Like Judaism, Christianity regulates many aspects of life, such as birth, marriage and divorce, albeit with a more limited level of 'control' over the life of the community.

There are different Christian traditions worldwide including Catholics, Protestants and Orthodox. There is no single system of Christian Law similar to Jewish Law or Islamic Law which broadly applies to all members of the faith. Instead, each Church has its own laws and regulations based on their interpretation of the Bible. There are however strong similarities between the various Christian traditions as laws mainly derive from the Bible and the dominant teaching of Christianity, namely that salvation through Christ is a matter of human faith and divine grace.[87] Most Churches have laws and regulatory instruments which together with the Bible contribute to the life of the Church as an institution. These laws govern notably internal and external relations of church ministry, worship, ritual, ecumenism and property. The laws of the Church are designed to facilitate and order the life of the Church and fulfil its divine mission.[88]

All the Christian Churches provide for rites of passage such as baptism, the profession of the faith, the Eucharist, the Holy Communion, marriage and divorce, but not all Christian traditions classify them as sacraments. Sacraments are seen as conveying spiritual grace while ordinances have a symbolic function. Nearly all Christian denominations (not Quakers) see baptism as a sacrament, which symbolises the incorporation of a person into the Church of Christ. It is administered with water in the name of the triune God.[89]

The life of Jesus Christ is at the heart of Christian symbolism and most Christian rituals serve to remember and celebrate the life, death and resurrection of Christ. There is a special meaning associated with it as Christ is seen as the embodiment of God's words and the Saviour.[90] Symbolically, Jesus Christ's dying reveals that life can come out of death and therefore gives meaning to death, hence Christians' belief in the afterlife. The main symbol of Christianity is the Latin cross (see Figure 3.13) which reminds Christians of the crucifixion. The fish sign which was discussed above is another symbol of Christianity and can sometimes be seen displayed on car bumpers. It is believed that the symbol was used as early as the first century by Early Christians who made an acrostic out of the Greek word for fish – *ichthys* which was used as a coded message for *Iesous Christos, Theou Yios, Soter* (Jesus Christ, Son of God, Saviour).[91]

Christian rituals serve to formalise the commitment to faith as shown in the Eucharist – bread and wine stand for the body and blood of Christ as per the

Figure 3.13 Latin cross

Gospel 'Unless you eat my flesh and drink my blood, you cannot have life in you' (John 6:53). Baptism, communion and marriage are further prophetic rituals showing a commitment to God and in anticipation of God's promise of life after death. As such, then, those rituals provide a source of hope to the community. But one could also argue that those rituals as any religious rituals may be perceived as fear-inducing for some individuals as they send the message that unless those rituals are performed the promise of life after death may not be fulfilled. This relates to religion as a coercive force and is linked to another function of rituals and symbols which is to fight evil. This concept of evil is perpetuated in part from the unknown and in part from the message of the Bible just as in Judaism. The message that the root of evil in human life is the abuse of freedom is one that many religions perpetuate[92] and this can be seen as limiting for those individuals who do not adhere to religious principles. Many religious rituals therefore are a way of countering evils by making a commitment to avoid a life of sin.

Islam

Like Jewish Law, Islamic Law is a religious legal system which governs every aspect of life and which is believed to be divinely revealed. It is an unquestioned assumption in modern Islam that theology and legal reasoning are permissible only to assert God's will as expressed in the Koran and the Sunnah.[93] The Koran is the Muslim Holy book which is believed to be a compilation of the verbal revelations of God (*Allah*) to the Prophet Mohammed while the Sunnah are believed to be God's revelations but conveyed in the words and practice of the Prophet Mohammed. The Koran is more generic while the Sunnah provide more details as to how the Koran is to be implemented. The Koran and the Sunnah constitute the basis of Islamic Law.[94]

There are five main schools of thought in Islam (*madhahib*), each named after their founders, namely Ja'fari (23% of Muslims), Hanafi (31% of Muslims), Maliki (25% of Muslims), Shafi'i (16% of Muslims) and Hanbali (4% of Muslims). The remaining percentage follows minority schools.[95] All of the schools are based on the Koran but differ in their interpretation.

In Islam as in Judaism, there is a prohibition against portraying living beings and depicting Allah or the Prophet Mohammed would amount to blasphemy. The Koran does not specify a symbol for Islam but some symbols became associated with Islam – they stem from artistic imagination rather than the holy book itself. The colour green for instance is usually associated with Islam – this is a cultural heritage from the Ottoman Empire.[96] We also tend to see geometric patterns in mosques and Islamic art – this is in keeping with the Islamic tradition of aniconism which is the prohibition in Islam on the representation of human and animal figures although some schools of thought believe that inanimate forms of life such as plants are acceptable for art work.[97] Islamic art avoids anything that could be an idol for men and distract them from God (Allah); as such it creates a void and conveys the spiritual message of Islam. As Burckhardt puts it, 'This void which Islamic art creates by its static, impersonal and anonymous quality enables man to be entirely himself, to repose in his ontological center where he is both the slave (*abd*) of God and His representative (*khalīfah*) on earth.'[98]

Islam controls every aspect of daily life including food and clothing – Islamic symbols and religious manifestation are also visible through clothing and as in Judaism, the Islamic dress code is focused on the concept of modesty. The dress code applies to both men and women and as in Judaism its purpose is to keep distance between the sexes but also to keep modesty as prescribed by the Koran:

> Say to the believing men that they should lower their gaze and guard their modesty: that will make for greater purity for them: and God is well acquainted with all that they do. And say to the believing women that they should lower their gaze and guard their modesty; that they should not display their *zeenah* (charms, or beauty and ornaments) except what (must ordinarily) appear thereof; that they should draw their *khimar* (veils) over their bosoms and not display their *zeenah* except to their husbands, their fathers … and that they should not strike their feet so as to draw attention to their hidden *zeenah* (ornaments).
>
> (Koran 24:31–32)

> O Prophet! Tell your wives and daughters and the believing women that they should draw over themselves their *jilbab* (outer garments) (when in public); this will be more conducive to their being recognized (as decent women) and not harassed. But God is indeed oft-forgiving, most merciful.
>
> (33:59)

There are different interpretations of these requirements and the various schools of thought differ on more 'technical' issues, such as what exactly constitutes *awra*, the part of the body that is inviolable or what body parts should be covered in the presence of *maharim* (relatives and next of kin with whom marriage is prohibited) but they all centre on the concept of modesty and contact between men and women.[99] In modern pluralist societies, Islamic dress has also become a political symbol and there is much controversy and stigma around Muslim head covering especially for women. This will be discussed further in Part II.

In addition to dress, Islam has rules for every aspect of daily life and therefore much like Judaism it is a way of life as well as a religion. As in Judaism, there are strict laws in relation to dress as well as daily rituals which make the faith highly visible (this is discussed further below), especially since it is part of a minority both in Europe and North America. In addition, the Muslim population is far from homogenous as it originates from a wide geographical spread. Immigration of Muslim populations in France, the UK and the US mirrors former colonies. As a result, French Muslims typically originate from North Africa while British Muslims are largely from Asia and Muslim Americans are very diverse but tend to be of African descent. Those populations bring with them their cultural as well as religious baggage. This is visible in relation to customs of clothing and food for instance. The perpetuation amongst those groups of religious, cultural and traditional customs provides them with a sense of identity. This is discussed in detail in the next chapter.

In modern religions, as in ancient civilisations, rituals and symbols have been omnipresent. Historians and archaeologists have made and continue to make sense of the nature of our ancestors' life through symbols and rituals. The above historical overview is a testimony to the centrality of symbols and rituals for religious communities. In the next section, we look at the development of religion law, the law of the state which concerns itself with religion and religious manifestation in order to understand how symbols and rituals came to attract 'special' protection from the law.

3.6 Origin of Religious Freedom as a Human Right

As demonstrated by the above brief historical overview of symbolic manifestation within both ancient and modern forms of religions, symbols and rituals are key to the development and maintenance of religious group identity. Religious symbols however are not directly protected by the law. What is protected rather is the freedom of thought, conscience and religion and by extension the manifestation of such beliefs, although the latter can be subjected to restrictions. It is paradoxical that religious freedom is born out of persecutions and religious intolerance, the very ideas that it purports to protect against. The road to religious freedom was indeed long and chaotic and it was not until the 16th and 17th centuries that the concept of religious freedom started to emerge, following years of religious wars and persecution both in Europe and the United States.[100]

The idea of religious freedom was alien to religions throughout history because the essence of religion was to contain the truth and, as discussed above, life outside the 'microcosm' was deemed dangerous and therefore human beings were dominated by the idea of fear of anyone different. Religious wars were marked by conquest and the urge for expansion as the idea that different ethnic and religious groups could share a territory was alien to our ancestors. Religion was also used to control the masses and became a potent tool for power especially when religion and state were merged and the former was used by the latter to gain legitimacy.

The development of freedom of religion as a human right is an important step towards the end of absolutism and states' religious compulsion[101] and is closely linked to the separation of religion from the state fuelled by the French revolution of 1789 or the American War of independence (1775–1783). The human right to religious freedom as enshrined in article 18 of the UDHR and subsequent international treaties acknowledges the freedom of thought, conscience and religion both individual and collective as well as the freedom to change one's religion and belief.[102] It respects belief and unbelief, religion and non-religion. In that sense it is a potent symbol of liberalism and has become a key feature of modern pluralist democracies.

What initially gave religion special protection by the law therefore is the historical context of intolerance and persecution. Religious symbols by their very nature have always been at the receiving end of the expression of intolerance. They are vulnerable to the expression of hatred and intolerance because they serve to define a group just as race, colour or ethnicity do.

Indeed, over the years, symbols established themselves as strong markers of identity. Religious symbols even today are vulnerable and are a target for racism, religious and racial discrimination. When a pig's head is left outside a mosque or a swastika painted on the walls of a synagogue, it is the community that is targeted through its symbols.[103] Similarly, when a Sikh man is assaulted because he is wearing a turban it is his symbol that is making him a target.[104] Yet the devoutly religious do not give up their symbolic markers to avoid persecution. On the contrary, religious symbols at times become political and are worn to make a point. This was the case with the Muslim headscarf in France following the head-scarf affair (*l'affaire des foulards* 1989) in the late 1980s.[105] Religious symbols therefore are a prime target for the expression of racial and religious hatred as well as discrimination.[106] They are very vulnerable to a given political climate. The resurgence of racial hatred targeted at minorities such as anti-Semitism or Isla-mophobia typically follows the pattern of national or international events. As such, anti-Semitism peaks tend to follow the Israeli-Palestinian conflict[107] while Isla-mophobia tends to rise in the aftermath of a terrorist attack.[108] As Gunn puts it, religion is not merely about the expression of faith, it is also the focus of pre-judice.[109] Gunn highlights the close connection between religion, ethnicity, family, culture, tradition and history; when a religious symbol is attacked therefore it is all of those aspects that are being targeted; 'the chief reason why religion becomes the focus of prejudice is that it usually stands for more than faith – it is the pivot of the cultural tradition of a group.'[110]

Religious persecution, discrimination and prejudice have taken different facets. Entire religious groups have been persecuted by states as in the case of Jews in Nazi Germany, states have prohibited the exercise of minority religions as in some Islamic countries like Saudi Arabia and Iran where religious minorities can only practise their faith in private.[111] Religion in those states can have coercive powers on individuals, people may be forced to comply with religious rules against their will. This can be seen in Saudi Arabia for instance where women are bound by a strict religious dress code. Similarly, communism as an ideology rejects religion and in the Soviet Union, religious properties were confiscated and those who practised a religion were harassed.[112] In modern pluralist states, religious groups may be the subject of discrimination especially if their religion is more than a belief and is associated with actions, rituals and traditions which are different from those of the majority. Some of those practices may not be accommodated by the law of the particular state, resulting in religious discrimination. The French law banning religious symbols at school for instance may result in adherents of minority faiths having to attend private faith schools or remaining in state school but giving up their religious garb.[113] This will be discussed further in Part II of the book.

Religions and religious groups have also been persecuted by other religious groups mainly because persecutors see the attacked religion as a threat to their own identity.[114] Gunn highlights three different facets of religion including reli-gion as belief, religion as identity and religion as a way of life. The last two categories are more likely to be targeted because they are more visible than religion as belief. Religion as identity and as a way of life go beyond doctrines and link religion to ethnicity, family, culture, tradition and history.[115] Christianity, which is the dominant faith in Europe and the United States, is more likely to fall under the category of religion as belief mainly because as a religion it does not impose a specific dress code on its participants and therefore it is less visible. Judaism, Islam and Sikhism on the other hand tend to be more visible because of the religious requirement that followers dress in a certain way.

Finally, persecution and prejudice can also come from the religions themselves when individuals are being coerced into joining a particular religious movement. This is often with the aim of converting or rallying participants. People as a result may be forced to comply with religious rules against their will. This is a common occurrence in those countries where the law of the land is the religious law and mainly affects women. This is the case in Islamic countries like the Kingdom of Saudi Arabia or Iran where women's rights are severely restricted by religious precepts.[116]

It is clear therefore that religion and its many facets has been both the subject and the cause of the expression of hatred, prejudice and discrimination. As such, it has merited special legal protection alongside other categories such as sex, gender or ethnicity but it has also become necessary for states to limit the exercise of religious expression especially when a specific practice infringes upon someone's else's freedom. The relationship between law and religion will be examined in subsequent chapters.

3.7 Concluding remarks

Religious or cultural symbols and rituals throughout history have shaped human consciousness in the sense of being aware of one's individual and collective identity. Symbols and rituals emerged as a means of making sense of the then seemingly inexplicable forces of nature and conferred power, status and reassurance by acting as a bridge to the sacred. In contemporary pluralist societies, despite Western culture being mostly dominated by rationalism and consumerism, human beings continue to use religious symbols to articulate their interconnection with divine forces.[117] This will be explored in the next chapter. Religious minorities typically adopt a different style of dress, shared by their community, which serves to bind the community together as well as distinguishing it from others. Religious dress provides the wearer with a sense of identity and belonging while also reminding her or him of the history of the community. Rituals and sacred spaces contribute to community building and reinforcing group identity. Religion as belief is a category that is relatively easier for the adjudicator to grasp but as rightly put by Gunn, it is religion as identity and religion as a way of life which the adjudicator should seek to understand since it is the underlying cause of religious persecution and discrimination.[118] In modern pluralist states, it can be argued that contemporary non-religious symbols and rituals which relate to national culture, social class, sports or politics play an equally important role in the expression of identity and as such may also qualify for protection by the law. As discussed above in Chapter 2, international human rights law acknowledges this by protecting religion and belief more generally. Yet, in modern pluralist states, individuals and groups are rarely discriminated against based on their political affiliation or what football team they support while religion continues to be a strong marker of identity and religious groups are still a vulnerable category which is why the law drew parameters around religion in the first place. In this context, the next chapter explores the functionality of religious symbols in modern pluralist states.

Notes

1   Emerson 1836. Ch. 1.
2   Human nature is fear-driven and anything that is unfamiliar can be a source of fear, questioning or rejection. See further Ehrlich 2000.
3   By 'preoccupation' I refer to the increased visibility of symbols and the renewed interest that law makers, politicians, judges and the media dedicate to the issue as well as the increase in academic literature on the issue. As argued by M. D. Evans 2010: '...few issues have attracted as much attention as the wearing or visibility of religious symbols in public institutions, public spaces and in the workplace', at 291.
4   James 1956.
5   Oxford Dictionary [online] Available from www.oed.com
6   Moritz and Goldammer n.d.
7   Idem.
8   Tambiah 1979, cited in Bowie 2006. 141–42.
9   *R (on the application of Williamson and others)* v. *Secretary of State for Education and Employment* [2005] UKHL 15.
10   Scharffs 2012. 44.
11   Scharffs 2012. 42.
12   Scharffs 2012. 44.
13   *Mount Soledad Memorial Association v. Trunk*, No. 11–998 (2012).
14   Prehistoric religion refers to religious beliefs and practices of prehistoric peoples. It includes Palaeolithic, Mesolithic, Neolithic and Bronze Age religion.
15   See further James 1957.
16   See for instance Monte Circeo in Italy in a grotto discovered in 1939 and which dates back to Neanderthal man, 70 to 100,000 years ago, in James 1957, op. cit. 17–33.
17   Idem.
18   James 1957, op. cit. 97. See also Lurker 1980.
19   James 1957, op. cit. 109.
20   Ibid. 144.
21   Gibson 2009. 10.
22   James 1957, op. cit. 229.
23   Idem.
24   Adkinson 2009.7.
25   See further Kenner 2006.
26   Lambek 2008. 129.
27   Adkinson 2009, op. cit. 7.
28   See for instance the Egyptian hieroglyphs – hieroglyphs are the ancient Egyptian language which used ideograms to signify entire words and as such had symbolic value. The sign for heaven for instance was a roof, the sign for life and soul was a bird, two legs signified to walk, etc. See further Lurker 1980. op. cit.
29   Kenner 2006, op. cit. 133 onwards.
30   Kenner 2006, op. cit. 133.
31   Gibson, 2009, op. cit. 36.
32   Lurker 1980, op. cit. 9.

33   Idem.
34   Eliade 1991. Chapter 1.
35   In history and archaeology, the Archaic Period is the period ranging from 8000 to 1000 BC.
36   Eliade 1991, op. cit. 37 onwards.
37   Op. cit. 39.
38   Idem.
39   See further Christie and Herold 2016.
40   Eliade 1959. 12.
41   Ibid. 29.
42   Ibid. 12.
43   See further Craig, Yung and Borrie 2012.
44   Yucatan Today n.d. La Ceiba: Sacred Maya Tree [online].
45   Dadosky 2010. 145.
46   Idem.
47   National Geographic Channel n.d. Scarification.
48   Kenner 2006, op. cit. 122.
49   Gibson 2009, op. cit. 30 onwards.
50   Lurker 1980. 9.
51   Gibson 2009, op. cit. 196.
52   Coffman 2008.
53   A dreidel is a four-sided spinning top with a letter of the Hebrew alphabet on each side. Together those letters (Nun, Gimmel, Hei and Shin) form the acronym for *Nes Gadol Haya Sham* which means a great miracle happened there.
54   I & II Maccabees (1 Macc 4:36–59; 2 Macc 10:1–8).
55   Rosier-Catach 2006. 54.
56   Ancient Egypt is a period in history which extended between c. 3,000 to 332 BC and preceded the Greco-Roman period.
57   Gibson, 2009, op. cit. 58.
58   Adkinson 2009, op. cit. 8.
59   Lurker 1980, op. cit. 8.
60   Maat was the daughter of Re the sun god.
61   Lurker 1980, op. cit. 78.
62   See the Pyramids which were used for the cult of the King.
63   See for instance ritual regicides performed to provide divine power to the King; see further Lurker 1980, op. cit. 2.
64   For examples of Egyptian symbols see Ziegler 2002.
65   Ziegler 2002, op. cit.
66   See further Lurker 1980, op. cit. at 24 onwards.
67   Lurker 1980, op. cit. 27.
68   Adkinson 2009, op. cit. 61.
69   Ziegler 2002, op. cit. 481, Fig. 244.
70   Adkinson 2009, op. cit. 192.
71   Ibid. 170 onwards.
72   Adkinson, 2009, op. cit. 192.
73   Ibid. 183.
74   Ibid. 182.
75   Exodus 20:4.
76   King David, according to the Hebrew Bible, was a very important figure of Jewish History.
77   On Jewish symbols, see further Frankel and Teutsch 2004.

78 See Rabbi Ganzfried 1927.
79 Code of Jewish Law, Chapter IX, Vol 1. Laws Relating to Fringes, 19.
80 Rabbi Hayim Yosef David Azulai, Israel, 1724–1806.
81 Rabbi David Halevi 1586–1667.
82 Green 2001. 89 onwards.
83 Frankel and Teutsch 2004, op. cit.
84 British Medical Association 2006.
85 See Barkham 2012.
86 See for example *L and B* (Children: Specific Issues: Temporary Leave to Remove from the Jurisdiction: Circumcision) [2016] EWHC 849 (Fam).
87 See further Doe 2013.
88 Ibid. 384–387.
89 Idem.
90 Cooke and Macy 2005. 40.
91 See further Coffman 2008, op. cit. as discussed above.
92 Cooke 2005, op. cit. 49.
93 Picken 2011.
94 Ibid.
95 Al-Islam.com n.d.
96 See further Esposito 1999. 260–61.
97 Kozac 2014.
98 Burckhardt 1970.
99 Maghniyyah n.d.
100 On the history of religious freedom in Europe see Blei 2002For North America see Bittker, Idleman and Ravitch 2015.
101 Olsen and Toddington 2007.178.
102 The international human rights framework for protection of religion and belief is discussed above in Chapter 2.
103 Incidents of this type have occurred in Europe as well as North America. See for instance: The Telegraph 2012and Jerusalem Post 2017.
104 See for instance Phillips 2016.
105 See further Bacquet 2012. This will be discussed further in Chapter 5.
106 See for instance the case of minarets in Switzerland (see further Wyler 2017). See also burqa bans in France discussed in Chapter 5.
107 See further Bacquet 2004.
108 Marsh 2018.
109 Gunn 2003. 202.
110 Gordon W. Allport, *The Nature of Prejudice* 446 (Addison-Wesley Pub. Co. 1979) (1954), cited in Gunn 2003. 203.
111 See Amnesty International n.d. 'Iran 2017/18'.
112 See generally Kraemer 2015.
113 Loi n° 2004–228 du 15 mars 2004 encadrant, en application du principe de laïcité, le port de signes ou de tenues manifestant une appartenance religieuse dans les écoles, collèges et lycées publics (Law of 2004 on religious symbols in primary and secondary state schools). This is discussed in Chapter 5.
114 Gunn 2003, op. cit. 203.
115 Ibid. 200 onwards.
116 See further Human Rights Watch 2015; on Saudi's recent proposal to remove women's ban on driving see: Human Rights Watch 2017.
117 Adkinson 2009, op. cit. 7.
118 Gunn 2003, 200 onwards.

References

Books

Adkinson, R., 2009. *Sacred Symbols: Peoples, Religions, Mysteries.* London: Thames and Hudson.

Bittker, B. I., Idleman, S. C., and Ravitch, F. S., 2015. *Religion and the State in American Law.* Cambridge: Cambridge University Press.

Blei, K., 2002. *Freedom of Religion and Belief: Europe's Story.* Assen, The Netherlands: Van Gorcum.

Bowie, F., 2006. *The Anthropology of Religion.* Oxford: Blackwell Publishing.

Christie, N. and Herold, H. ed., 2016. *Fortified Settlements in Early Medieval Europe: Defended Communities of the 8th–10th Centuries.* Oxford: Oxbow Books.

Cooke, B. and Macy, G., 2005. *Christian Symbol and Ritual: An Introduction.* Oxford: Oxford University Press.

Doe, N., 2013. *Christian Law, Contemporary Principles.* Cambridge: Cambridge University Press.

Eliade, M., 1959. *The Sacred and the Profane.* New York: Harvest Book.

Eliade, M., 1991. *Images and Symbols.* Princeton: Princeton University Press.

Emerson, R. W., 1836. *Nature.* Cambridge: James Munroe and Co.

Ehrlich, P., 2000. *Human Natures: Genes, Cultures, and the Human Prospect.* USA: Island Press.

Esposito, J. L. ed., 1999. *The Oxford History of Islam.* Oxford: Oxford University Press.

Frankel, E. and Teutsch, P., 2004. *The Encyclopedia of Jewish Symbols.* Oxford: Rowman & Littlefield Publishers, Inc.

Gibson, C., 2009. *How to Read Symbols.* Lewes, East Sussex: Ivy Press.

Green, R. M., 2001. *A Brief History of Jewish Dress,* London: Safira.

James, E.O., 1956. *History of Religion,* London: Hodder and Stoughton.

James, E.O., 1957. *Prehistoric Religion.* London: Thames and Hudson.

Kenner, T.A., 2006. *Symbols and Their Hidden Meanings: The Mysterious Significance and Forgotten Origins of Signs and Symbols in the Modern World.* London: Carlton.

Kraemer, S., 2015. *Inside the Cold War from Marx to Reagan: An Unprecedented Guide to the Roots, History, Strategies, and Key Documents of the Cold War.* Lanham, MD: University Press of America.

Lambek, M. ed., 2008. *A Reader in the Anthropology of Religion,* 2nd ed. Oxford: Blackwell Publishing.

Lurker, M., 1980. *The Gods and Symbols of Ancient Egypt,* New York: Thames and Hudson.

Olsen, H. P., and Toddington, S., 2007. *Architecture of Justice: Legal Theory and the Idea of Institutional Design.* London: Routledge.

Picken, G. N. ed., 2011. *Islamic Law.* London: Routledge.

Rabbi Ganzfried, S., 1927. *Code of Jewish Law* (Translated by Hyman E. Goldin). New York: Star Hebrew Book Company.

Rosier-Catach, I., 2006. *Les sacrements comme signes qui font ce qu'ils signifient: signe efficace vs. efficacité symbolique.* Paris: Institut Catholique de Paris.

Tambiah, S. J., 1979. *A Performative Approach to Ritual.* London: Oxford University Press.

Ziegler, C., 2002. *The Pharaohs.* London: Thames & Hudson.

Articles, book chapters and conference papers

Bacquet, S., 2012. 'Religious Freedom in a Secular Society: an Analysis of the French Approach to Manifestation of Belief in the Public Sphere', in CumperP. and LewisT. eds. *Religion, Rights and Secular Society.* Cheltenham: Edward Elgar. 147–168.

Craig, D. R., Yung, L., and Borrie, W. T., 2012. 'Blackfeet Belong to the Mountains: Hope, Loss, and Blackfeet Claims to Glacier National Park, Montana'. *Conservation and Society,* 10(3): 232–242.

Dadosky, J. D., 2010. 'Sacred Symbols as Explanatory. Geertz, Eliade and Lonergan'. *Fu Jen International Religious Studies,* 4(1) Summer: 137–158.

Evans, M. D., 2010. 'Religious Symbols: An Introduction', in FerrariS. and CristoforiR. Eds. *Law and Religion in the 21st Century; Relations between States and Religious Communities.* Farnham: Ashgate. 291–296.

Gunn, J., 2003. 'The Complexity of Religion and the Definition of "Religion" in International Law'. 16*Harv. Hum. Rts. J.,* 189, 202.

Scharffs, B. G., 2012. 'The role of judges in determining the meaning of religious symbols', in Temperman, J., ed. *The Lautsi Papers: Multidisciplinary Reflections on Religious Symbols in the Public Classroom.* Leiden: Martinus Nijhoff, 35–58.

Wyler, D., 2017. 'The Swiss Minaret Ban Referendum and Switzerland's International Reputation: A Vote with an Impact'. *Journal of Muslim Minority Affairs,* 37(4): 413–425.

Websites

Attributed author

Bacquet, S., 2004. 'An Analysis of the Resurgence of Anti-Semitism in France'. *Journal of Diplomatic Language.* 4, https://papers.ssrn.com/sol3/papers.cfm?abstract_id=1337662 [Accessed 17 August 2018]

Burckhardt, T., 1970. 'The Void in Islamic Art', *Studies in Comparative Religion,* 4(2), http://www.studiesincomparativereligion.com/public/articles/The_Void_in_Islamic_Art-by_Titus_Burckhardt.aspx [Accessed 17 August 2018]

Barkham, P., 2012. 'Circumcision: The Cruellest Cut', *The Guardian,* 28 August. https://www.theguardian.com/world/2012/aug/28/circumcision-the-cruellest-cut [Accessed 17 August 2018]

Coffman, E., 2008. 'What is the Origin of the Christian Fish Symbol?' *Christianity Today,* August. http://www.christianitytoday.com/history/2008/august/what-is-origin-of-christian-fish-symbol.html [Accessed 17 August 2018]

Kozac, J. 2014. 'Aniconism in Islamic Art', http://islamic-arts.org/2014/aniconism-in-islamic-art/ [Accessed 18 August 2018]

Maghniyyah, A. M. J., n.d. 'The Rules of Modesty According to Five Islamic Schools of Law'. Al-Islam.org, https://www.al-islam.org/shiite-encyclopedia-ahlul-bayt-dilp-team/rules-modesty-according-five-islamic-schools-law [Accessed 31 August 2018]

Marsh, S., 2018. 'Record Number of Anti-Muslim Attacks Reported in UK Last Year'. *The Guardian,* 20 July. https://www.theguardian.com/uk-news/2018/jul/20/record-number-anti-muslim-attacks-reported-uk-2017 [Accessed 31 August 2018]

Moritz, K. and Goldammer, A., n.d. 'Religious Symbolism and Iconography', Encyclopaedia Britannica, https://www.britannica.com/topic/religious-symbolism/Influence-of-religion-on-symbolism-and-iconography [Accessed 16 August 2018]

Phillips, K., 2016. 'A Sikh Man Was Brutally Attacked by a Group who Removed his Turban, Cut off his Hair'. *The Washington Post*, 8 October. https://www.washingtonp ost.com/news/acts-of-faith/wp/2016/10/08/a-sikh-man-was-brutally-attacked-by-a -group-who-removed-his-turban-cut-off-his-hair/?utm_term=.41e59a85fcf8   [Accessed 17 August 2018]

No attributed author

Al-Islam.com, n.d. 'The Five Schools of Islamic Thought', https://www.al-islam.org/ inquiries-about-shia-islam-sayyid-moustafa-al-qazwini/five-schools-islamic-thought [Accessed 18 August 2018]

Amnesty International, n.d. 'Iran 2017/18', https://www.amnesty.org/en/countries/m iddle-east-and-north-africa/iran/report-iran/ [Accessed 26 October 2018]

British Medical Association, 2006. 'The Law and Ethics of Male Circumcision', June. http s://www.bma.org.uk/advice/employment/ethics/children-and-young-people/ma le-circumcision [Accessed 17 August 2018]

Human Rights Watch, 2015. 'Women's Rights in Iran', October. https://www.hrw.org/ news/2015/10/28/womens-rights-iran [Accessed 17 August 2018]

Human Rights Watch, 2017. 'Saudi Arabia: As Women's Driving Ban Ends, Provide Parity', September.   https://www.hrw.org/news/2017/09/27/saudi-arabia-womens-driving-ba n-ends-provide-parity [Accessed 17 August 2018]

Jerusalem Post, 2017. 'Chicago Synagogue Plastered with Swastikas in Antisemitic Attack', 5 February.   http://www.jpost.com/Diaspora/Chicago-synagogue-plastered-with-swa stikas-in-antisemitic-attack-480598 [Accessed 18 August 2018]

National Geographic Channel, n.d. 'Scarification', https://youtu.be/Lfhot7tQcWs [Accessed 17 August 2018]

Yucatan Today, n.d. 'La Ceiba: Sacred Maya Tree', http://yucatantoday.com/la-ceiba-sa cred-mayan-tree/?lang=en [Accessed 17 August 2018]

The Telegraph, 2012. 'Anger as Pig Heads Dumped outside French Mosque', 1 August. http://www.telegraph.co.uk/news/worldnews/europe/france/9445453/ Anger-as-pig-heads-dumped-outside-French-mosque.html   [Accessed   17   August 2018]

Others

Loi n° 2004–228 of 15 March 2004 encadrant, en application du principe de laïcité, le port de signes ou de tenues manifestant une appartenance religieuse dans les écoles, collèges et lycées publics (Law of 2004 on religious symbols in primary and secondary state schools.)

4 Religious symbols in contemporary pluralist states

4.1 Introduction

> We live in a society that has ... become both increasingly secular but also increasingly diverse in religious affiliation.
>
> Munby LJ Johns Case [2011][1]

Having looked at symbols in a historical and religious context, this chapter now turns to the issue of symbols in contemporary pluralist states. Despite what sociologists have called 'the secularisation thesis',[2] it is now generally accepted that modernisation has not led to the demise of religion and that we are instead witnessing in 21st century modern democracies, a revival of religion.[3] In this chapter, we attempt to elucidate some of the reasons behind this revival of religion which led to symbols becoming more visible in the public sphere as discussed in previous chapters. Doing this requires an understanding of religious symbols' relationship with individuals and their role in the making of modern individual and collective religious identities. As a consequence of symbols' visibility in the public sphere, they have come into close encounter with the law and the courts. Judges are increasingly called upon to adjudicate on disputes related to symbols and rituals; in particular, courts are asked to rule on whether a particular symbol or practice ought to be tolerated in the name of religious freedom. In recent years, courts have had to decide inter alia on whether having a religious symbol in a state school classroom is a breach of the principle of state neutrality,[4] whether state schools are allowed to ban certain religious symbols such as a purity ring,[5] kara bangle,[6] jilbab,[7] niqab[8] or cornrows[9] in order to satisfy their uniform policy and whether banning the full face cover in the public sphere amounts to a breach of article 9 of the ECHR on freedom of religion.[10] These are only a few examples of the range of situations courts have had to deal with and those issues will be explored in more detail in subsequent chapters. This interference of the law with symbols has resulted in some bans in the name of neutrality, health and safety or security, leaving some minority groups unable to manifest their religion in the public sphere.

As discussed in Chapter 3, symbols historically developed as a coping mechanism in order to fulfil human desire to control and contain external forces which were sources of fear. As such, symbols had an explanatory and comforting function. Throughout history, symbols evolved as a form of language, a code which only made sense on the intellectual level of its creator. In modern pluralist societies, science can provide an explanation for nature's phenomena and language is developed to an extent that symbols are not needed as much as they used to be in order to fulfil those functions. Yet as we will see in this chapter, individuals and groups cling to symbols and rituals. In this chapter we attempt to understand this phenomenon by taking a sociological approach to manifestation of belief. This will lay the basis for the legal analysis that follows and allow us to draw some conclusions as to the impact that restrictions on manifestation of belief have on faith minorities.

4.2 The revival of religious symbols: from secularisation to pluralism

Despite the proposition made by sociologists in the latter half of the 20th century, that religion would fade away, we are witnessing in 21st century modern democracies what the Australian sociologist Bouma calls a 'revitalisation' of the role of religion in the public sphere.[11] The secularisation thesis was based on the idea that science would replace religion. The theory was used by social scientists and historians who argued that modernity would result in the decline of religion. Proponents of the secularisation thesis advanced in the 1950s that modernisation had eroded the dominance of religion in society.[12] Reality has in fact shown that there is a resurgence of religion in the public sphere and some like Berger who were advocates of the secularisation thesis now prefer to use the concept of 'pluralism' to explain religion in the modern world.[13] Berger now argues that modernity in fact produces pluralism, the coexistence in the same society of different worldviews and value systems, not secularisation.[14] Berger sees pluralism not as undermining religion but as changing the way it operates.[15] This does not mean however that the secularisation thesis should be discarded altogether. As discussed by Sandberg, it provides a useful explanation of the changing role of religion in society. If the hypothesis that religion would disappear from the public sphere proved to be flawed, what is certain is that some form of societal secularisation has taken place, and this has had a profound impact on the social role played by religious institutions.[16] Indeed, we have seen a transfer of social functions from religious to state institutions as other agencies are now fulfilling roles previously performed by religious institutions, such as in the field of education and welfare. In Europe, church and state have mostly separated. There remain a few exceptions such as England where there is no formal separation between church and state and where the Church of England has the 'privileged'[17] position of Established Church but even then, the Church has a minor role in government affairs. As Sandberg puts it, the key relationship is now between the state and the individual rather than between religion and the individual as legal systems are no longer run by religious communities.[18] This is true of modern pluralist democracies but not countries where religion and politics are merged as in Islamic Republics.

What is sure therefore is that secularisation has contributed if not to the decline at least to the transformation of the place of religion in the public sphere. In addition to secularisation, what the German sociologist Max Weber called 'rationalisation' also contributed to this changing role of religion. Rationalisation involves 'challenging the intellectual basis for truth claims made on the strength of sacred and/or revealed knowledge' and 'calling into question the authority of religious specialists.'[19] This phenomenon has meant that religions are no longer regarded as the only source of authority as natural phenomena can now be explained with science. Efficiency and predictability become more important than spirituality and technology as opposed to religion comes to control human behaviour and therefore religion no longer takes centre stage in society. As Wallis and Bruce put it, religion has become a 'privatized, individual experience', a 'leisure activity' rather than 'a matter of necessity'.[20] In the legal sphere this is evidenced by the separation of church from state and by the diminishing role of organised religion. In modern liberal democracies, citizens are no longer dependent on religion for the provision of education, welfare or medical care as those functions have been taken over by the state.

Like Berger and Bouma, the French political scientist Olivier Roy maintains that secularisation has not eradicated religion but instead has produced a religious revival. This revival however is a transformation of religion rather than a comeback of religion as such. For Roy, this religious transformation could be a reaction to modernity or a reflection of individual freedom and diversity.[21] Roy argues that secularisation has provided religions with autonomy from territories, culture and politics, giving them the freedom to reconstruct themselves.[22] This means that religions are no longer confined to geographical territories and as such they are exposed to a wider public. It also means that religions have to 'market' themselves to a wider audience if they wish to attract followers. Religious freedom has meant that religions are in competition with each other. We therefore witness a transformation of the religious landscape which some call 'religious revival', but the term 'religious revival' may be misleading because it tends to suggest that society might have become more religious. We will see in this chapter that this is not necessarily the case and that what we witness is a transformation of religion rather than a revival as such. Roy describes 'religious revivalism' as a product of secularisation rather than a reaction against it. He points out that this increased religious visibility is not necessarily a sign of increased 'religiousness' but rather the emergence of new forms of religious visibility.[23] While some religions like Christianity are in decline, others, such as minority faiths, are rising and those faiths that are on the rise tend to be more practice based and thus more visible. This will be discussed further below.

The English sociologist of religion Grace Davie explains the continued presence of religion in British society and beyond despite the secularisation thesis by what she calls 'believing without belonging' and 'vicarious religion'.[24] She argues that religions have become more individualised and that people may have stopped attending church, but this does not mean that they do not have a religious belief. Instead, we witness what Davie calls a form of 'vicarious religion' whereby religion is being practised by professional religious personnel on behalf of believers who experience religion at second hand or vicariously.[25] Davie's thesis applies to Christianity and certainly goes some way towards explaining the decline of Christianity both in Europe and in the United States but the same cannot necessarily be said about minority faith and non-religious movements which tend to be on the rise. In the United States for instance research by the Pew Institute indicates that while a large majority of Americans continue to identify as Christians, the numbers have dropped from 78.4% in 2007 to 70.6% in 2014. Meanwhile, those who describe themselves as 'religiously unaffiliated' have increased from 16.1% to 22.8% and those who are 'non-Christians' including Jewish, Muslims, Hindus and other faith have also increased from 4.7% to 5.9%. Europe follows a similar pattern, with Christianity expected to decline and non-religious groups and minority faiths expected to grow.[26] Roy points out that more charismatic and fundamentalist forms of religion are emerging as well as new religious movements (NRMs) such as the Seventh Day Adventists or the Jehovah's Witnesses.[27] Traditional forms of religion therefore give way to less traditional ones such as Evangelicalism, Pentecostalism, Salafism, Lubavitch.[28] Christian Pentecostalism for instance is currently the fastest growing religion in the world, together with Mormonism.[29] Those religions that are on the rise tend to be more extreme forms of religions, hence their more acute visibility. We witness therefore a changing religious pattern whereby some religions are in decline and others are on the rise.

4.3 The influence of religion in the public sphere

As society becomes more religiously diverse, it causes religion to resurface in public discourse.[30] Religious communities are now more likely to take part in public debate and smaller religious communities now have a voice on public policy matters and are demanding more recognition as well as rising up against state laws and policies which conflict with their ideologies. This is visible through the urban landscape with religious minorities demanding recognition through religious edifices that represent their community. By demanding to share a part of the public landscape, religious minorities are seeking official recognition. While in the 1960s religious minority groups would be content with using existing buildings for their gathering such as for instance houses or church halls hired for the day, those same communities in the 1990s began to demand their own purpose-built buildings. In England, the London Neasden Temple built between 1992 and 1995 is evidence of the pluralistic religious landscape. The Shri Swaminarayan Mandir was hand-crafted in India and shipped and assembled in London to build an imposing temple off London's North Circular road.[31] Data published by Peach and Gale show a clear increase in Muslim, Hindu and Sikh registered places of worship in England and Wales between 1964 and 1998.[32] Europe is no longer dominated by churches but also sees the presence of minarets, temples and synagogues in the urban landscape.[33] Public display of diversity legitimises religious communities who feel part of society when their symbols are part of the urban landscape, hence the increase in planning permissions for religious edifices. Similarly, religious voice is heard in politics, as exemplified by the Catholic Church rising against abortion, contraception or gay marriages even though Pope Francis, who represents the Catholic Church, adopts a softer stance.[34] Some religious minorities also demand their own legal system which suits their religion and culture. We are seeing Sharia Courts, Beth Dins, Islamic and kosher mortgages.[35] States have needed to make provisions in the law to allow religious marriages, burials or slaughtering of animals.[36] In England for instance Muslims and Jews are allowed to slaughter animals without pre-stoning which is a legal requirement in order to preserve animals' welfare.[37] This religious transformation therefore has made religion more salient and as a result, religious symbols are resurfacing in the public domain. There are a number of reasons for this increased visibility of religious symbols, which we now turn to.

Immigration and globalisation have led to the rise of minority faiths such as Islam, Judaism, Hinduism and Sikhism which have a more salient manifestation element than Christianity, which is mainly belief-based. This goes some way to explaining this increased visibility. As discussed by Modood and Calhoun, not all religions are based on belief like Christianity. For many religious groups, religion is not understood as belief but rather as practice. Some believe that they have a religious duty to behave a certain way, adopt a particular diet, or perform certain rites in order to belong to a particular faith.[38] For them, following religious law plays a major part in their life. Religious minorities have to negotiate a majoritarian culture which sees religion as a private affair. As a result, religious minorities are making claims of public recognition and respect for religious symbols plays a big role in the negotiation and the strengthening of identity. Roy argues that this religious revival in the public sphere is a 'display of religious purity' or 'reconstructed traditions'.[39] This can be seen in relation to the way people display their faith. Individuals in Europe and North America are increasingly caught up between two cultures and traditions and there is not one way of expressing this identity crisis. The visible display of religion is a testimony to this complex identity crisis. People are caught between conforming to their religion and fitting in with modern culture. In Britain, for instance, we are seeing this in the way Jewish and Muslim women display their faith. Their clothing, which is a mixture of traditional and religious norms with more Western dress, shows a clear attempt to belong to the religious community but also to fit in with Western culture.

In addition, as boundaries between religious groups become more fluid, boundary markers within symbols become more significant. Some people use religious and cultural symbols to feel part of the group rather than purely for religious reasons. Since September 11, 2001, Hindus and Sikhs have often for instance been mistaken for Muslims and as a result become victims of hate and prejudice.[40] They have therefore been keen to assert their own identity. Religion as a result has become more visible in Europe and the United States but increased visibility is not necessarily a sign of increased religiosity. What we witness is more akin to a transformation of religion.

4.4 The transformation of religion

While the religious landscape has transformed, we cannot say that religion has disappeared altogether. As Berger puts it, 'God is not dead, it is rather that there are too many gods.'[41] There is still a need for spirituality, but it is not necessarily in the shape of traditional religions. Christianity has declined in Europe and in the USA or at least church attendance has declined, but as revealed by the UK Kendal

Project, other forms of spirituality are on the increase. This empirical project was carried out over a period of two years and sought to track down every form of religion and spirituality in the English town of Kendal. The project found that the 'congressional domain', which included more traditional forms of religious spirituality, still outnumbered what they called the 'holistic milieu' which included activities with a spiritual dimension but not religious in the traditional sense. However this latter category was on the rise, leading the project to predict an increase in other forms of spirituality and a decrease in more traditional forms of religion.[42] This religious transformation can be attributed to what the American philosopher Charles Taylor describes as 'a massive subjective turn of modern culture'.[43] According to Taylor it is important to live one's humanity as opposed to conforming with a model imposed from outside by society, the previous generation, religious or political authority. The subjective turn is a shift from ascribed to achieved status whereby identities are no longer determined by birth but instead achieved through dialogue and subjective experiences.[44] The subjective turn therefore explains the growth of more individualised forms of religiosity such as conversions and the rise of NRMs discussed above. What this shows therefore is that religion as such may be decreasing but people are not less spiritual. In the globalised secularised society, there remains a demand for spirituality, just not necessarily of a purely religious nature. This transformation poses new challenges to judicial personnel and law makers. The broad approach taken by the courts in relation to defining religion and belief reflects this change. As will be discussed in Part II, religion and belief tend to be interpreted broadly by the courts. However, when it comes to manifestation of belief judges have a tendency to be more conservative and are not readily prepared to declare that: one, religious freedom is engaged and two, that there has been an interference which such. This will be examined further in Part II in relation to the three jurisdictions under scrutiny.

The literature uses the market metaphor to explain the religious transformation and a situation where religion is part of a 'consumer-oriented' market where individuals can choose according to their own preferences. As Roy puts it, this theory of a market, which is borrowed from economics, presupposes that there is a demand for religion and that human nature still has a 'religious need'.[45] People have choice in the globalised religious market as there is no longer a political constraint demanding that people share the religion of the sovereign. The individual who is free from ethnic, cultural, social and historical constraints can freely choose the religious product that best suits him, hence the rise of conversions and NRMs identified above.[46] This of course presupposes that individuals are indeed free from social and cultural constraints, which is not necessarily the case amongst some community faiths such as radical Islam, Ultra-Orthodox Judaism or radical Hinduism. Yet, even amongst those communities, transformations are taking place and some individuals leave the faith or on the contrary embrace it in a more extreme fashion than their families.[47] This is discussed below in relation to modern identities.

The transformation of the religious landscape is not without consequences for social interactions. There are tensions as some feel threatened by the decline of their own group and the rise of others and therefore try to limit the presence of symbols of faith. We witness the expression of hate through annihilation of religious symbols such as Koran burning, Jewish cemeteries being desecrated,[48] attacks on mosques[49] and Jewish sites; attacks on African American churches are also rising in the US.[50] This opposition according to Bouma is a reaction against the rise of diversity. Bouma argues that history has conditioned us to fear diversity and to see it as a problem needing to be overcome. He argues that religious events such as the Spanish Inquisition or European religious wars in the 16th and 17th centuries created a negative presumption of religion as a source of violence and conflict. Bouma uses the concept of 'competitive piety' to describe the internal rivalry within religious groups. He describes the rhetoric of 'negative othering' which leads to negative stereotyping.[51] This is something we have seen in relation to the Muslim minority post-September 11, 2001 and which continues today with the rise of ISIS. Muslims' portrayal in the media leads to stereotyping and antagonises individuals and groups. As Roy puts it, globalisation places religions in competition with each other.[52] We face situations where groups compete to shape the society according to their view.

In addition, visual religious symbols are often perceived as threatening.[53] Visual symbols provoke fear in those not belonging to the tradition in question. When displayed in public settings, religious symbols may be perceived as divisive, suggesting recognition by the state of a particular minority group and this is likely to cause discomfort in a society which expects the assimilation of minorities.[54] The public display of religious symbols can also create tensions between religious groups as it may be perceived as endorsement from the state of one faith over another. It is those tensions that have led to legal intervention with religion, belief and religious manifestation. In the next section we look at the interaction between symbols and the law.

4.5 Symbols' encounter with the law: the 'juridification' of symbols

Since the second half of the 20th century, we have witnessed what Sandberg has called a 'juridification' of religion whereby religion has come into close encounter with the courts.[55] In particular, there have been many cases involving manifestation of beliefs. Individuals being denied the right to wear a religious symbol which they deem crucial for the maintenance of their religious identity have used the courts to defend their right to manifest their religion. Judges have been confronted with such issues as whether governments are allowed to display religious symbols in the public sphere – this has notably been the case in secular states such as France and the US. There have also been many court cases involving prohibitions of religious symbols including head coverings and religious artefacts. Such cases have arisen in all three jurisdictions under review namely, France, England and Wales and the United States. Court cases have been brought by both minority and majority faiths to defend their religious commitments. Defendants have included governments, public bodies such as schools and private employers. Cases are being brought on the basis of human rights and/or non-discrimination. This is explored in depth in Part II.

The right to freedom of thought, conscience and religion is guaranteed under international human rights law by article 18 of the ICCPR of which all three countries under review are a party. At the regional level, freedom of thought, conscience and religion is guaranteed by article 9 of the ECHR which both the UK and France are a party to. In addition, freedom of religion is guaranteed by the French and American Constitutions. Non-discrimination on the grounds of religion and belief is enshrined in all three legal systems. However, while the right to freedom of thought, conscience and religion is absolute, the freedom to manifest the same is subject to limitations. As such, states can limit the exercise of freedom of religion and belief when there is a justification based on the law of that state, public safety, order, health, morals or the freedom of others. Often courts find governments' and public bodies' as well as private entities' justification for suppressing a particular symbol valid despite the absence of evidence that it would cause harm to society.[56] Political scientist A. D. Renteln argues that the principle of religious liberty has not served minorities well in the United States;[57] this argument could be extended to Europe. UK courts found justifications for banning religious symbols in cases like *R (on the application of Begum) v. Headteacher and Governors of Denbigh High School*,[58] *R (on the application of Playfoot) v. Governing Body of Millais School*[59] or *Eweida v. British Airways.*[60] Similar outcomes were found in France in cases surrounding head coverings especially Muslim hijabs and Sikh turbans as well as in the United States with cases like *Menorah vs Illinois*[61] in relation to the Jewish yarmulke. These cases will be discussed further in Part II.

At times therefore, religious minorities are faced with the dilemma of either violating state law by displaying their religious symbol or violating religious law by complying with state law and not displaying their faith, leading them to challenge policies denying them the right to wear symbols which they consider important for their identity. Faced with such dilemma the outsider may question whether it would not simply be easier to discard the conflicting religious symbol. Why cannot a Muslim woman remove her veil, a Sikh man remove his turban or a Jew his yarmulke? Those who raise those questions fail to appreciate the significance of symbols for members of a religious group. As discussed in the previous chapter, symbols are deeply connected to individuals' and groups' identities, but their function tends to be misunderstood by judges and policy makers, hence the need to explore this further. In the next section, we explore the special relationship between religious symbols and individuals.

4.6 Religious symbols, individuals and the building of contemporary identities

As discussed above, religious markers have become an important part of modern identities. Religious symbols are more visible in the public sphere and modern identities have become complex and fluid as a result of globalisation and migrations. As argued by Olivier Roy, religions seem to be engines that drive the reformulation of identity.[62] For believers, therefore, the preservation of their symbol plays a crucial part in their lives. Yet, in secular society, we have seen that conflicts are emerging about the place of those symbols in the public sphere. Some governments and judicial personnel have tended to adopt a Western ethnocentric conception of visual religious symbols and their assessment tends to be based on the idea that they do not matter. This is mostly apparent in legislation and policies seeking to ban the display of religious symbols in public and in judicial approaches that uphold those bans. This approach fails to understand the complexities of the nature of the relationship between religious symbols and individuals. This section discusses the findings from an empirical research project I undertook in 2011/12 exploring the impact of religious symbols on the making of contemporary religious identities.[63] The research sought to understand the nature of this relationship and the extent to which religious symbols contribute to the making of modern identities.

My participants were Higher Education students and staff at the University of Westminster in London aged between 18 and 35 years old, from a range of ethnic, religious and cultural backgrounds. Religious as well as non-religious groups were represented and while the study was qualitative and as such there was no requirement for the sample to be representative,[64] the sample obtained was nonetheless robust and reflected the University's multicultural environment. Not all of the 25 participants manifested their faith or their belief visually and as the terms 'religion' and 'belief' were left up to the participants to define, they were given a very broad meaning. As a result, 'religious symbols' included crosses, fish pins, stones, tattoos, strings, hijabs, niqabs, kara bangles, turbans and a ceremonial dagger. Some carried multiple symbols such as three crosses. Others also referred to symbols kept in the home.

The empirical study focused on the meaning and significance of religious symbols and their place in the lives of individuals. The study entailed questioning the role and significance of religion in the making of individual and collective identity. Five main findings emerged from the data, namely that the way symbols are perceived is based on individuals' personal experience with religion and culture; that religiosity is ascribed by birth through ancestors' history but evolves and crystallises via family upbringing, education and spiritual journey of an individual; that the reasons why people wear religious symbols are therefore highly intimate; that one's relationship with symbols is ultimately dependent on one's relationship with religion and that given the special nature of one's relationship with symbols, state intervention with any religious symbol (either through Parliament or the courts) should be kept to the minimum necessary to protect other citizens.

The study revealed that those who wear symbols consider them as sacred and those symbols form an intrinsic characteristic of their personality, whereas for most of those who do not wear them,[65] symbols are mostly insignificant: they do not matter. In other words, the same object could be part of someone's attributes and be a mere object for others. Those who did not wear symbols questioned their relevance and emphasised the importance of belief as opposed to wearing a symbol. Some described symbols as 'a political statement' or 'a way to be seen', whereas most of those who wore a religious symbol linked it to practising their religion and viewed religion and symbols as a very important part of their lives.

I'll never say what religion do you belong to? I just say do you believe in God? Belief is more important. ... wearing any symbol doesn't make you religious ...'

(SF10–11)[66]

You are meant to consider them like another body part – like your hand, you should never part from them (the 5Ks).

(SM1–1)

Whether symbols matter therefore is tightly linked to whether individuals choose to consider them as sacred. Once they have entered the realm of the sacred, those symbols take on a very personal and intimate significance, often linked to childhood, family history, tradition and one's spiritual journey. Ultimately, they are part of an individual's identity while at the same time reinforcing belonging in a particular group or culture. Participants described their relationship with their symbol in a very sentimental way. It is clear that those symbols had more than a religious significance.

This cross was a present from my father to my mum when they were engaged ... she gave it to me as an encouragement to pass my exam.

(SM9–10)

I have worn this for about 20 years [a cross]. My husband gave it to me for my birthday soon after we got married.

(AF1–6)

It [a cross] became more like something that's there. If it wasn't a cross I would still wear it.

(SF7–8)

Religiosity of an individual is both acquired through birth status (ascribed) and developed throughout upbringing and family history (acquired); therefore, it can be argued that in some cases, religion and any associated symbols are to be considered as *intrinsic* characteristics of individuals as opposed to extrinsic values or 'labels' that could be added on, gained from the external environment. For these participants, religion could not be seen as separate from individuals:

A religion is more like land that you inherit because my dad was Muslim so I was born Muslim.

(SF15–18)

... it's true that in Islam if someone is a Muslim, they remain a Muslim ...

(FG2–17)

I don't think religion is a choice.

(SF11–12)

… because in Asian families, family is central, you go by the religion of your parents and often that of your father.

(SM8–9)

Religion is not necessarily something that people choose – what they choose is whether to embrace or reject the faith they were brought up in. So, someone could be intrinsically Muslim but extrinsically secular or agnostic. In other words, a person may have been born in a Muslim family and have grown up surrounded by Muslim culture, tradition and religious practice but over the years, they might have decided to abandon the faith – they would no longer class themselves as religiously Muslim but Islam would still inevitably be a part of their identity. Some people describe themselves as ex-Muslims, secular Jews, ex-ultra-Orthodox Jews. Atheists are usually formerly religious and converts have moved from one religion to another. Religious history in contemporary pluralist states is a journey as opposed to something fixed. It is usually the increased understanding of faith that leads people to embrace it or reject it.[67] One can argue therefore that an individual may reject his or her faith but religion remains nonetheless part of his or her cultural and family heritage; somewhere down the line it relates to who they are and where they have come from. What makes them embrace or reject their faith is a matter of belief. This became evident in this study amongst participants who had either converted, stopped practising their religion or became non-believers. This conception of religion as a fluid concept assumes an autonomous being who is able to make choices rather than being oppressed and coerced by a particular religion. Even in modern pluralist states, there are instances where this individual autonomy is being curtailed by traditional family values and where breaking away from those religious values may entail breaking away from the family altogether. In such a case, the individual may be displaying visual symbols of a faith that they do not fully embrace simply in order to 'fit in' the community and for fear of being shunned. Whether the state banning those symbols, as in France, or failing to accommodate for symbols, as is the case in the UK and the US, is an effective way towards addressing those problems however is questionable. What such approaches tend to produce is more isolation than autonomy for those concerned as it removes them from mainstream society. This will be discussed in subsequent chapters.

Despite the direct relationship between the religion of an individual and his or her family upbringing, very few participants (one did) complained of pressure to follow the religion of their parents. On the contrary, many young Muslim women revealed that they had taken up their headscarf against the will of their parents.

My best friend doesn't wear hijab at all. She wants to but because of family restrictions she can't. … My other friend who started wearing the niqab, her mum stopped speaking to her.

(SF16–21)

> I was so scared I didn't want to tell her [mother] because I knew she wouldn't like it (niqab) so one day I said I want to wear it and she said no.
>
> (SF18–23)

This goes against the frequent assumption that Muslim women are forced into wearing a headscarf. The French full-face cover ban, for instance, is based on the assumption that women are oppressed into wearing a niqab.

Female Muslims admitted to being inspired but not pressurised by seeing others wear the hijab:

> I have always wanted to wear a jilbab and headscarf but I was kind of embarrassed or ashamed ... I didn't feel comfortable because my friends didn't wear it at secondary school but when I left secondary school and went to a different environment where we all mixed ... loads of girls wore jilbab and headscarf so I felt more comfortable and I started wearing it.
>
> (SF3–3)

However, it is interesting that when it came to how the participants would raise their children, many admitted that they would not force their own religion onto them but would somehow be disappointed if they converted or did not follow their religion and practices. A Muslim participant described the feelings she would have with any of her future children should they decide to remove their headscarf once they reach the age of 20:

> Disappointed. I would persuade them again, take them to classes, lectures ... I'll do what I can to make them understand the importance of wearing it and if they still don't wear it I don't know what I would do then.
>
> (SF3–3)

Some (a minority amongst the most practising individuals) were keen to let their (future) children decide when they become the right age. This desire from parents to transmit what they see as basic values is a further testimony to the direct relationship between religiosity and upbringing. It is clear therefore that religion and symbols are deeply rooted in family history and form an integral part of an individual's personal history. It is the interplay between what can be considered as ascribed religion and what can be termed achieved religion that shapes contemporary religious identities. Similarly, religiosity is tightly linked to cultural background and some religious practices are imbued with cultural practices. Symbols therefore are not solely about religion per se but also reflect belonging to a particular cultural, religious or ethnic group.

The qualitative study further looked into the reasons why people display religious symbols and it was found that those reasons were very intimate in nature. Participants who wore a religious symbol did so for the following reasons: because they believed that it is a requirement of their faith; as a sign of respect for their religion; as part of religious tradition; as a statement/reminder of their faith; for practical reasons; for protection; to please their Lord; or to show that they are proud of who they are and of their religion. They felt that their symbol gave them a sense of belonging to a group, a sense of comfort, support, protection and security. The concept of 'religious emotion' described by Riis and Woodhead[68] supports this finding. Riis and Woodhead describe sacred symbols as a 'powerful stimulus' for the expression of emotions such as anger, hatred, worship or joy which assist in the cultivation of personal emotions.[69] Religious emotion therefore is associated with religious and cultural symbols such as objects but also sacred space such as temples, shrines, landscapes. As such, symbols help to consolidate new solidarities, but they can also become the object of rebellion. As discussed in Chapter 3 above, symbols can be used as a means of gaining power, criticising established power or they can be desecrated by enemies. Symbols' tight connection with identity can also become a source of conflicts between majority and minority cultures when majority cultures perceive a minority symbol or practice as violating their own identity. This is the case in some countries with the Islamic face cover (the burqa or niqab) which is often perceived as an infringement of the principle of equality between men and women. This is discussed in Chapter 5 in relation to France and the burqa ban.

The above findings also confirm Day's thesis that belief is a social phenomenon allowing people to express their collective sense of belonging.[70] She argues that belief plays a role in shaping identities which individuals create to fit in social situations. This is what Day calls 'believing in belonging'. Religion, she argues, is a subset of belief. Day developed the concept of 'performative belief' to describe a phenomenon whereby people who would not otherwise be religious can have a collective religious identity.[71] As discussed in Chapter 2, Durkheim in his work also highlighted the importance of religious gatherings and the collective enthusiasm which they generate.[72]

My study further revealed that the 'decision'[73] to display one's faith is a deeply intimate one which is dependent on one's conception of religiosity. In some cases, it is part of one's identity as a religious being, while in others it is a manifestation of being part of a group. For all the participants, it is an expression of belief and is driven by their own interpretation and understanding of religious doctrines but it generally does not matter whether co-religionists share their beliefs. What came out of the findings is a general sense of respect for individuals (although some participants expressed their disagreement with the niqab) and an acknowledgment that spiritual journeys are personal and cannot be imposed. Had the study been conducted in a different geographic location or in a different environment this latter aspect might have been different. As participants were in Higher Education it does presuppose a certain degree of freedom and autonomy.

Most participants described religion as one of three categories: a relationship with God, a way of life or a set of rules. Those who fell into the first category were those who tended not to wear a symbol and gave priority to belief over manifestation (these were mostly Christians but not exclusively). Those in the second category generally displayed their faith but were less strict in their religious practice. Religion was described as 'a guide', 'part of who you are', 'part of your identity', while those in the third category saw their religion as the driving force behind their life and were usually stricter in their practice, linking their symbols to 'full submission to God' or following 'what is in the teachings'. There was also a minority amongst participants who did not value religion or symbols and described the former as: 'man made tradition', 'a shield for people to hide behind', some kind of dogma imposed by an institution. These people were keen to part with their ascribed religious background even if it involved a troubled relationship with their families.

Participants were questioned about the level of interference they would be prepared to take from the state and the responses varied depending on their view of religion. Whether one is prepared to remove his or her symbol therefore depends on one's view of the role of symbols and, as described above, views of symbols are determined by one's religiosity. If an individual wears a symbol as an absolute requirement of their faith then they are less likely to be prepared to remove such symbol than if they merely wear it as an expression of faith.

It appears therefore that the degree of interference an individual is prepared to take with his or her symbol is fully dependent on why they wear a symbol in the first place. If they consider it as a religious requirement, then any unjustified request by the state that the individual in question should remove their symbol will be seen as a violation of the individual's identity. Given the special nature of the relationship between individuals and their symbols, they are not objects that can be merely taken on and off in the way that one removes a hat for instance or folds one's umbrella upon entering a building. This should certainly be the primary consideration for anyone attempting to interfere with one's religious symbols.

4.7 Concluding remarks on the function of symbols in contemporary pluralist states

The public display of religious symbols in contemporary pluralist states therefore is a reflection of the changing religious landscape. A number of factors have contributed to those changes, including geopolitical factors and modernity. As the role of religion in society has transformed, individuals have not lost their sense of spirituality and religion and belief can fulfil that need. There is a sense that, in the globalised world, individuals' identities are increasingly being absorbed within the pluralist environment and individuals feel more and more detached from their religious and cultural identity. They turn to religious symbols in order to get the sense of belonging and comfort that they lack in an increasingly individualised world. The relationship between individuals and their religious symbols is a deeply intimate one, driven by religious and cultural emotions. For some, religious symbols are a religious requirement, for others they are a link to their community or a way of life. In all cases, for those who display them, symbols are charged with emotional and spiritual meaning and are part of one's identity. Yet, for secularists symbols should be kept away from the public sphere as they are reminiscent of a time when religion dominated society.

The extent to which people are able to display their faith in public within modern secular society is one which is very controversial, as some religious precepts conflict with modern principles of equality and neutrality. The state and the law have been called upon to arbitrate conflicts involving display of faith. In addition, with the transformation of religion and the secularisation of society as discussed in early chapters, new religious movements have emerged and non-religious movements at times fulfil a similar function to religion, thus highlighting the need for a less traditional approach to manifestation of belief. In the next three chapters, we explore this interaction between manifestation of belief and the law and the extent to which individuals are free to manifest their belief in pluralist modern societies such as France, the UK and the United States.

Notes

1 *Johns v Derby City Council and Equality and Human Rights Commission (intervening)* [2011] EWHC 375 (Admin).
2 The secularisation thesis is the idea that modernisation contributes to the decline of religion and religious activity such as attending religious service. This will be discussed in further detail below.
3 See for instance Cranmer, Hill and Kenny 2016, xvii. See also, Kirsch and Turner 2016.
4 *Lautsi and Others v. Italy*, Application no. 30814/06. 18 March 2011.
5 *R (on the application of Playfoot) v Governing Body of Millais School* [2007] EWHC 1698 (Admin).
6 *R (on the application of Watkins-Singh) v Governing Body of Aberdare Girls' High School* [2008] EWHC 1865 (Admin).
7 *R (on the application of Begum (by her litigation friend, Rahman)) v. Headteacher and Governors of Denbigh High School* [2006] UKHL 15
8 *X v Y School & Ors* [2007] EWHC 298 (Admin).
9 *SG v St Gregory's Catholic Science College* [2011] EWHC 1452 (Admin).
10 *SAS v France* (Application no. 43835/11). 1 July 2014.
11 Bouma 2011.
12 Thuswaldner 2014.
13 See Berger 1999.
14 Thuswaldner 2014, op. cit.
15 See Davie, Catto and Woodhead 2016. 530.
16 Sandberg 2014. 160.
17 The term 'privileged' refers to the different legal status of the Church of England in comparison to other religious groups. This is discussed in detail in Chapter 6.
18 Sandberg 2014, op. cit. 67.
19 Beckford 2003. 48.
20 Wallis and Bruce 1992. 13.
21 Roy 2013. 2.
22 Idem.
23 Roy 2013, op. cit. 4.
24 Davie 1994.
25 Idem.
26 Pew Research Institute 2015
27 Roy 2013, op. cit. 4.
28 Idem.
29 Idem.
30 Bouma 2011, op. cit.
31 See for example the Hindu temple in Neasden, London, BAPS n.d.
32 Peach and Gale 2003.

33 Idem.
34 See Goodstein 2013.
35 See in the UK the Islamic Sharia Council n.d.; for Beth Dins see TheUS.org n.d.
36 Bouma 2011, op. cit.
37 See Part 4 of The Welfare of Animals (Slaughter or Killing) Regulations 1995. This is further discussed in Part II.
38 Modood and Calhoun 2015.
39 Roy 2013, op. cit. 5.
40 See for instance, Bascu 2016. This also became apparent through my empirical research Bacquet 2016.
41 Berger's 'Is God Dead' refers to the cover of *Time Magazine* in April 1966. See also Bruce 2002.
42 See further Heelas and Woodhead 2005.
43 Taylor 1991, quoted in Sandberg 2014, op. cit. 161–162.
44 Sandberg 2014, op. cit. 161–162.
45 Roy 2013, op. cit. 159.
46 Ibid. 160.
47 The Sunday Times 2017. See also Saleem and Mughal 2018.
48 See for instance in the US, BBC News 2017.
49 See for instance in the UK, Roberts 2017.
50 See for instance Gill 2017.
51 Bouma 2011, op. cit. 33.
52 Roy 2013, op. cit. 160.
53 Renteln 2004.
54 Ibid. 574.
55 Sandberg 2011.
56 Renteln 2004. op. cit. 1576.
57 Idem.
58 [2006] UKHL 15.
59 [2007] EWHC 1698 (Admin).
60 [2010] EWCA Civ 80 CA.
61 683 F.2d 1030 (7th Cir. 1982).
62 Roy 2013, op. cit. 2.
63 The full paper has previously been published in Bacquet 2016.
64 See Webley 2010. 926.
65 Some of the non-symbol wearers nonetheless acknowledged the importance of symbols for others.
66 These references were generated to preserve the anonymity of the participants. S refers to a student, A refers to Academic. F is for female, M is for male and FG is for focus group. The numbers refer to the various interviews and transcripts. So, for example: SF10–11 means student female – interviewee 10 and transcript 11.
67 Religion in Education (n.d.). A contribution to Dialogue or a factor of Conflict in transforming societies of European Countries (REDCo) – a project sponsored by the European Commission which focused on how European citizens of different religious and cultural background can live together.
68 Riis and Woodhead 2010.
69 Ibid. 8.
70 Day 2011.
71 Ibid. 194.
72 Durkheim 1915.
73 The extent to which displaying one's faith is a decision is debatable and varies according to individuals and how they define religion. This is apparent from the empirical data, hence the use of inverted commas. It is also relative in relation to children who may be compelled to display their faith.

References

Books

Beckford, J. A., 2003. *Social Theory and Religion*. Cambridge: Cambridge University Press.
Berger, P. L. ed., 1999. *The Desecularisation of the World in Resurgent Religion and World Politics*. Washington: William B Eerdmans Publishing Co.
Bouma, G. D., 2011. *Being Faithful in Diversity: Religions and Social Policy in Multifaith Societies*. Hindmarsh, SA: ATF Press.
Bruce, S., 2002. *God is Dead – Secularisation in the West*. Oxford: Wiley-Blackwell.
Cranmer, F., Hill, M. and Kenny, C. eds, 2016. *The Confluence of Law and Religion, Interdisciplinary Reflections on the Work of Norman Doe*. Cambridge: Cambridge University Press.
Davie, G., 1994. *Religion in Britain since 1945: Believing Without Belonging*. Oxford: Blackwell.
Day, A., 2011. *Believing in Belonging*. Oxford: Oxford University Press.
Durkheim, E., 1915. *The Elementary Forms of the Religious Life*. London: George Allen and Unwin.
Heelas, P. and Woodhead, L., 2005. *The Spiritual Revolution: Why Religion is Giving Way to Spirituality*. Oxford: Blackwell.
Kirsch, T. and Turner, B., eds., 2016. *Permutation of Order: Religion and Law as Contested Sovereignties*. Abingdon, Oxon: Routledge.
Riis, O. and Woodhead, L., 2010. *A Sociology of Religious Emotion*. Oxford: Oxford University Press.
Roy, O., 2013. *Holy Ignorance: When Religion and Culture Part Ways*. Oxford: Oxford University Press.
Saleem, A. and Mughal, F., eds., 2018. *Leaving the Faith Behind: The Journeys and Perspectives of People who Have Chosen to Leave Islam*. London: Darton, Longman and Todd Ltd.
Sandberg, R., 2011. *Law and Religion*. Cambridge: Cambridge University Press.
Sandberg, R., 2014. *Religion, Law and Society*. Cambridge: Cambridge University Press.
Taylor, C., 1991. *The Ethics of Authenticity*. Cambridge, MA: Harvard University Press.

Articles, book chapters and conference papers

Bacquet, S. 2016. 'Religious Symbols and the Making of Contemporary Religious Identities' in SandbergR. ed., *Religion and Legal Pluralism*. Abingdon: Ashgate. 113–130.
Davie, G., Catto, R. and Woodhead, L., 2016. 'Secularisation and Secularism' in Woodhead, L., Partridge, C. and Kawanami, H. eds. *Religions in the Modern World: Traditions and Transformations*. London and New York: Routledge. 551–570.
Modood, T. and Calhoun, C., 2015. 'Religion in Britain: Challenges for Higher Education, Stimulus Paper', Leadership Foundation for Higher Education. June.
Peach, C. and Gale, R., 2003. 'Muslims, Hindus, and Sikhs in the New Religious Landscape of England', *The Geographical Review*, 93(4): 469–490.
Renteln, A. D., 2004. 'Visual Religious Symbols and the Law', *American Behavioural Scientist*, 47(12): 1573–1596.
Thuswaldner, G., 2014. 'A Conversation with Peter L. Berger "How My Views Have Changed"', *The Cresset*, Lent, 77(3): 16–21.
Wallis, R. and Bruce, S., 1992. 'Secularisation: The Orthodox Model', in BruceS. ed. *Religion and Modernization: Sociologists and Historians Debate the Secularization Thesis*. Oxford: Clarendon. 8–30.

Webley, L., 2010. 'Qualitative approaches to empirical legal research', in CaneP. and Krit-zerH. M. eds., *The Oxford Handbook of Empirical Legal Research*. Oxford: Oxford University Press. 926–950.

Websites

Attributed author

Bascu, M., 2016. '15 Years after 9/11, Sikhs Still Victims of Anti-Muslim Hate Crimes', CNN, 15September. https://edition.cnn.com/2016/09/15/us/sikh-hate-crime-victims/index.html [Accessed 18 August 2018]

Gill, L., 2017. 'Five Black New Jersey Churches Attacked, Police Investigating As Hate Crimes', *Newsweek*, 26 November. http://www.newsweek.com/vandals-attack-five-black-new-jersey-churches-722565 [Accessed 18 August 2018]

Goodstein, L., 2013. 'Pope Says Church Is "Obsessed" with Gays, Abortion and Birth Control', *The New York Times*, 19 September. https://www.nytimes.com/2013/09/20/world/europe/pope-bluntly-faults-churchs-focus-on-gays-and-abortion.html [Accessed 18 August 2018]

Roberts, R., 2017. 'Hate Crime Targeting UK Mosques More than Doubled in Past Year, Figures Show', *The Independent*, 8 October. http://www.independent.co.uk/news/uk/home-news/hate-crime-muslims-mosques-islamist-extremism-terrorism-terror-attacks-a7989746.html [Accessed 18 August 2018]

No attributed author

BBC News, 2017. 'Hundreds of US Jewish Graves Attacked in Philadelphia', 27 February. https://www.bbc.com/news/world-us-canada-39082013 [Accessed 18 August 2018]

TheUS.org, n.d. 'Beth Dins', https://www.theus.org.uk/article/about-london-beth-din [Accessed 22 March 2019]

BAPS, n.d. 'The Mandir', http://londonmandir.baps.org/the-mandir/ [Accessed 18 August 2018]

Islamic Sharia Council, n.d. http://www.islamic-sharia.org/ [Accessed 22 March 2019]

Pew Research Institute, 2015. 'America's Changing Religious Landscape', 12 May. http://www.pewforum.org/2015/05/12/americas-changing-religious-landscape/ [Accessed 18 August 2018]

Religion in Education n.d. A contribution to Dialogue or a factor of Conflict in trans-forming societies of European Countries (REDCo) – a project sponsored by the European Commission which focused on how European citizens of different religious and cultural background can live together, http://www.redco.uni-hamburg.de/web/3480/3481/index.html [Accessed 18 August 2018]

The Sunday Times, 2017. 'Meet the British Jew who Escaped from the Haredi Commu-nity', 2 July. https://www.thetimes.co.uk/article/meet-the-british-jews-who-escaped-from-the-strict-haredi-community-75b9cvlwp [Accessed 18 August 2018]

Others

Part 4 of The Welfare of Animals (Slaughter or Killing) Regulations 1995.

Part II

Religious Symbols and the Law in 21st Century Pluralist States

5 France and *laïcité* [1]

5.1 Introduction

Article 10 of the 1789 Declaration of the Rights of Man and Citizen provides that '[n]o one may be disturbed on account of his opinions, even religious ones, as long as the manifestation of such opinions does not interfere with the established Law and Order'. Freedom of religion is also afforded constitutional protection. Article 1 of the Constitution of 4 October 1958 states 'France shall be an indivisible, secular, democratic and social Republic. It shall ensure the equality of all citizens before the law, without distinction of origin, race or religion. It shall respect all beliefs.' It appears therefore that freedom of thought is positively protected, in compliance with Article 9 (1) of the European Convention on Human Rights (ECHR).

Manifestation of religion in the public sphere however is subject to a number of limitations caused by the French tradition of *laïcité*. *Laïcité* is a form of secularism which tends to be active and militant as opposed to the more passive form of secularism that we may observe in some countries like England for instance. *Laïcité* is a feature of French republican theories which originated in the Enlightenment century and crystallised with the French Revolution in 1789. Before the revolution, church–state relations in France had a long history of power struggle which resulted in a rejection of religious authority held by the Catholic priests. This power struggle is what gave way to the current system which is designed to guarantee freedom of conscience, religion and belief but which puts a strong emphasis on freedom from religion and tends to advocate so-called religious neutrality. *Laïcité* therefore came as a reaction to the imposition of moral authority by the Catholic Church. In addition to the Constitution, there are mainly three laws which govern the relationship between church and state and manifestation of belief. We shall firstly explore the Constitution before moving on to those laws.

5.2 The French Constitution and republicanism

Article 1 of the French Constitution of 1958 which is the current French Constitution provides that: 'France shall be an indivisible, secular, democratic and social Republic. It shall ensure the equality of all citizens before the law, without distinction of origin, race or religion. It shall respect all beliefs.'[2]

The Constitution is based on three pillars – *Liberté* (freedom), *Egalité* (equality), *Fraternité* (citizenship) that are rooted in republican theories. The French philosophers of the Enlightenment considered individual autonomy as key to realising the right to *liberty* since, according to them, real freedom could not be achieved without freedom from religion and tradition. They saw school education as vital in contributing to the learning of individual autonomy,[3] and it is not surprising therefore that the term *laïcité* was first used in the context of schools in the preamble to the Constitution of 1946.[4]

With this in mind, state schools have the role of developing children's autonomy so that they may exercise their right to liberty through distancing themselves from their original affiliation.[5] It follows therefore that *equality* is achieved by putting cultural differences aside rather than via the recognition and reinforcement of cultural differences as in multiculturalism. *Fraternity* comes from a common inclination of citizens to participate actively in the free political community.[6] As Laborde puts it '[t]he bond of citizenship would be eroded if society were fragmented into a collection of identity groups seeking recognition rather than work [ing] towards the public interest'.[7] Thus fraternity requires autonomy, in order to flourish. What Laborde describes however is akin to English multiculturalism which recognises and values differences rather than seeking to hide them away.

While it may indeed be important to distance oneself from cultural, social and religious affiliation in order to achieve a certain level of autonomy and ultimately exercise one's right to liberty (including the freedom to choose one's religion, or choose none), the goal of creating a universal community of citizens that share a single culture sits uneasily with the diverse social reality in France. As Jennings points out, the French Republic is ambivalent in nature. It is a culturally and ethnically diverse society (in part due to the large population of immigrants of North African origin) but yet is not one that describes itself as a pluralist society. Instead, the republican tradition still holds strong within French society and in particular within the field of education.[8] French social policy has tended to focus on integration rather than on the recognition of collective rights that is essential to multiculturalism. In fact, republicanism focuses on the recognition of the individual, rather than the group and its ability to exist outside its historical, social, cultural and religious affiliation. Secularism therefore is a prerequisite for republicanism since autonomy can only be achieved if religion is kept separate from the state. This church–state separation is enshrined within the Law of 1905.

5.3 The Law of 1905 separating church and state: from neutrality to *laïcité*

While the law of 1905 established the separation between church and state, which is key to *laïcité*, it did not make any explicit reference to the word *laïcité*. *Laïcité* as a constitutional principle came to be recognised later in both the 1946 and 1958 constitutions. The law of 1905 is based on two key principles: freedom of conscience and the separation of church and state, and these provide the foundations for *laïcité*. Freedom of conscience is guaranteed under Article 1 and includes freedom of worship provided that this does not interfere with public order. Critics of this article argue that it is the result of a war against Catholicism and that freedom of worship alone does not guarantee freedom to practise one's religion.[9] Indeed, this approach privileges orthodoxy over orthopraxy faith and is a recurrent theme with judicial approaches to religion, not just in France. Yet, Article 1 was adopted by a large majority in both chambers of the French Parliament. Separation of church and state is governed by Article 2 of the Law of 1905, which provides that the state does not recognise, remunerate or fund any religion. As such, the state becomes religiously neutral.

As rightly pointed out by Jacques Robert, though, the law of 1905 is quite outdated since it does not take into account those religious groups that were absent from France at the time of drafting.[10] In particular, Muslims are not taken into account. Moreover, despite the French claim to *laicité*, the calendar of the Republic is essentially Christian. Except for the national holidays such as Bastille Day, all holidays are Christian (Ascension, Easter, Christmas). Thus, it can be said that, although the state aspires to be neutral, Catholics are put in a more favourable position in that they can practise their religion more freely than Muslims, Jews and Sikhs since it is facilitated by the calendar. For instance, going to Church on Sunday is possible whereas attending Friday prayers or respecting the Sabbath may not be possible if one is employed. Sunday remains the official day of rest and this is still reflected in tight Sunday trading laws despite some relaxations in the past few years.[11]

This neutrality of the state is essentially what later became known as *laicité*. Three main principles govern the principle of *laicité*: neutrality of the state, freedom of conscience and pluralism.[12]

Neutrality of the State is the main prerequisite to *laicité*. In order to fulfil the Constitution's guarantee of equality before the law, the state not only has to be separated from religion but in addition it needs to appear religiously neutral in the provision of public services. Thus, the principle of neutrality of the agents of the state (*neutralité des agents du service public*)[13] stipulates that manifestation of beliefs or the wearing of religious symbols are forbidden for those working on behalf of the state, including the police, school teachers, government ministers, local council workers, public medical personnel etc. This injunction against the display of religious symbols preserves the public sphere as a secular space, while allowing the private sphere to be imbued with religious identity, free from interference by the state.

This principle implies a clear division between a citizen's private life on the one hand and the public sphere on the other. It becomes difficult for citizens to practise their religion outside the private sphere. At a time when the dominant religion was Christianity, the distinction between belief and practice might not have been viewed as an infringement to one's freedom of religion; Christianity is mainly a belief-based religion which does not generally require a public display of faith. In today's diverse French society however, it is necessary to distinguish between those religions that are belief-based such as Christianity and others that are more practice-based and, as such, require that their members publicly display their faith, such as Sikhism, Islam and Judaism (in its most Orthodox form). The turban for instance is an essential element of the Sikh faith, members of the Sikh religion are required to wear it by the *Sikh Code of Conduct* as promulgated by the various Gurus.[14]

With the principle of neutrality of the agents of the state, a Sikh man or a practising Muslim woman are faced with the choice of either manifesting their religion or working for the French Government. If they choose the latter, they must give up on their religious practice, at least while they are on duty. This inevitably leads to religious discrimination as it excludes certain religious groups from certain professions unless they are prepared to renounce their religious practice while in service.[15] Those who support the principle of neutrality of the state argue that public administration must remain neutral and that those working for the public sector are free to manifest their beliefs, only not while they are at work. This conception views religious symbols as add-on objects which people wear or display as they please just like a fashion accessory. This approach fails to take into account the historical and social context of religious symbols which is discussed in Chapter 4.

The laic state guarantees *freedom of conscience*: individuals are free to choose, or not choose, a religious or spiritual position, to change it, or even cease to adhere to it. The state aims to ensure that no single group or community is allowed to impose on anyone their particular faith. It seeks to protect individuals from any physical or moral pressure on religious or spiritual grounds.[16] This is particularly important at school where the state has a duty to protect school children from any social pressure but at the same time allows them to form their own opinion on the various religions. In the laic state, therefore religious freedom is guaranteed by protecting the individual from religious pressure particularly during childhood when the individual is most vulnerable.[17] This provides the rationale for the 2004 legislation on manifestation of belief at school which will be discussed further below.

Pluralism, the third pillar of *laïcité* is enshrined in article 2 of the law of 1905. By renouncing the idea of a state religion, the republic places all religions on the same level. No single religion will have a special status and as such the old distinction between those official and non-official religions is abolished.[18] The state therefore has a duty to protect those minority religions against any forms of discrimination just as the majority.

Over a century after the law of 1905, the French *laïcité* keeps being debated and has been a source of controversy especially since the law of 2004 which took *laïcité* even further by banning religious symbols at school. In the next section, we look at the more recent legislation on *laïcité* and how religious minorities have been accommodated.

5.4 The Law of 2004 on manifestation of belief at school

In France, manifestation of belief at school is subject to limitations as provided by the Law of 15 March 2004 on the display of signs or clothing manifesting religious belonging at primary and secondary state schools (*Port de signes ou de tenues manifestant une appartenance religieuse dans les écoles, collèges et lycées publics*). This law which was voted in February 2004 by the French National Assembly with a large majority (494/36) bans the wearing of conspicuous signs of religious affiliations in state primary and secondary schools. As a result of this law, Article L141-5-1 of the Education Code was amended to provide that: 'Dans les écoles, les collèges et les lycées publics, le port de signes ou tenues par lesquels les élèves manifestent ostensiblement une appartenance religieuse est interdit.' (In primary and secondary public education, the wearing of conspicuous signs of religious affiliation is forbidden.)

The law is particularly short but there is an accompanying application decree which specifies that the signs or dress that are forbidden are those that would lead one to be affiliated with a particular religion such as the Islamic veil (in all its forms), the Jewish yarmulke or a large cross. The Sikh turban also falls under this category. Discreet religious signs are allowed and the law does not forbid any attire or symbol worn by pupils without any religious significance.[19] In case of a breach, the application decree recommends that a dialogue is opened between the student and all those involved and provides that exclusion must be used as a last resort.[20]

The Law of 2004 was enacted following a report by the Stasi Commission.[21] The report reaffirmed the strong tradition of *laïcité* and recalled its importance within the Republic, especially for schools and public services. The Commission acknowledged that *laïcité* was confronted with a new religious and spiritual diversity and noted that reasonable adjustments had already been made, notably in relation to planning permission for new religious buildings, accommodation of religious holidays, dietary requirements linked to religious belief and incorporating some religious studies in the school curriculum.[22]

The report provides examples of infringements of *laïcité* that the Commission considered to be a threat to the neutrality of public services and of the state. In schools, for instance, the Commission noted that disruption was caused by repeated absences for prayer, or fasting, or young girls refusing to take part in PE lessons. Exams were also disrupted when female Muslim students refused to go through identity checks or to be examined by a male examiner. In public hospitals, similar problems had occurred with husbands or fathers refusing to have their daughter or wife treated by a male doctor. The same kinds of difficulty were also reported in prisons.[23]

The Commission considered that these infringements were responsible for what they called '*repli communautaire*' (communitarism). In France, this term is used to describe a situation in which minorities live in self-sufficient communities rather than integrate with the majority.[24] The report highlighted that schools or sports no longer helped to improve the situation. The Commission noted for instance that community sports teams had developed that no longer took part in competitions at federation level; women also tended to be automatically excluded by faith communities from local swimming pools and stadiums.[25] The Commission pointed out that the concept of *mixité*, which in France advocates mixed access to public places such as sporting facilities, was being compromised by those practices, which in turn resulted in a reduction of equality between the sexes.[26]

Moreover, the Commission noted that women's rights in those communities were in decline – '*la situation des filles dans les cités relève d'un veritable drame*' (the situation of young women on estates is a real concern).[27] The report notes that young women were victims of sexism and were at the receiving end of verbal, psychological and/or physical pressure and violence. Some were forced to wear modest clothing and the report noted that, while some women willingly choose to wear the headscarf, others are put under pressure to wear it. Pressure usually comes both from within the family (for example from a brother or father) and from the wider community, the perception is that, were they not to wear a veil, young women would be regarded as indecent or unfaithful.[28] These findings were gathered through interviews with various stakeholders including Muslim young women.

Finally, the Commission noted the rise of racism and xenophobia especially targeted at Muslims, as well as the rise of anti-Semitism,[29] and made a number of recommendations in addition to outlawing conspicuous signs of religious affiliation at school. These included the drawing-up of a Charter on *laïcité*, [30] the establishment of a national school for Islamic studies,[31] the creation of Muslim chaplaincies in the army, alternatives to pork and fish on Friday in public service cafeterias,[32] and the recognition of some Muslim and Jewish holidays.[33]

In a speech on 17 December 2003, President Chirac announced that a law banning conspicuous religious signs at school would be put before Parliament, but the proposal to add additional public holidays to the school calendar to accommodate important religious festivals was rejected at the outset by the President. However, Chirac recommended that exams should not be set on those days. In relation to hospitals, he noted that nothing could justify a patient refusing to be treated by a doctor of the opposite sex and advocated a law to this effect. The proposal to create a Charter on *laïcité* was retained and the President also insisted on the need to protect women's rights and the principle of *mixité*. [34] The Charter on *laïcité* was eventually adopted in 2007 and disseminated to public service establishments such as hospitals and universities.[35] In February 2016, the 'Laïcité Watchdog' (*Observatoire de la Laïcité*)[36] published guidelines on how to deal with religion in public health establishments. The guidelines are directed to both medical personnel and patients and remind medical personnel that they are not allowed to display any signs of religious affiliations while performing their functions. The guidelines also apply to patients and stipulate that religious beliefs are respected as well as dietary requirements, however in an emergency situation the guidelines recall that it is not possible for patients to choose their doctor, including asking for a doctor of the same sex. It is also not possible for parents to refuse medical treatment for their children in a life emergency situation. The guidelines do not prohibit a Christmas tree being displayed in hospitals though, as they recall that it is a pagan custom devoid of religious meaning.[37]

While the Law of 2004 targets all religious signs, it is clear that it was primarily a reaction to the Muslim headscarf following the late 1980s headscarf affairs. In the next section, we look at the political context leading to the Law of 2004.

5.5 Socio-political context: Law of 2004

Following decolonisation of North Africa, France found itself with a large population of North African immigrants who are now well established in France and whose children are often French citizens.[38] It is estimated that there are currently around 4.7 million Muslims living in France (7.5% of the population), which makes it the largest Muslim community in Europe together with Germany.[39] This influx of immigrants and their establishment in France has resulted in an increasingly diverse and multi-cultural French society that perhaps conflicts to a certain extent with the underlying principle of universalism that has dominated French ideology during the various republican regimes.[40]

French Muslims have indeed remained largely part of a poorer minority, mostly uneducated and marginalised, generally living on the outskirts of big cities in what have become known as *banlieues*. Strictly '*banlieue*' means 'suburb' but over the years it has come to be used pejoratively to denote those poorer suburbs, mainly populated by immigrants who mostly live in council estates (called '*cités*') and receive state benefit often linked to unemployment. Allegedly as a result of poverty and unemployment, the poorer suburbs have become a breeding ground for street crime, making them even less attractive to small businesses and private housing schemes. Also, local public schools have tended to achieve poorer success rates than city centres which adds to the stigma associated with the *banlieues*.[41] It is no surprise, then, that in the late 1990s some suburban schools became the theatre of a series of incidents involving Muslim headscarves.[42] These later became known as *l'affaire des foulards* (the headscarves affair) and eventually led to the adoption of the law of 2004 discussed above.

L'affaire des foulards started in October 1989 when three Muslim girls were expelled from a school in one of the poor, marginalised Parisian suburbs. The girls had refused to remove their headscarves, which the school principal alleged were in contravention of the principle of *laïcité*. In November 1989 the Conseil d'Etat (French constitutional court) ruled that the wearing of religious symbols was not incompatible with the principle of *laïcité* as long as the said symbol was not worn in a polemical or ostentatious manner.[43] The decision whether a particular symbol would be considered ostentatious was left to schools.[44] These events attracted a lot of media coverage at a time when international attention was already turned towards Islam,[45] with the start of the first Palestinian *intifada* as well as the Iranian *fatwa* against Salman Rushdie.[46] As a result, what began as a small school incident grew into a wider national debate on the place of Muslims in France. The headscarf became a symbol of Muslim identity in the secular Republic. More and more young Muslims took to wearing the headscarf and protests claiming the freedom to wear a headscarf in the classroom were organised in the schools of various French cities.[47] In September 1994 following more school incidents Francois Bayrou, then Minister of Education, issued a decree prohibiting ostentatious signs of religious affiliation at school, although discreet ones were permitted.[48] The decree suggested that schools revise their rules and regulations to take this into account but, following the decree, more protests ensued and there were a number of exclusions from schools that gave rise to various court decisions.[49] In deciding whether to overturn an exclusion the courts had to look at whether the wearing of the religious symbol in question amounted to an act of proselytism or propaganda. If so, then exclusion could be upheld. A number of exclusions were overturned, for instance when pupils had been excluded solely on the ground of their wearing a headscarf that the school had deemed incompatible with *laïcité*. Moreover, in a decision of 26 July 1996 the Conseil d'Etat overturned the decision of a university to deny access to female students wearing headscarves on the ground that the university had received an anonymous security threat.[50] The court held that the security threat could have been addressed without the need to deny access to those students. On the other hand, in a decision of 27 November 1996,[51] the Conseil d'Etat confirmed 17 exclusions of students who had organised protests against a change in their school's rules and regulations following the decree. The Conseil considered that the students had gone beyond their right to manifest their religion by disrupting the normal functioning of the school.

Over the years, there were more and more cases of exclusion and more and more litigation as schools were left with the responsibility of deciding whether the wearing of a particular religious symbol could be seen as proselytism.[52] This led to much confusion and inconsistency, and in 2003, in order to clarify the situation, the then President Jacques Chirac decided to introduce a law that would ban all religious symbols at school. He commissioned the Stasi report on *laïcité* in the Republic,[53] which eventually led to the adoption of the Law of 2004.

Those in favour of the law argued that the headscarf is a symbol of oppression of women and that in order to guarantee their freedom of religion (including freedom from religion), they need to be able to take it off if they so choose. French schools cannot endorse what might constitute a symbol of repression against women.[54] As such, the law is seen as promoting equality and protecting the secular state and pupils from any social and religious pressure. The detractors of the law have argued that the law was enacted to target the French Muslim minority[55] as part of a fear of the rising Islamic fundamentalism.[56] They have also argued that the law will reinforce France's already strong policy of assimilation and integration.[57] Saxena argues that minority groups are required to surrender their identity in the name of assimilation.[58] It is true that with *laïcité*, it becomes difficult for minorities to manifest their identity outside the private sphere, especially those who follow a practice-based religion.

The law has also frequently been accused of breaching human rights, in particular, article 9 and 14 of the ECHR and Article 2 of Protocol 1 (right to education) as well as article 18 of the International Covenant on Civil and Political Rights (ICCPR). The European Court of Human Rights however has never so far declared the French law incompatible with the ECHR since the prohibition is 'prescribed by law' and therefore falls within the state's margin of appreciation. The right to belief is absolute, but the right to manifest that belief is considered to be qualified and thus capable of restriction as long as that restriction is prescribed by law, in defence of a legitimate aim and proportionate. In July 2009, the European Court upheld a number of exclusions for failure to comply with the law.

The Court recognised that the law of 2004 placed a restriction on the manifestation of religion but since the law carried the legitimate aim of protecting the rights and freedom of others as well as public order, it was a justified interference and the expulsions were not disproportionate. The claims based on article 14 were rejected because the law applies to all religious symbols and the claim that the exclusions were an infringement on the right to education was also rejected since distance learning was available.[59] The HRC on the other hand found France to be in breach of its obligations under Article 18 of the International Covenant on Civil and Political Rights (ICCPR) following a communication concerning the exclusion of a Sikh pupil from school for wearing a mini turban or *keski*. [60] In its decision the Committee recognised that the prohibition on the applicant wearing his turban at school according to the Law of 2004 places a restriction on his right to freedom of religion (para 8.3) and concluded that France had not provided enough evidence to show that the applicant wearing his turban would pose a threat to the rights and freedom of other pupils and that accordingly his expulsion from school was not proportionate. According to the Committee, France had not shown 'how the sacrifice of those persons' rights is either necessary or proportionate to the benefits achieved' (para 8.7). The HRC therefore acknowledged the contribution of the law in responding to a series of incidents compromising the safety of school children (para 8.6) but condemned although not explicitly the blanket ban on religious symbols at schools which the Committee sees as simplifying 'the administration of the restrictive policy' (8.7). While the HRC remains general in its view on the Law of 2004 it is clear that the law was implemented as a reaction to the headscarf affairs but that it has as a result deprived all religious communities in displaying their faith even though there is no record of particular incidents with those faith groups. On the other hand, France asserts that allowing some symbols and not others may be discriminatory (para 5.8). In addition, one could argue that the presence of a number of private schools, including religious ones that are subsidised by the French government, provides an accessible alternative to state-secular schools and thus the right to education is not compromised by the Law of 2004.[61]

However, for the minority of Muslim girls, Sikhs and Jewish boys who consider that wearing a veil, turban or kippa is an obligation of their religion, the law forces them to choose between their religion on the one hand and *laïcité* on the other. It appears therefore that openly practising their religion is not compatible with *laïcité*. If they wish to continue to display their faith, they can continue to do so only in private or in limited public spaces. As a result, many religious students have moved to religious schools or opted for distance learning which will isolate them even more, thus making the process of integration even more difficult. While the law focused on all conspicuous religious symbols, the impact of the law is mostly felt by those who belong to a practice-based religion such as Islam, Sikhism and Judaism. The Catholic majority in France is unlikely to be affected: Catholics seldom wear large crosses and there is no such requirement in Catholicism – the wearing of a religious symbol is not considered an article of faith but rather an expression of faith. In that sense, the allegation that the legislation is discriminatory can be seen as well founded. Indeed, the reference to large Catholic crosses in the decree has been accused of being a 'symbolic gesture' to avoid the charge of discrimination.[62]

5.6 The impact of the Law of 2004

In July 2005, the Ministry of Education published a research report on the application of the Law of 2004.[63] The report provided both a quantitative and qualitative study of the implications of the Law of 2004. In 2004–2005, 639 signs were recorded in the country or a decrease of over 50 per cent in comparison to the previous year. Ninety-six cases of students opted for alternative solutions including attending a private school, leaving school for those above 16 or registering on a distant learning programme. Forty-seven exclusions were made. There were nine court cases and all of the decisions upheld exclusions. Overall therefore the figures seem encouraging, showing a decrease in the number of incidents, but the report fails to refer to those students who simply did not get back to school at all in September 2004. Inevitably, the Law led to some young Muslim students having to renounce their education while others eventually gave in to the law in order to continue to study, knowing that once they reached university they would be free to dress how they wished. The law was deemed to be a success by the French Government as seen in the above report as well as for instance the Laïcité Watchdog report of 2013[64] which highlights that since the school year 2008–2009 there are no records of judicial actions against a school exclusion. Again we must question the extent to which this can actually be deemed a success for the law as the report fails to mention those students who left school altogether or chose an alternative route for their education. The law remains contested and opposition groups continue to voice their concerns and to denounce the negative side effects of the law such as the exclusion of parents wearing a hijab from school[65] or the wearing by certain Muslim students of long skirts which have been deemed too ostentatious by some schools and against the Law of 2004.[66] There have also been some issues with bandanas which as confirmed by the Conseil d'Etat are not permitted in schools under the Law of 2004 if worn in a manner that is ostentatious and motivated by a religious aim.[67] So if the bandana is worn to bypass the prohibition on the headscarf at school then that would not be acceptable but if a bandana was to be worn as a fashion accessory it would be tolerated.

5.7 The Law of 11 October 2010: prohibition of full face covers in public spaces

The Law of 2004 on manifestation of belief at schools has permeated many aspects of French society, such as employment, higher education as well as more generally the public sphere where the restriction is limited to garments which cover the full face. The law of 2010 was mainly aimed at the minority of Muslim women who wear a burqa or a niqab covering the entire face except for the eyes. The debate on the full face cover was launched by then President Nicolas Sarkozy in 2009 in a speech at the Palace of Versailles when he declared that the burqa was not welcome in France and described it as a 'sign of subservience', and contrary to the Republic's principle of women's dignity.[68] Following Sarkozy's comments, the French National Assembly commissioned a special inquiry into the wearing of the full face cover in France and whether it undermines secularism. The report of the inquiry which comprises over 600 pages was published after a very thorough examination of the practice and concluded that wearing a full face cover was an infringement of the liberty and dignity of women. The report indicated that the inquiry had concluded that the practice of wearing a full face cover is not pre-scribed by religion but instead constitutes a cultural custom, and amounts to excluding women from social life and is therefore against republican values. It recommended that the practice be outlawed in public places.[69] This being said, the report is based on empirical evidence collected from stakeholders including academics, politicians, religious leaders, feminist organisations, laicists' organisa-tions but not those individuals who are concerned by the practice.

Whether a particular practice is prescribed by religion is often a criterion used by courts and law makers to determine the extent to which a practice should be permitted. This has been the case with UK courts as will be discussed in the next chapter. While it bears some relevance, it should be looked at with caution because, as we have seen in Chapter 4, religious symbols are highly personal and intimate and it is up to the wearer to decide the importance they wish to give to a particular symbol. It should not be for the state or for the law to interfere with individuals' spiritual connection with a particular sacralised object unless of course it poses a threat to others or to public order. The presumption of the French Government as shown by Sarkozy's speech as well as the inquiry is that the niqab is synonymous with submission of women. While the full face cover is a practice that may well seem at odds with Western practice, it is difficult to ascertain whe-ther a particular individual wears it voluntarily or not. The empirical research that I have carried out with young females wearing the niqab found that all were wear-ing it voluntarily and often against the will of their parents rather than the oppo-site.[70] My findings are supported by empirical research carried out in France,[71] England,[72] Belgium[73] and the Netherlands.[74] All the research confirmed that bans on full face covers are based on false assumptions that the niqab is imposed on women and that the bans are counterproductive as they often do not have the intended effect of dissuading woman from wearing such face covering. Perhaps the most convincing argument advanced by the French special enquiry described above is that the niqab is incompatible with the principle of 'living together' since hiding one's faith is hiding one's identity.[75] The issue with the ban is that by interfering with one's dress, the state is adopting the very paternalistic behaviour it seeks to prevent. It is unrealistic to think that banning a particular religious attire will lead those who wear it to remove it.[76] The efficiency of the law therefore is highly questionable, especially given that it targeted a very small proportion of women within the French Muslim population.[77]

Consulted on the issue, the rector of the Grand Mosque of Paris condemned the wearing of the burqa in France, saying that French Islam must be open and liberal, and that there is no need for French Muslims to hide behind a burqa.[78] The Head of the French Council of Muslim Faith indicated that while he supported taking action to discourage women from wearing a full face cover, a legal ban would stigmatise a vulnerable group.[79] The general Muslim public was also divided on the issue, although it would appear that a majority were against the burqa.[80]

In June 2010, the Rapport Garraud[81] noted that the face is synonymous with identity and thus the uniqueness of an individual and that dialogue can only come from the face. To hide one's face is to exclude oneself from the social contract which allows citizens to live together (*'le vivre ensemble'*).[82] Acknowledging that outlawing the practice carries some risks, the report discusses the possibility that a law might result in the stigmatisation of Muslim women dressing this way and of Islam more generally. Moreover, for those women who refuse to give up the practice, it may mean that they will be forced to remain at home which will lead to them being even more isolated. Despite those reservations, the report recommended that a law be adopted, and on 14 September 2010 the French Parliament voted in favour of the law prohibiting the full face cover. Article 1 provides that 'nul ne peut, dans l'espace public, porter une tenue destinée à dissimuler son visage'[83] (no one can in the public domain, wear a garment intended to fully cover one's face). The new law includes all forms of head covers, not just the burqa, but it is clear from the way the law came to be enacted that it was a reaction to the proliferation of full face covers (burqa or niqab) which are worn by a minority of French Muslims.

Public space for the purpose of the law is defined at article 2 and includes: all public places including places open to the public or delivering a public service. This includes the streets and is thus wider in scope than previous bans on religious symbols in public service or public schools.[84] Exceptions to the ban include instances when a face cover is prescribed by law for health reasons, sports or when worn during traditional or artistic manifestations.[85] In addition, the *Conseil Constitutionnel*, asked to review the law by Parliament in accordance with article 61 of the French Constitution, has held that it conforms to the constitution but added a reservation to the effect that the law could not apply in places of worship open to the public.[86] Presumably this would mean that women have to cover their face immediately before entering the place of worship, as travelling from their home in a full face cover would constitute an infringement to the law.

The law provides that breaches will result in fines of 150 euros for those caught wearing the veil and that anyone who forces a person to cover their face risks penalties of up to 30,000 euros and a one-year jail term.[87] In the autumn of 2016, the Ministry of the Interior published a report on the impact of the Law of 2010. The report indicates that over a 6 year period over 1,600 offences have been recorded with the number of offences decreasing over the years. While there were 392 offences recorded in 2013, the number went down to 278 in 2015.[88] However, those women who are fined rarely pay the fines by themselves as an Algerian businessman called Rachid Nekkaz has set up a fund to cover those fines.[89] The number of woman affected by the law in France was estimated at about 2,000 in 2016;[90] this shows no decrease from 2009 and therefore confirms the inefficacy of the law. As with the Law of 2004 discussed above, the figures published by the

Government paint a positive picture of the Law but in reality, the press as well as police trade unions report that the law is difficult to enforce with some women being arrested and reoffending on a regular basis and one single woman receiving as many as 33 fines.[91] Rather than having the expected deterrent effect, the law has led some women to wear the niqab as a reaction to the law and to society, which they see as hostile.[92] Many of the women who were interviewed by a journalist from *Le Monde* were either single or declared wearing the niqab despite opposition from their husband, which again contradicts the presumption of the French Government according to which the niqab is a symbol of submission of women to men.[93]

Those who oppose the law argue that it is an overreaction to a minor problem since the practice only concerns a small number of Muslim women and that it is part of a crusade against Islam which, in France, does not fit with *laïcité*. Those who support it, on the other hand, argue that the law was not enacted to address a religious problem since the burqa is not a religious requirement of Islam.[94] It is, they argue, a sectarian practice which is encouraged by a minority of Muslims, called the Salafi movement, who interpret the Koran to the letter. It is argued that the law aims to address national security issues and respect for women. In an age where CCTV has become the norm, there is a gap between the practice of covering one's face and issues of security. For instance, how can a teacher safely allow a child to leave school when picked up by someone with a full face cover – it may be difficult to be sure of the identity of the person coming to collect the child.[95] Yet, the proportionality of the measure to the aim is highly questionable.

The legality of the Law of 2010 was tested before the ECHR in the case of *SAS v. France* [96] in which a French Muslim alleged that the Law of 2010 was violating a number of provisions of the ECHR including the right to freedom of religion under Article 9. While the Court made a case against a general ban of the full face cover, in this particular case they did not find any violation because they accepted the French Government's argument that the law fulfilled the legitimate aim of 'living together' ('*vivre ensemble*'). The outcome of the case did not come as a surprise as the Court usually applies a wide margin of appreciation[97] in order to preserve the sovereignty of member states. The outcome of the case was widely criticised by commentators and the case was described as a 'dangerous precedent'.[98] Yet, France is not the only European country to have banned the niqab. Belgium, some parts of Italy, Switzerland and The Netherlands also have laws banning the full-face cover[99] while Germany has announced plans to ban the garment.[100] The problem with those laws is that it further stigmatises the Muslim minority and risks withdrawing Muslim women from public life altogether.[101]

Recently, the UN Human Rights Committee (HRC) found France to be in violation of two women's religious freedom by fining them for wearing the niqab in 2012.[102] This was the first time the UN HRC had been called to consider burqa bans. It remains to be seen whether France will follow the recommendations of the HRC, which is not legally binding on its member states.

5.8 *Laïcité* and employment

While the principle of *laïcité* in France is primarily one that applies to the state and the public sphere, secular currents have permeated the private domain such as employment. In June 2014, the French 'Cour de Cassation' which is a last resort court upheld a decision by a private nursery, Baby Loup,[103] to dismiss the Deputy Director following her refusal to take off her hijab. The Court held that it was permissible for a private company or an organisation to limit the freedom of its employees to manifest their religion provided it can be justified by the nature of the job and that it is proportionate to the aims sought. In this case, the nursery had an internal policy highlighting that the freedom of conscience and religion of its personnel could not compromise the principles of *laïcité* and neutrality applicable to the activities of the nursery. The Court therefore found that the restriction on the right of the employee to manifest her freedom of religion was justified since the applicant was in direct contact with children and their parents. The court took into consideration the fact that the nursery was a small unit with only 18 employees. While the decision was taken on the facts of the case and does not therefore set a general precedent in relation to the hijab at work, it raises serious issues about the purpose of *laïcité* and one cannot help but wonder what the impact of this decision will be on the French Muslim minority, which is likely to feel increasingly unwelcome.

This approach is reflected in recent changes to the employment law. Law n° 2016–1088 of 8 August 2016, also called Law El-Khomri, modified the Employment Code to include a provision on neutrality within the work environment. Article L1321–2-1 of the Employment Code now provides that private companies with at least 20 employees are entitled to limit religious expression as part of their internal regulations. Limitations must be justified by the nature of the tasks to be performed by the employees, respond to a determining and essential professional requirement and proportionate to the aim sought. The new law therefore creates an exception to the existing non-discrimination provision in Article L1132–1 of the Employment Code.

Recently the European Court of Justice was asked to deliver an opinion on yet another case involving a French Muslim woman who was dismissed by her employer, a French private company for refusing to remove her headscarf while on customer visits after the company had received complaints from customers.[104] Mrs Bougnaoui's dismissal had been upheld by the French Court of Appeal and she had appealed her decision to the Cour de Cassation who stayed the appeal and asked for a preliminary ruling by the European Court of Justice. The ECJ was asked to rule on whether article 4 of Directive 2000/78 on equal treatment within employment should be interpreted as meaning that the wish of a customer of an information technology consulting company no longer to have the information technology services of that company provided by an employee, a design engineer, wearing an Islamic headscarf, is a genuine and determining occupational requirement, by reason of the nature of the particular occupational activities concerned or of the context in which they are carried out. The ECJ held that a difference of treatment based on an internal neutrality policy of the employer may not constitute indirect discrimination if it is justified by a legitimate aim. However, in the present case, there was no such neutrality policy and the court considered that a customer's request that an employee does not wear a headscarf cannot be considered as 'a genuine and determining occupational requirement' for the purpose of the Framework directive. The ECJ therefore leaned towards the employee. However, in a case that was decided at the same time and concerned Belgium, the ECJ took a different view and sided with the employer. In *Achbita* [105] which concerns Belgium, on the other hand the company in question had a neutrality policy in place when an employee started wearing a headscarf, leading to her dismissal for breach of the company's neutrality policy. The court held in that case that Ms Achbita's dismissal did not constitute direct discrimination because the neutrality policy applied to all and was proportionate to the aims of the G4S security company.

Some French Muslim women undeniably have to choose between practising their religion, which for some might include wearing a form of head covering that they may consider to be prescribed by the Koran, and taking an active part in French public life, as the two are not compatible. Private religious schooling has also been encouraged which further creates communitarism or '*repli comunautaire*' as discussed above.

As a result, minorities find themselves more stigmatised and this leads to more exclusions thus undermining the initial aim of the legislation which was 'integration'. *Laïcité* is taken to such an extreme that it can be seen as the 'religion' of the republic. The idea that, in order to be a French citizen, one must detach oneself from any religious and cultural background is one that may lead to ignorance and segregation rather than integration. It might also allow religious practice, relegated to the private sphere, to go unchallenged once it is hidden from view and from public debate. While it is important to support freedom from religion and the state has to protect its citizens from factional pressure, religion and culture are often intertwined and for certain minorities giving up their culture amounts to surrendering their identity.

The French neutrality therefore is protective of freedom of conscience but negates the importance of manifestation of belief as a key aspect of identity, especially for religious minorities who are expected to adapt to the majority practices. Non-religious practices however are not discouraged. This sends the message that the 'secular' deserves more protection than the 'religious'. In the next chapter, the French approach is contrasted with the English approach which does not insist on a separation between church and state.

Notes

1 An earlier version of this chapter was published in Bacquet 2012.
2 '*La France est une République indivisible, laïque, démocratique et sociale. Elle assure l'égalité devant la loi de tous les citoyens sans distinction d'origine, de race ou de religion. Elle respecte toutes les croyances…*' The full text is available from: https://www.legifrance.gouv.fr/affichTexteArticle.do;jsessionid=CEB85AA7B9DCE37F66B935464E7E4149.tpdila18v_2?idArticle=LEGIARTI000019240997&cidTexte=

JORFTEXT000000571356&categorieLien=id&dateTexte [accessed 18 August 2018].

3   Laborde 2001.
4   Art 13 '... *L'organisation de l'enseignement public gratuit et laïque à tous les degrés est un devoir de l'Etat*' (... the organisation of public and free education at all levels is a duty of the State).
5   Kintzler 1996.
6   Ibid.
7   Laborde 2001, op. cit. 720.
8   Jennings 2000. 576.
9   Conseil d'Etat 2004.
10   Robert 2003.
11   See Loi Macron n° 2015–990 of 6 August 2015 *pour la croissance, l'activité et l'égalité des chances économiques* which relaxes the existing legislation concerning work on Sunday. [online] Available from: https://www.legifrance.gouv.fr/affichTexte.do?cidTexte=JORFTEXT000030978561&categorieLien=id [accessed 28 December 2018]. See further: Editions Tissot, 21 July 2015. 'Loi Macron: les nouvelles règles du travail le dimanche' [online]. Available from: https://www2.editions-tissot.fr/actualite/droit-du-travail/loi-macron-les-nouvelles-regles-du-travail-le-dimanche [accessed 18 August 2018].
12   Conseil d'Etat 2004, op. cit. 272–278.
13   Conseil d'Etat 3 May 1950 Demoiselle Jamet in Stasi 2003. para 2.2.
14   See further Gohil and Sidhu2008; Nayar 2004.
15   This is argued by Clarke 1986. 283.
16   Stasi 2003, op. cit. para 1.2.2.
17   Olsen and Toddington 2007. 165.
18   Before the law of 1905 only Catholicism, Protestantism and Judaism were recognised religions and therefore in receipt of state funds. See Robert 2003. 640.
19   Circulaire n° 2004–084 of 18 May 2004 JO of 22 May 2004. [Online] Available from: http://www.legifrance.gouv.fr/affichTexte.do?cidTexte=JORFTEXT000000252465&dateTexte [accessed 18 August 2018].
20   Ibid.
21   Stasi 2003 op. cit.
22   Ibid., para 3.1.1.
23   Ibid., para 3.2.1.
24   See generally Wallach-Scott 2007.
25   Stasi 2003, op. cit. para 3.3.1.
26   Ibid., para 4.1.2.2.
27   In the words of the head of an association; ibid., para 3.3.2.1.
28   Ibid.
29   Ibid., para 3.3.2.2. On anti-Semitism in France see Bacquet 2004.
30   Stasi 2003, op. cit. para 4.1.1.1.
31   Ibid., para 4.3.2.
32   Ibid., paras 4.3.3ff.
33   Ibid., para 4.4.
34   Chirac 2003.
35   Charte de la Laïcité dans les services publics, April 2007, [online] Available from: http://solidarites-sante.gouv.fr/IMG/pdf/charte_laicite-2.pdf [accessed 18 August 2018].
36   L'Observatoire de la Laïcité is a Government advisory body on *laïcité*. It assists the Government in implementing *laïcité* policies by doing research, collecting data, preparing reports as well as making recommendations. See further their webpage available from: http://www.gouvernement.fr/missions-de-l-observatoire-de-la-laicite [accessed 18 August 2018].

37 Observatoire de la Laïcité, 2016. 'Laïcité et gestion du fait religieux dans les établissements publics de santé'. [online] Available from: http://www.gouvernement.fr/sites/default/files/contenu/piece-jointe/2016/02/laicite_et_gestion_du_fait_religieux_dans_les_etablissements_publics_de_sante_1.pdf [accessed 18 August 2018].

38 See generally Freedman 2004. 7–9.

39 Hackett 2017.

40 For an account of the history of immigration and its resonance on *laïcité* see Wallach-Scott 2007, op. cit. 21–41.

41 See generally statistics published by the French Ministry of Education [online] available from: http://www.education.gouv.fr/cid3014/les-indicateurs-de-resultats-des-lycees.html. For instance, in Lycée Henri Wallon in Aubervilliers, north of Paris, largely populated by immigrants, the pass rate at the Baccalaureate in 2017 was 70 per cent whereas Lycée Victor Hugo in central Paris achieved 99 per cent.

42 See generally Freedman 2004, op. cit. 7–10.

43 Conseil d'Etat, 27 November 1989. Avis n° 346.893 relatif au port de signes d'appartenance religieuse.

44 Conseil d'Etat, 2 November 1992. Décision n° 130394.

45 See generally Tévanian 2006.

46 Wallach-Scott 2007, op. cit. 71–2.

47 See for example Rueff 1989.

48 Circulaire n° 1649 du 20 Septembre 1994, [online] Available from: http://www.assemblee-nationale.fr/12/dossiers/documents-laicite/document-3.pdf [accessed 19 August 2018.]

49 See for example, Depalle 1995.

50 Requête n° 170106 du 26 Juillet 1996.

51 Requêtes n° 170207 et 170208 du 27 Novembre 1996.

52 See for example, Monnot and Ternisen 2003.

53 Stasi 2003, op. cit.

54 Olsen and Toddington 2007, op. cit. 163.

55 Wallach-Scott 2007, op. cit. 1.

56 Fourneret 2006.

57 See Freedman 2004, op. cit.

58 Saxena 2007. 767.

59 See for instance the cases of *Aktas v France* App no 43563/08, *Bayrak v France* App no 14308/08, *Gamaleddyn v France* App no 18527/08, *Ghazal v France* App no 29134/08, *J. Singh v France* App no 25463/08 and *R. Singh v France* App no 27561/08.

60 Communication No. 1852/2008.

61 La documentation française, 'L'école républicaine'. [online] Available from: http://www.ladocumentationfrancaise.fr/dossiers/france-50-ans-transformations/ecole-republicaine.shtml [accessed 19 August 2018].

62 Saxena 2007, op. cit. 767 and Wallach-Scott 2007, op. cit. 3, 4.

63 Chérifi 2005.

64 Observatoire de la Laïcité 2013.

65 See Circulaire Chatel No. 2012–056 of 27 March 2012 which provides that any parent accompanying children on school outings falls within the provisions of the Law of 2004 and thus must not wear any ostentatious signs. However, Education Minister Vallaud-Belkacem had declared in October 2014 that parents accompanying children did not have to comply with the 2004 legislation and administrative courts have given conflicting decisions on the issue. See: Tribunal Administratif (Administrative Court) de Montreuil – Decision No 1012015 of 22 November 2011. [online] Available from: http://media.education.gouv.fr/file/11_novembre/26/3/TA_Montreuil_22.11.11_200263.pdf [accessed 19 August 2018] as opposed to Decision No 1305386 of 9 June 2015 of Tribunal Administratif de Nice [online] Available from: http://

nice.tribunal-administratif.fr/content/download/43508/377042/version/1/file/
1305386.pdf [accessed 28 December 2018].

66   Battaglia M. 12 May 2016. Refusée au lycée pour une jupe 'trop longue': y a-t-il eu
     discrimination? *Le Monde.* [online] http://www.lemonde.fr/education/article/
     2016/05/12/refusee-au-lycee-pour-une-jupe-trop-longue-y-a-t-il-eu-discrimination_
     4918360_1473685.html [Accessed 19 August 2018].
67   5 décembre 2007, Monsieur et Madame GHAZAL, requête n°295671.
68   BBC News 2009.
69   Assemblée Nationale 2010.
70   This is discussed in further detail in Chapter 4. For the full paper see: Bacquet 2015.
71   Open Society Foundation 2011.
72   Inge 2016.
73   Human Rights Centre of Ghent University 2015.
74   Ibid.
75   Garraud 2010.
76   This is backed up by the Open Society Justice Initiative research of September 2013.
     Bouteldja 2013.
77   Women wearing the full face cover in France were estimated at 2000 in 2009 or
     0.03% of the French population, see Nunès 2010. There is no evidence to suggest
     that the percentage of French Muslim women wearing the burqa has either increased
     or decreased since the ban; see further BBC News 2018.
78   Lemonde.fr with AFP 2009.
79   BBC News 2010.
80   Bidar 2009.
81   This is the equivalent of the Stasi report but for the 2010 law proposal.
82   Garraud 2010, op. cit.
83   Loi n° 2010–1192 of October 2010 interdisant la dissimulation du visage dans
     l'espace public.
84   Things that are already forbidden in the streets of France include walking around
     naked and protesting with a hood.
85   Article 2(ii).
86   Décision n° 2010–613 DC of 7 October 2010.
87   Article 4.
88   La Parisienne 2016.
89   Le Parisien.fr 2016.
90   La Parisienne 2016.
91   Cigainero 2016.
92   De Féo 2016.
93   Pascual 2015.
94   Copé 2009.
95   Ibid.
96   *SAS v France* (Application no. 43835/11). 1 July 2014.
97   See for instance the case of *Lautsi and Others v. Italy*, (Application no. 30814/06) 18
     March 2011.
98   Smet 2015.
99   Sanghani 2017.
100 Dearden 2017.
101 See for instance: Zerouala 2014.
102 Sonia Yaker CCPR/C/123/D/2747/2016 and Miriana Hebbadj CCPR/C/123/
     D/2807/2016 of 17 July 2018.
103 Arrêt du 25 juin 2014 n° 612, Assemblée plénière n° de pourvoi: E1328369.

104 *Asma Bougnaoui and Association de défense des droits de l'homme (ADDH) v Micro-pole SA*, Request for a preliminary ruling from the Cour de cassation, Case C-188/15, 14 March 2017.
105 *Samira Achbita and Centrum voor gelijkheid van kansen en voor racismebestrijding v G4S Secure Solutions NV*. Request for a preliminary ruling from the Hof van Cassatie, Case C-157/15, 14 March 2017.

References

Books

Inge, A., 2016. *The Making of a Salafi Woman*. Oxford: Oxford University Press.
Kintzler, C., 1996. *La république en question*. Paris: Minerve.
Olsen, H. P. and Toddington, S., 2007. *Architectures of Justice*. Farnham: Ashgate.
Wallach-Scott, J., 2007. *The Politics of the Veil*. Princeton: Princeton University Press.

Articles, book chapters and conference papers

Bacquet, S., 2012. 'Religious Freedom in a Secular Society: An Analysis of the French Approach to Manifestation of Beliefs in the Public Sphere', in CumperP. and LewisT., eds. *Religion, Rights and Secular Society*. Cheltenham: Edward Elgar. 147–168.
Bacquet, S., 2015. 'Religious Symbols and the Making of Contemporary Religious Identities' in SandbergR. ed. *Religion and Legal Pluralism*. Farnham: Ashgate. 113–130.
Clarke, D. M., 1986. 'Freedom of Thought in Schools: a Comparative Study'. *International and Comparative Law Quarterly*, 35(2): 271–301.
Depalle, P., 1995. 'Deux élèves portant le foulard islamique sont exclues d'un lycée de Nevers', *Le Monde*, 24 October. Archives.
Fourneret, J., 2006. 'France: Banning Legal Pluralism by Passing a Law'. *Hastings Intl. & Comp. L. Rev*. 29: 223.
Freedman, J., 2004. 'Secularism as a Barrier to Integration? The French Dilemma', *International Migration*, 42(3): 5–27.
Gohil, N. S. and Sidhu, D.S., 2008. 'The Sikh Turban: Post-9/11 Challenges to this Article of Faith', *Rutgers J. L. & Religion*, 1(9).
Jennings, J., 2000. 'Citizenship, Republicanism and Multiculturalism in Contemporary France', *British Journal of Political Science*, 30(4): 575–598.
Laborde, C., 2001. 'The Culture(s) of the Republic, Nationalism and Multiculturalism in French Republican Thought', *Political Theory*, 29(5): 718.
Monnot, C. and Ternisen, X., 2003. 'L'exclusion de deux lycéennes voilées divise l'extrême gauche', *Le Monde*, 9 October. Archives.
Robert, J., 2003. 'Religious Liberty and French Secularism', *Brigham Young Law Review*, 2003(2): 637.
Rueff, J., 1989. 'Le défilé des intouchables', *Le Monde*, 24 October. Archives.
Saxena, M., 2007. 'The French Headscarf Law and the Right to Manifest Religious Belief'. *Det Mercy L Rev*, 84: 765.
Tévanian, P., 2006. 'Le voile médiatique. Un faux débat: "l'affaire du foulard islamique"', *Communication*, 25(1): 362.

Websites

Attributed author

Bacquet, S. 2004. 'An Analysis of the Resurgence of Anti-Semitism in France', *Journal of Diplomatic Language*, 1(4). https://papers.ssrn.com/sol3/papers.cfm?abstract_id= 1337662 [Accessed 17 August 2018]

Battaglia, M., 2016. 'Refusée au lycée pour une jupe "trop longue": y a-t-il eu discrimination?' *Le Monde*, 12 May. http://www.lemonde.fr/education/article/2016/05/12/ refusee-au-lycee-pour-une-jupe-trop-longue-y-a-t-il-eu-discrimination_4918360_ 1473685.html [Accessed 19 August 2018]

Bidar, A., 2009. 'La burqa, une pathologie de la culture musulmane'. *Libération*, 29 June. http://www.liberation.fr/societe/0101576805-la-burqa-une-pathologie-de-la-cul ture-musulmane [Accessed 26 November 2010]

Bouteldja, N. 2013. 'After the Ban: The Experiences of 35 Women of the Full-Face Veil in France'. Open Society Justice Initiative. September. https://www.opensocietyfounda tions.org/sites/default/files/after-the-ban-experience-full-face-veil-france-20140210. pdf [Accessed 16 January 2019]

Chérifi, H. Ministère de l'éducation nationale de l'enseignement supérieur et de la recherche, 2005. 'Application de la loi du 15 mars 2004 sur le port des signes religieux ostensibles dans les établissements d'enseignement publics', July. http://www.ladocum entationfrancaise.fr/var/storage/rapports-publics/064000177.pdf#page=1&zoom=a uto,0,849 [Accessed 19 August 2018]

Chirac, J., 2003. 'Discours relatif au respect du principe de laïcité dans la république', *Fil-info-France*, 17 December. http://www.fil-infofrance.com/actualites-monde/discours-chira c-loi-laicite.htm [Accessed 18 August 2018]

Cigainero, J., 2016. 'Five Years into Ban, Burqa Divide Widens in France'. *Deutsche Welle*, 10 April. http://www.dw.com/en/five-years-into-ban-burqa-divide-widens-in-france/a -19177275 [Accessed 19 August 2018]

Copé, J. F., 2009. 'Voile intégral: une loi indispensable', *Le Figaro.fr*, 15 December. http://www.lefigaro.fr/editos/2009/12/15/01031-20091215ARTFIG00654-voi le-integral-une-loi-indispensable-.php [Accessed 14 November 2018]

Dearden, L., 2017. 'German Parliament Votes in Favour of Partial Burqa Ban', *The Independent*, 28 April. http://www.independent.co.uk/news/world/europe/germa ny-burqa-ban-law-vote-favour-angela-merkel-islam-muslim-civil-servants-judges-milita ry-a7706781.html [Accessed 20 August 2018]

De Féo, A., 2016. 'Le niqab, une revanche des femmes?' *Slate.fr*, 11 October. http://www.sla te.fr/story/125391/niqab-inversion-de-domination [Accessed 19 August 2018]

Garraud, J.P., 2010. 'Rapport n° 2648 sur le projet de loi interdisant la dissimulation du visage dans l'espace public', 23 June. http://www.assemblee-nationale.fr/13/rapports/ r2648.asp#P418_115159 [Accessed 19 August 2018]

Hackett, C., 2017. '5 Facts about the Muslim Population in Europe'. Pew Research Center, 29 November. http://www.pewresearch.org/fact-tank/2016/07/19/5-facts-a bout-the-muslim-population-in-europe/ [Accessed 18 August 2018]

Nayar, R., 2004. 'French Sikhs Defend the Turban'. BBC News, 17 January. http://news. bbc.co.uk/1/hi/world/europe/3403775.stm [Accessed 18 August 2018]

Nunès, E., 2010. 'Le doute subsiste sur le nombre de femmes portant le voile integral', *Le Monde*, 28 April. http://www.lemonde.fr/politique/article/2010/04/27/le-doute-subsiste-sur-le-nombre-de-femmes-portant-le-voile-integral_1343410_823448.html [Accessed 2 November 2018]

Pascual, J., 2015. 'Loi sur le voile intégral: On a créé le monstre qu'on voulait éviter', *Le Monde*, 10 October. http://www.lemonde.fr/religions/article/2015/10/10/loi-sur-le-voile-integral-on-a-cree-le-monstre-qu-on-voulait-eviter_4786934_1653130.html [Accessed 19 August 2018]

Sanghani, R., 2017. 'Burqa Bans: The Countries where Muslim Women Can't Wear Veils', *The Telegraph*, 17 August. http://www.telegraph.co.uk/women/life/burqa-bans-the-countries-where-muslim-women-cant-wear-veils/ [Accessed 20 August 2018]

Smet, S., 2015. 'The Results Are In: Poll on Best and Worst ECtHR Judgment of 2014', 12 February. https://strasbourgobservers.com/2015/02/12/the-results-are-in-poll-on-best-and-worst-ecthr-judgment-of-2014/ [Accessed 20 August 2018]

Stasi, B., 2003. 'Commission de réflexion sur l'application du principe de laïcité dans la République: rapport au Président de la République', December. https://www.la documentationfrancaise.fr/var/storage/rapports-publics/034000725.pdf [Accessed 18 August 2018]

Zerouala, F., 2014. 'Headscarf Ban Turns France's Muslim Women towards Home-working', *The Guardian*, 3 October. https://www.theguardian.com/world/2014/oct/03/france-muslim-women-home-working [Accessed 20 August 2018]

No attributed author

Assemblée Nationale. 'Rapport d'information au nom de la Mission d'information sur la pratique du port du voile intégral sur le territoire national', http://www.assemblee-nationale.fr/13/rap-info/i2262.asp#P24348 [Accessed 19 August 2018]

BBC News. 2010. 'French MPs Vote to Ban Islamic Full Veil in Public', 13 July. http://www.bbc.co.uk/news/10611398 [Accessed 2 November 2018]

BBC News. 2009. 'Sarkozy Speaks out against Burqa', 22 June. http://news.bbc.co.uk/1/hi/8112821.stm [Accessed 19 August 2018]

BBC News. 2018. 'The Islamic Veil across Europe', 31 May. https://www.bbc.co.uk/news/world-europe-13038095 [Accessed 2 November 2018]

Charte de la Laïcité dans les services publics, 2007. April. http://solidarites-sante.gouv.fr/IMG/pdf/charte_laicite-2.pdf [Accessed 18 August 2018]

Circulaire n° 2004–084 of 18 May 2004 JO of 22 May 2004, http://www.legifrance.gouv.fr/affichTexte.do?cidTexte=JORFTEXT000000252465&dateTexte [Accessed 18 August 2018]

Circulaire n° 1649 of 20 September 1994, http://www.assemblee-nationale.fr/12/dossiers/documents-laicite/document-3.pdf [Accessed 19 August 2018]

Conseil d'Etat, 2004. Rapport public: jurisprudence et avis de 2003 – un siècle de laïcité, http://lesrapports.ladocumentationfrancaise.fr/ BRP/044000121/0000.pdf [Accessed 18 August 2018]

Editions Tissot, 2015. 'Loi Macron: les nouvelles règles du travail le dimanche', 21 July. https://www2.editions-tissot.fr/actualite/droit-du-travail/loi-macron-les-nouvelles-regles-du-travail-le-dimanche [Accessed 18 August 2018]

French Constitution, Article 1, https://www.legifrance.gouv.fr/affichTexteArticle.do;jsessionid=CEB85AA7B9DCE37F66B935464E7E4149.tpdila18v_2?idArticle=LEGIARTI000019240997&cidTexte=JORFTEXT000000571356&categorieLien=id&dateTexte [Accessed 18 August 2018]

Human Rights Centre of Ghent University, 'Submissions to the ECHR in the case of SAS v France Application no. 43835/11', http://www.hrc.ugent.be/wp-content/uploads/2015/11/SAS.pdf [Accessed 19 August 2018]

La documentation française, L'école républicaine. http://www.ladocumentationfrancaise.fr/dossiers/france-50-ans-transformations/ecole-republicaine.shtml   [Accessed   19 August 2018]

Loi n° 2010–1192 of October 2010 interdisant la dissimulation du visage dans l'espace public, http://legifrance.gouv.fr/affichTexte.do?cidTexte=JORFTEXT000022911670&categor ieLien=id [Accessed 19 August 2018]

Loi Macron n° 2015–990 of 6 August 2015 pour la croissance, l'activité et l'égalité des chances économiques, https://www.legifrance.gouv.fr/affichTexte.do?cidTexte=JORF TEXT000030978561&categorieLien=id [Accessed 28 December 2018]

La Parisienne, 2016. 'Loi sur le voile intégral : un peu plus de 1600 verbalisations en six ans', 11 October. http://www.leparisien.fr/laparisienne/societe/loi-sur-le-voile-integral-un-peu-p lus-de-1600-verbalisations-en-six-ans-11-10-2016-6194487.php [Accessed 19 August 2018]

Le Parisien.fr. 2016. 'Il paie les amendes anti-burkini', 17 August. http://www.leparisien. fr/espace-premium/val-de-marne-94/il-paie-les-amendes-anti-burkini-17-08-2016-6046703.php [Accessed 11 November 2018]

Lemonde.fr with AFP, 2009. 'Des députés réclament une commission d'enquête sur le port de la burqa', 18 June. https://www.lemonde.fr/politique/article/2009/06/17/des-deputes-re clament-une-commission-d-enquete-sur-le-port-de-la-burqa_1207794_823448.html [Acces- sed 2 November 2018]

Observatoire de la Laïcité, 2013. 'Rapport d'Etape', http://www.ladocumentationfranca ise.fr/var/storage/rapports-publics/134000405.pdf [Accessed 19 August 2018]

Observatoire de la Laïcité, 2016. 'Laïcité et gestion du fait religieux dans les établissements publics de santé', http://www.gouvernement.fr/sites/default/files/contenu/piece- jointe/2016/02/laicite_et_gestion_du_fait_religieux_dans_les_etablissements_publics_de_ sante_1.pdf [Accessed 18 August 2018]

Open Society Foundation, 2011. 'Unveiling the Truth: Why 32 Muslim Women Wear the Full-Face Veil in France', April. https://www.opensocietyfoundations.org/reports/unvei ling-truth-why-32-muslim-women-wear-full-face-veil-france [Accessed 18 August 2018]

Others

Circulaire Chatel No. 2012–056 of 27 March 2012.

6 England and the established church

6.1 Introduction

The UK[1] does not have a written constitution and therefore there is no guarantee of rights in the shape of an entrenched Bill of Rights as in France or in the US. England however has a long tradition of religious toleration and human rights protection, including religious freedom which has been guaranteed by civil liberties – the ability for citizens to do what they like provided it is not prohibited by law – up until the coming into force of the Human Rights Act (HRA) 1998 in 2000. The HRA incorporated the rights contained in the European Convention on Human Rights (ECHR) into UK law, allowing individuals to invoke their Convention rights directly with UK courts rather than having to petition the European Court of Human Rights in Strasbourg. Article 9 of the ECHR therefore, which guarantees freedom of conscience, religion and belief, is now part of English Law. Freedom from discrimination on the ground of religion is also protected by the Equality Act 2010 (EA). In addition, English law has granted religious exemptions to minority groups including Jews, Sikhs and Muslims. This chapter will start by discussing the relationship between the state and religion in England and will move on to examining how manifestation of religion is protected both under the Human Rights Act 1998 and the Equality Act 2010 with a particular emphasis on schools and employment in order to draw a comparison with France.

6.2 Church–state relations in England

There is no formal separation of church and state in England. The Church of England has the privileged position of established church[2] which means that it has a different legal status from other religious groups. As a result, the Queen is the Head of the Church of England[3] and there is a requirement that the Monarch must be a Protestant in communion with the Established Church.[4] In addition, the presence of the Established Church is felt within the UK Parliament as the House of Lords, which is the unelected upper house of Parliament, counts 26 Bishops known as the Lords Spiritual. The Lords Spiritual do not belong to any political parties and there is a constitutional convention suggesting that they do not take part in political debates. As such, their ability to influence legislation remains extremely minimal, which has led some to question the extent to which their presence is necessary.[5] As a result of establishment, the internal laws of the Church which can be termed religious laws are subject to Royal Assent by the Monarch and in certain circumstances Parliament's approval. The law of the Church of England therefore is also part of the law of England. The extent to which establishment is compatible with religious freedom has been much debated[6] but the ECHR has not held mild forms of establishment to be incompatible with Article 9 of the Convention. In *Darby v. Sweden* [7] for instance, it was held that 'A State Church system cannot in itself be considered to violate Article 9 of the Convention ... However, a State Church system must, in order to satisfy Article 9, include specific safeguards for the individual freedom of religion.'

Despite the official position of the Church of England, there are occasional references in the case law to the separation of church and state beyond the established position of the Church of England and the autonomy of the Church remains protected in key areas. In *R. v. Chief Rabbi, ex parte Wachmann* [8] for instance, Simon Brown J in the QBD of the High Court recalled that:

> The state has not surrendered or delegated any of its functions or powers to the Church. None of the functions that the Church of England performs would have to be performed in its place by the state if the Church were to abdicate its responsibility. The relationship which the state has with the Church of England is one of recognition, not of the devolution to it of any of the powers or functions of government.

The case concerned the jurisdiction of the court to review a decision of the Chief Rabbi to terminate a rabbi's employment contract. It was held that: the court would never be prepared to rule on questions of Jewish law'. In relation to the determination of whether someone is morally and religiously fit to carry out the spiritual and pastoral duties of his office, the court 'must inevitably be wary of entering so self-evidently sensitive an area, straying across the well-recognised divide between church and state.'

Despite England's ceremonial recognition of the role of religion therefore, it is considered to be a secular state and its approach to regulating religious symbols in the public sphere can be seen as generally relaxed when contrasted with the French policy of *laïcité*. English secularism is what is known as passive secularism as opposed to France's more militant *laïcité*, as it does not prevent the accommodation by the state of religious minorities through exemptions to the law. This will be discussed in the next section.

6.3 Religious freedom in England before the Human Rights Act

Up until the coming into force of the HRA, religious symbols were afforded a de facto level of protection, based on Britain's multicultural and pluralist policy. Indeed, Britain has an admirable legislative track record since the 1960s in promoting policies of tolerance aimed at what would now be called multiculturalism and 'social inclusion'.[9] Cultural differences have typically been accommodated in the public sphere and regulations concerning school uniforms, for example, have generally been permissive. Sikhs have, since 1976, been exempt from wearing crash and safety helmets and allowed to wear turbans. Moreover, in October 2015, the Deregulation Act extended the initial protection offered to Sikhs by the Employment Act 1989. While the 1989 Act provided Sikhs with an exemption to wearing safety helmets on 'construction sites', the 2015 legislation extends this to the 'workplace' in general.[10] Similarly, s. 139A of the Criminal Justice Act 1988 was amended by S.4 of the Offensive Weapons Act 1996 in order to provide a defence to having an article with blade or offensive weapon on religious grounds. This is to accommodate the Sikh minority who as part of the five Ks[11] believe that they are required to wear a kirpan, which is a short sword or knife with a curved blade. Finally, part 4 of the Welfare of Animals Regulations 1995 allows for the slaughtering of animals by religious methods in order to accommodate Jews and Muslims with the requirements of their respective religions. These exemptions to the law to accommodate religious minorities are something that in France could not be allowed because they would be considered as a breach of the neutrality principle with the state indirectly showing support to a particular faith group. Those religious exemptions in English law signify that religious differences are recognised and valued and this is also reflected in the context of schools.

6.4 Religious symbols in English Schools

Unlike France, most English schools have a uniform policy or dress code in place. There is no legislation on school uniforms in England, and it is left to schools' governing bodies to decide whether their school needs a policy and, if so, what that policy should be. This is in accordance with section 21 of the Education Act (as amended by section 38 of the Education and Inspections Act 2006) which places responsibility for the conduct of the school on the governing body. The DCSF strongly encourages schools to have a uniform policy as:

> ...it can instil pride; support positive behaviour and discipline; encourage identity with, and support for, school ethos; ensure pupils of all races and backgrounds feel welcome; protect children from social pressures to dress in a particular way; and nurture cohesion and promote good relations between different groups of pupils. Above all, many schools believe that school uniform supports effective teaching and learning.[12]

School uniform policies have traditionally been flexible enough to allow for the expression of cultural and religious diversity with schools consulting with community religious leaders to ensure that a particular uniform is suitable for pupils attending the school. In the famous *Begum* case[13] for instance, Denbigh High School, the Defendant, went to great lengths to accommodate religious differences. It offered three uniform options; the school appointed a working party to review its policy, and it consulted with local religious leaders, parents and students to ensure that it fulfilled the Islamic requirement that women wear modest dress

(*Begum* para. 6 and 7). This was particularly important since the school in this case had a large proportion of Muslim students, yet this still provoked the charge by one pupil that the uniform policy was unduly restrictive and infringed her right to manifest her religious freedom protected under Article 9 of the ECHR. This case will be explored in further detail below.

When a school uniform policy discriminates against a particular ethnic group on the basis of race or religion, the courts have tended to adopt a pluralist stance. In *Mandla v. Dowell Lee*, [14] the Court of Appeal, relying mainly on the Race Relations Act 1976 (RRA) (now repealed by the EA 2010) held that a school uniform requiring short hair and caps for boys was discriminatory to Sikhs who wear a turban as part of their identity. But the courts have been reluctant to undermine the authority of a school's governing body, and in more recent case law have reaffirmed the authority of head teachers and school governors, and their right to insist on uniform policy. As a result of this approach, some school children have been unable to manifest their faith. This will be discussed in the next section.

6.5 The Human Rights Act 1998 and schools

Section 6 of the HRA provides that 'it is unlawful for a public authority to act in a way which is incompatible with a Convention right.' Public authorities include anyone who is performing a 'public function'. This includes Government departments, local authorities, the National Health Service and state schools. [15] The Human Rights Act does not apply to private bodies such as private companies unless they are performing a public function. Breaches of the right to freedom of religion by private entities are normally dealt with under the EA 2010 which prohibits discrimination (direct and indirect), victimisation and harassment on the protected characteristics which include religion. [16] The bulk of the case law on Article 9 of the ECHR involves manifestation of belief at schools.

Under the HRA, state schools, as public authorities, are under an obligation to comply with the ECHR. In relation to human rights, schools are required to act reasonably in accommodating religious requirements. Guidance produced by the Ministry of Education provides that:

> Where a school has good reason for restricting an individual's freedoms, for example, the promotion of cohesion and good order in the school, or genuine health and safety or security considerations, the restriction of an individual's rights to manifest their religion or belief may be justified. The school must balance the rights of individual pupils against the best interests of the school community as a whole. Nevertheless, it should be possible for most religious requirements to be met within a school uniform policy and a governing body should act reasonably through consultation and dialogue in accommodating these. [17]

Different schools are, therefore, entitled to adopt their own uniform policies, in accordance with the needs of local communities while respecting cultural and religious diversity.

6.6 English courts' approach to manifestation of belief at school

This section examines a number of court decisions which have shaped the courts' approach to religious manifestation at school.

In *Begum* [18] and *X* v. *Y*, [19] the claimants challenged a school's uniform policy which prevented them from wearing, respectively, a full body garment (jilbab) and full face cover (niqab). In *Playfoot* [20] and *Watkins-Singh* [21] the claimants challenged the school 'no jewellery' policy which prevented them from wearing, respectively a 'purity ring' (as a symbol of commitment to chastity before marriage) and a *kara* bangle as a manifestation of the Sikh faith.[22]

Overall, the courts' approach has been one of deference to the Executive. Judges are reluctant to get involved in 'religious' matters such as deciding what item of religious clothing should or should not be worn at school. Lord Bingham recalled that:

> The House is not, and could not be, invited to rule on whether Islamic dress, or any feature of Islamic dress, should or should not be permitted in the schools of this country. That would be a most inappropriate question for the House in its judicial capacity.
>
> (*Begum* para. 2)

This is not an isolated sentiment, Justice Silber in *Watkins-Singh* warned:

> This judgement is fact-sensitive and it does not concern or resolve the issue of whether the wearing of the Kara should be permitted in the schools of this country. Indeed, that is not a question that a court could or should be asked to resolve.
>
> (para. 1)

This is also apparent in both *R v. Secretary of State for Education and Employment* [23] para. 22:

> ...emphatically, it is not for the court to embark on an inquiry into the asserted belief and judge its 'validity' by some objective standard such as the source material upon which the claimant founds his belief or the orthodox teaching of the religion in question or the extent to which the claimant's belief conforms to or differs from the views of others professing the same religion. Freedom of religion protects the subjective belief of an individual[24]

and in *X* v. *Y* [25] para. 1:

> This judgment is fact-sensitive and it does not concern or resolve the issue of whether the wearing of the niqab should be permitted in the schools of this country. That is not a question that a court could or should be asked to resolve.[26]

In addition to the reluctance to be perceived as arbiters of faith, courts also have a tendency to defer to what Vakulenko calls 'local knowledge'.[27] This approach is based on the idea that the sovereign Parliament has given local authorities decision making power for the very reason that they are better experienced to make those decisions. If the courts were to overrule those decisions, it would amount to overstepping their role. This is reiterated by Lord Bingham in *Begum*:

> It would in my opinion be irresponsible of any court, lacking the experience, background and detailed knowledge of the head teacher, staff and governors, to overrule their judgement on a matter as sensitive as this. The power of decision has been given to them for the compelling reason that they are best placed to exercise it. And I see no reason to disturb their decision.
>
> (para. 34)

This trend originates in the 'margin of appreciation' doctrine developed by the European Court of Human Rights (ECHR) in order to preserve state sovereignty. The court assumes that, given the diversity of national systems amongst members of the Council of Europe, national courts are in a better position to decide on issues that concern their citizens.[28] Despite this trend, the High Court in *Playfoot* had to rule on whether the silver ring[29] was a requirement of the claimant's faith. Using the test in *Williamson*, the judge concluded that the act of wearing a purity ring was not 'intimately linked' to the belief in chastity before marriage: 'If the belief takes the form of a perceived obligation to act in a specific way then, in principle doing that act pursuant to that belief is itself a manifestation of that belief in practice' (para. 32).

Ms Playfoot, however, belonged to the Silver Ring Thing Movement, a movement that originated in the US and which at the time had a strong presence in the UK.[30] The ring is clearly a key element of the movement and the website clearly states that the ring is not a piece of jewellery but rather a symbol of one's faith to God and it cannot be bought without participating in one of the SRT courses.[31] It appears that the court in *Playfoot* adopted a traditional legal approach to looking at the evidence rather than a more contextual approach which may have given the judge more leeway. In order to conclude that the ring was not a manifestation of the claimant's belief, the court relied on the absence of evidence of a specific requirement within the Catholic faith (para. 23) – 'the claimant was not obliged by her religious faith to wear the ring ...' (para. 38 iii). This is a quasi-legal approach to looking at the evidence, which seems to privilege traditional religious symbols over what Gereluck calls social symbols.[32] This is also apparent in *Watkins-Singh* even though the case was mainly decided on the basis of the RRA (now repealed by the EQ 2010). The outcome is 'consistent' with *Playfoot* in that the *kara* bangle is a recognised symbol of the Sikh faith. The outcome of those two cases is discussed in further detail below.

The court's approach has generally been consistent, with most of the cases on Article 9 using a threefold approach. First, the court determines whether Article 9 is engaged by looking at the seriousness and legitimacy of the belief as well as for some evidence of that belief as seen above. Then it asks whether the freedom to manifest that belief is subject to interference by the public authority's decision. Finally, if this is answered in the affirmative, it considers whether such interference is justified under Article 9(2). In order to determine whether Article 9 is engaged, the courts look at the seriousness of the belief. In *Kalac v. Turkey*, [33] the European Court of Human Rights pointed out that Article 9 does not protect every act motivated or inspired by a religion or belief (para. 27). In *Williamson*, for instance, it was held that the claimants' beliefs were 'not sufficiently cogent, serious, cohesive or important' to fall within the remits of Article 9 (the claimants believed that teachers should be able to administer corporal punishment to children and claimed that this was part of their Christian faith). In *Playfoot*, the judge concluded that Article 9 was not engaged on the basis that the 'purity ring' was not a requirement of the Catholic faith (para. 23–24). On the other hand, in both *Begum* and *X v. Y*, the courts had no difficulty declaring that Article 9 was engaged and that the claimants' belief was sincere. Both cases concerned the Islamic headscarf. Lord Bingham recalled that 'any sincere religious belief must command respect, particularly when derived from an ancient and respected religion', even though Lord Hoffman later added that Article 9 does not require that one should be allowed to manifest one's religion at any time and place of one's choosing (*Begum* para. 50). This confirms the trend of privileging religious symbols over social and cultural ones as discussed above.

While the right to freedom of thought, conscience and religion under the ECHR (Article 9 (1)) is absolute, the right to manifest one's religion and belief (Article 9(2)) is subject to limitations. Article 9(2) provides:

> 2. Freedom to manifest one's religion or beliefs shall be subject only to such limitations as are prescribed by law and are necessary in a democratic society in the interests of public safety, for the protection of public order, health or morals, or the protection of the rights and freedoms of others.

The courts, therefore, look at whether the claimant's freedom to manifest her or his belief is subject to limitations or undue interference within the meaning of Article 9(2) and if so whether such limitation or interference is justified under that provision. In doing so, the courts apply the proportionality test *R (Daly) v. Secretary of State for the Home Department*, [34] taking into account the circumstances of the case (*Williamson* para. 38) – the disputed measure must be proportionate to the legitimate aim pursued. Lord Bingham recalled that the Strasbourg jurisprudence shows that interference is not easily established (*Begum* para. 24).

Both *Begum* and *X v. Y* failed on the basis that there was no interference with Article 9.[35] The court, in both cases, went on to look at whether if there was interference, that interference would be justified. In *Begum*, a number of factors were considered before deciding that the school did not interfere with the claimant's Article 9 rights: the school had been chosen by the claimant; the uniform policy had clearly been explained to parents and pupils; there were other schools that the claimant could attend and where she would be allowed to wear the jilbab; the school had designed its policy taking into account the needs of the Muslim community (para. 25 and 32). Similarly, in *X v. Y*, no interference was found since the claimant had been offered another place at a school where she could wear the niqab, and even if there had been an interference, that interference would have been justified despite the school's policy with regards to the disputed garment being less clear than in *Begum* (para. 39 and 93). The possibility of manifesting one's belief in another place or way as a justification for interference is, however, one which has received a number of criticisms from both judges and academics. Lord Nicholls in *Begum* pointed to the disruption caused to one's education by moving to another school (para. 41).[36]

If the courts' approach to religious freedom and school uniforms has been consistent in terms of the application of the law, the extent to which the above approach has produced logical decisions is debatable. In particular, it is difficult, *prima facie*, to reconcile the outcome in *Playfoot* with the outcome in *Watkins-Singh*, even if the latter was decided on the basis of the RRA as opposed to the HRA. For, what is the difference between a silver ring and a *kara* bangle? Both look like pieces of jewellery, both are discreet items that do not seem to present any particular health and safety risk. The judge in *Watkins-Singh* pointed to the nature of the *kara* bangle as being unlikely to create pressure based on difference in wealth. He referred to the unobtrusive nature of the *kara* (para. 92), but this description could easily apply to the silver ring. The only difference between the 'purity ring' and the *kara* bangle is that the purity ring is not an established symbol of the Catholic faith whilst there is evidence of the importance of the *kara* to Sikhs (see *Watkins-Singh* para. 23 to 30). In *Playfoot* on the other hand, the judge held that: 'The claimant was not obliged by her religious faith to wear the ring …' (para. 38(iii)). The judge in *Watkins-Singh* also pointed to the 'sharp distinction' between both *Begum* and *X v. Y* and *Watkins-Singh*, since the disputed garments in both *Begum* and *X v. Y* were extremely visible. The judge referred to their 'ostentatious nature' (para. 77); this clearly does not apply to the silver ring.

Moreover, the 'mandatory requirement' test used in *Playfoot* was deemed too high a threshold by Justice Silber in *Watkins-Singh* (para. 89). Instead, the judge found it sufficient that wearing the *kara* was of 'exceptional importance' to the claimant and that there was evidence that it had a 'deep significance for adherers of that religion' (para. 78d). The test used in *Playfoot* appears to be a very narrow interpretation of the test in *Williamson* which states:

> it is not for the court to embark on an inquiry into the asserted belief and judge its 'validity' by some objective standard such as the source material upon which the claimant's belief conforms to or differs from the views of others professing the same religion …
>
> (para. 58)

It would indeed be problematic for judges to instigate an inquiry into religious texts, even with the assistance of 'experts', for these issues are regularly riddled with controversy even amongst the followers of particular faiths. The requirement of the Koran, for example, that Muslim women wear modest dress is a source of contention within the Muslim community itself and is subject to a variety of interpretations. While some women choose simply to wear a headscarf, others prefer to wear the full body garment (jilbab), hence the controversy in *Begum* and *X v. Y*. The wearing of religious dress and symbols may reflect the wearer's understanding of the requirement prescribed in their tradition or belief. As pointed out by the Executive Committee of the Inter-faith Network for the UK, appropriate religious dress or symbols is an issue for followers of a particular tradition to discuss amongst themselves.[37]

The courts' approach in *Playfoot*, therefore, not only oversteps the realm of religion but also denies any importance to social and political symbols. Yet, it is difficult to foresee how the court in *Playfoot* could have decided differently without inviting litigation and undermining the authority of school governors. Had Miss Playfoot been granted an exemption to the uniform policy to wear the purity ring, what would prevent, let us say, 'Goths' requesting exemptions in order to wear black, or pupils seeking permissions to wear 'political' wristbands?

What is problematic with the courts' approach in those cases is that they have not been able to acknowledge that there has at least been an interference with a particular belief but that this interference may have been justified by a particular policy. More recent case law beyond the context of schools at both the domestic and regional level (Strasbourg) shows a shift from this approach which is to be welcome. The case of *Bashir, R (on the application of) v The Independent Adjudicator* [38] which concerned a devout Muslim prisoner is a testament to this shift in approach. Bashir had embarked, upon the advice of his Imam, on a 3-day fast prior to his upcoming hearing when prison officers invited him to drink water in order to provide a urine sample as part as a drug test based on reasonable suspicions. When Bashir refused, he was charged for failing to obey a lawful order and proceeded to challenge the charges, amongst others, on the ground of breach of the Human Rights Act as the decision interfered with his right to manifest his religion under Article 9 of the ECHR. The judge in the High Court held that 'there could be no real doubt that the claimant's fast was intimately linked to his religious belief' (para. 20) and that 'there is nothing within Article 9 that requires there to be a perceived, much less an objectively demonstrable obligation for the manifestation of religious belief to be protectable' (para. 21) and that 'to require him to provide a sample of urine which he was not able to provide without breaking his fast was an interference with the claimant's article 9' (para. 23). This shift of approach is to be welcomed as requiring something to be a requirement of a faith before it can attract the protection of Article 9 is failing to recognise the complexity of religion and belief in 21st century modern pluralist states.

The European Court of Human Rights' decision in *Eweida and others v. UK* [39] is consistent with this change of approach. Ms Eweida, who worked for British Airways in a customer facing role insisted that her Christian faith required her to wear a small cross on a chain visible around her neck. She was told by BA that it was a breach of its uniform policy but when asked to remove it, she refused. She also declined offers to be transferred to a non-customer facing role which would allow her to wear her cross visibly. BA later changed its uniform policy so that religious or charity symbols would be permitted and Ms Eweida was reinstated in her role, able to wear the desired cross. However, Ms Eweida brought claims of unlawful discrimination contrary to the Employment Equality (Religion or Belief) Regulation 2003 and claimed compensation for the period where she was left at home without pay. She notably claimed that she had been put at a disadvantage in comparison to colleagues with other beliefs who had been allowed to display their faith. Her claims were rejected by UK courts and she appealed to Strasbourg where she was successful. The ECHR concluded that:

> ...Given the importance in a democratic society of freedom of religion, the Court considers that, where an individual complains of a restriction on freedom of religion in the workplace, rather than holding that the possibility of changing job would negate any interference with the right, the better approach would be to weigh that possibility in the overall balance when considering whether or not the restriction was proportionate.
>
> (Para. 83)

and that: 'Eweida's insistence on wearing a cross visibly at work was motivated by her desire to bear witness to her Christian faith – her behaviour was a manifestation of her religious belief' (para. 89).

> Mrs Eweida's cross was discreet and cannot have detracted from her professional appearance. There was no evidence that the wearing of other, previously authorised, items of religious clothing, such as turbans and hijabs, by other employees, had any negative impact on BA's brand or image.
>
> (para. 94)

Strasbourg rejected the UK's argument that in order to attract the protection of Article 9 something has to be a requirement of that belief:

> In order to count as a 'manifestation' within the meaning of Article 9, the act in question must be intimately linked to the religion or belief. An example would be an act of worship or devotion which forms part of the practice of a religion or belief in a generally recognised form. However, the manifestation of religion or belief is not limited to such acts; the existence of a sufficiently close and direct nexus between the act and the underlying belief must be determined on the facts of each case. In particular, there is no requirement on the applicant to establish that he or she acted in fulfilment of a duty mandated by the religion in question.
>
> (para. 82)

The European Court of Human Right's judgment in *Eweida* was described by Sandberg as the rebirth of religious freedom because it criticised the approach in

Begum and advocated the 'justification' rather than the 'interference' approach.[40] As discussed above, it should not be for the courts to decide what constitutes interference with one's religious freedom. It remains to be seen whether English courts will follow the more relaxed approach of the ECHR or whether they will continue to give preference to those well-established religions. The approach that we have seen in the above cases follows a limiting definition of religion which fails to take into account the nature of modern religious identities and follows a narrow definition of religion.

6.7 The Equality Act 2010 and employment cases

Manifestation of belief at work is protected by the Equality Act 2010 which prohibits direct and indirect discrimination, victimisation and harassment on the ground of one or several of the protected characteristics (see section 4). The EA implemented EU Directive 2000/78 and repealed the Employment Equality (Religion or Belief) Regulations 2003. The outcome of employment cases in England is usually difficult to predict as courts tend to operate on a case by case basis. The main question for the court in employment cases usually revolves around the definition of religion and belief. The EA defines religion and belief in section 10 but in line with the rest of the legislation on religion remains relatively vague and is therefore subject to the courts' interpretation. The definition in s.10.1 and 10.2 provides that 'Religion means any religion and a reference to religion includes a reference to a lack of religion' and 'Belief means any religious or philosophical belief and a reference to belief includes a reference to a lack of belief.' The EA therefore protects religious as well as non-religious belief but religion as such is not defined. Generally, courts have been reluctant to find that the claimant has been discriminated against when they have signed a contract and are aware of any restrictions that may be placed on their religion and belief. For instance, someone who is contracted to work on Sunday who later complains of religious discrimination because she cannot attend mass is not likely to be successful in claiming discrimination.[41]

Since the EA came into force, there have been a large number of disputes where applicants have challenged their dismissals on the ground of religious discrimination. Cases include, asking for a specific day off for religious worship,[42] discussing religion at recruitment interviews,[43] requesting prayer breaks,[44] religious symbols and uniforms,[45] refusal to perform a duty due to religious belief,[46] talking about religion in the workplace[47] and being treated differently or being dismissed because of one's religion or belief.[48]

In determining whether a religion or belief attracts the protection of the EA, the courts apply the Grainger test.[49] In *Grainger v. Nicholson*, Mr Nicholson alleged that he was dismissed on the basis of his belief in climate change. He believed that carbon emissions needed to be cut urgently in order to avoid catastrophic climate change and his belief affected all aspects of his life. The Employment Appeal Tribunal held that Nicholson's beliefs about climate change and the environment were capable of being a belief for the purposes of the regulations, taking into account the case of *McClintock*,[50] where the EAT held that the test for determining whether beliefs can properly be considered to fall into the category of a philosophical belief is whether they have 'sufficient cogency, seriousness, cohesion and importance and are worthy of respect in a democratic society.'

At paragraph 24 of their judgment, the EAT also set out the criteria which must be satisfied for a belief to validly be deemed a philosophical belief, namely: the belief must be genuinely held; it must be a belief and not an opinion or viewpoint based on the present state of information available; it must be a belief as to a weighty and substantial aspect of human life and behaviour; it must attain a certain level of cogency, seriousness, cohesion and importance; and it must be worthy of respect in a democratic society, not be incompatible with human dignity and not conflict with the fundamental rights of others.

While in this case Nicholson's belief in climate change fulfilled the criteria to attract the protection of the EA, the case does not set precedent for a blanket protection of climate change as in certain cases the same belief may not pass the test.

Generally speaking, English courts and tribunals have been more sympathetic to accommodating religious belief in employment than in France unless the religious belief or practice in question conflicts with an occupational requirement. This was the case in both *Ladele v London Borough of Islington* [51] and *McFarlane v Relate Avon Ltd* [52] where claimants had refused to perform their duties under their contract, namely performing civil partnerships for same sex couples (Ms Ladele) and refusing to counsel gay couples (Mr McFarlane). Ladele who was a Registrar at Islington Borough Council and McFarlane who was a relationship counsellor at Relate lost their discrimination claims because they refused to perform a duty which was at the core of their function and allowing the claim would have been perceived as discrimination on the grounds of sexual orientation. Ladele had refused to perform civil partnership ceremonies for same sex couples while McFarlane had refused to counsel gay couples.

Health and safety also trumps religious freedom in employment cases. This was seen in *Chaplin v Royal Devon & Exeter Hospital NHS Foundation Trust* [53] where a nurse was not granted the right to wear a cross on a chain. All those decisions were upheld by the ECHR.[54]

While the UK has no express limitations on the right to manifest religion in the public sphere, some bans have been upheld in the context of school as described above and court buildings.[55] However, a law like the French one banning religious symbols at school or even banning a type of symbol in the public sphere is unlikely to be in line with the British tradition of multiculturalism.

Overall, England's lack of separation between Church and State has meant that religion is acknowledged and protected. This protection has extended to less traditional religious beliefs or non-religious beliefs. Even if there remain a number of areas where the rationale for the involvement of the Church of England is questionable, it has at least created a terrain for religious and non-religious groups to gain recognition.

Notes

1 The United Kingdom (UK) is a union of four countries namely England, Wales, Scotland and Northern Ireland. In this section, we shall only focus on England which is the largest of the four countries.
2 Canon A1 The Church of England is 'established according to the laws of this realm under the Queen's Majesty, belongs to the true and apostolic Church of Christ', in Sandberg 2012. 60.
3 Canon A7.
4 Sandberg 2012. op. cit. 61.
5 See for instance the campaign by the National Secular Society (2017) to abolish the Bishops' bench.
6 See for instance most recently Garcia Oliva and Hall 2018.
7 [1991] 13 EHRR 774.
8 [1992] 1 WLR 1036, QBD.
9 See Parekh 2006 and Modood 2007.
10 Deregulation Act 2015 s. 6.
11 The five Ks are the five outward signs required of a Sikh if they have been baptised.
12 DCSF guidance to schools on school uniform and related policies, October 2007. The Department for Education (2013) has since produced updated guidelines which focus on value for money. Support for uniform policies is maintained.
13 *R (Begum (by her Litigation Friend, Rahman)) v Headteacher and Governors of Denbigh High School* [2006] UKHL 15.
14 *Mandla (Sewa Singh) and another v Dowell Lee and others* [1983] 2 AC 548.
15 Note however that faith schools can discriminate on the basis of religion and therefore require their pupils to wear a specific school uniform in line with their religious ethos.
16 S. 4 of the Equality Act.
17 Department for Education 2013.
18 *R (Begum (by her Litigation Friend, Rahman)) v Headteacher and Governors of Denbigh High School* [2006] UKHL 15.
19 *X v Y School & Ors* [2007] EWHC 298 (Admin).
20 *R (Playfoot) v Governing Body of Millais School* [2007] EWHC 1698 (Admin), [2007] ELR 484.
21 *R (on the application of Watkins-Singh) v Governing Body of Aberdare Girls' High School* [2008] EWHC 1865 (Admin).
22 This is a thin bracelet that Sikhs wear as a manifestation of their belonging to the Sikh faith. The *kara* bangle is part of the five Ks described above.
23 *R (on the application of Williamson and others)* v. *Secretary of State for Education and Employment* [2005] UKHL 15. Thereafter *Williamson*.
24 Lord Nicholls of Birkenhead in *Williamson*.
25 [2007] EWHC 298 (Admin).
26 Justice Silber.
27 Vakulenko 2007.
28 Ibid. and Hutchinson 1999.
29 This is a silver band worn by members of the Silver Ring Thing Movement (SRT) as a symbol of their commitment to chastity before marriage. This is based on ch. 4 v.3-4 of the New Testament: 'God wants you to be holy, so you should keep clear of sexual sin. Then each of you will control your body and live in holiness and honour.'
30 At the time of writing, the UK website is no longer available nor can any details about the movement in the UK be found in the public domain.
31 For further details see https://www.silverringthing.com/ [accessed 01/04/2019].
32 Gereluck 2008. 86.
33 [1997] 27 EHRR 552.
34 *R (Daly)* v. *Secretary of State for the Home Department* [2001] UKHL 26.

35 In *Begum* however, both Lord Nicholls and Baroness Hale in the minority found that the claimant's rights under Article 9 had been interfered with by the school but they both agreed with the majority that the interference was justified.
36 For a discussion of this approach see also Leader 2007.
37 Executive Committee of the Inter Faith network for the UK (no date).
38 [2011] EWHC 1108.
39 Case of *Eweida and Others v. The United Kingdom* (Applications nos. 48420/10, 59842/10, 51671/10 and 36516/10), 15 January 2013.
40 Sandberg 2014. 217.
41 *MBA v The Mayor & Burgesses of the London Borough of Merton* [2013] UKEAT/ 0332/12/SM.
42 *Thompson v Luke Delaney George Stobbart Ltd* [2011] NIFET 00007_11FET.
43 *Rawson v University of the West of England* [2015] ET/1400524/09.
44 *Cherfi v G4S Security Services Ltd* [2011] *UKEAT/0379/10/DMS; Qureshi v Teknequip Ltd* [1999] ET/3203202/98.
45 *Eweida* [2013] op. cit.; *Chaplin v Royal Devon & Exeter Hospital NHS Foundation Trust* [2010] ET 1702886/2009.
46 *Ladele v London Borough of Islington* [2009] EWCA Civ 1357; *McFarlane v Relate Avon Ltd* [2010] EWCA Civ 880.
47 *Wasteney v East London NHS Foundation Trust* [2016] UKEAT/0157/15/LA; *Drew v Walsall Healthcare NHS Trust* [2013] UKEAT/0378/12/SM.
48 *Chandhok & Anor v Tirkey* [2014] UKEAT/0190/14/KN; *Grainger plc and others v Nicholson* [2010] EAT/0219/09.
49 *Grainger* 2010 ibid.
50 *A McClintock v Department of Constitutional Affairs* [2007] EAT/0223/07.
51 [2009] EWCA Civ 1357 CA.
52 [2010] EWCA Civ 771.
53 [2010] ET 1702886/2009.
54 See *Eweida* [2013] op. cit.
55 See *The Queen v. D (R)* [2013] EW Misc 13 (CC).

References

Books

Parekh, B.C., 2006. *Rethinking Multiculturalism: Cultural Diversity and Political Theory.* Basingstoke: Macmillan.
Garcia Oliva, J., and Hall, H., 2018. *Religion, Law and the Constitution: Balancing Beliefs in Britain.* London: Routledge.
Gereluck, D. 2008. *Symbolic Clothing in Schools.* London: Continuum.
Modood, T., 2007. *Multiculturalism: A Civic Idea.* Cambridge: Polity.
Sandberg, R., 2012. *Law and Religion.* Cambridge: Cambridge University Press.
Sandberg, R., 2014. *Religion, Law and Society.* Cambridge: Cambridge University Press.

Articles, book chapters and conference papers

Hutchinson, M. R., 1999. 'The Margin of Appreciation Doctrine in the European Court of Human Rights', *The International and Comparative Law Quarterly,* 48(3): 638–650.
Leader, S., 2007. 'Freedom and Futures: Personal Priorities, Institutional Demands and Freedom of Religion', *The Modern Law Review,* 70(5): 713–730.

Vakulenko, A., 2007. 'Islamic Dress in Human Rights Jurisprudence: a Critique of Current Trends', *Human Rights Law Review*, 7(4): 721.

Websites

No attributed author

Department for Education, 2013. 'School Uniform Guidance for Governing Bodies, School Leaders, School Staff and Local Authorities.' September, https://assets.publish ing.service.gov.uk/government/uploads/system/uploads/attachment_data/file/ 514978/School_Uniform_Guidance.pdf [Accessed 20 August 2018]

Executive Committee of the Inter Faith Network for the UK (no date). 'Reflections on Wearing of Religious Dress and Symbols', https://www.interfaith.org.uk/uploads/reli giousdress.pdf [Accessed 20 August 2018]

National Secular Society. 2017. 'Abolish Bishops' Bench to Reduce the Size of the House of Lords', 21 February. http://www.secularism.org.uk/news/2017/02/abolish-bishop s-bench-to-reduce-the-size-of-the-house-of-lords [Accessed 20 August 2018]

Others

Deregulation Act 2015
Equality Act 2010

7 The United States and tolerant neutrality

7.1 Introduction

'We are a religious people whose institutions presuppose a Supreme Being.'[1] This declaration made by the United States Supreme Court (US SC) in 1952 captures the essence of the United States (US) Government relationship with religion. While the US Constitution provides for complete separation between the state and religion and for government neutrality, religion remains an important aspect of the American social fabric and unlike in France, secularism does not mean that religion is completely relegated to the private sphere. As Chief Justice Burger observed in *Lynch v Donnelly*, 'There is an unbroken history of official acknowledgment by all three branches of government of the role of religion in American life from at least 1789.'[2] This chapter will explore the US constitutional arrangements for church–state relations by looking at the religion clauses[3] of the First Amendment of the US Constitution and their interpretation by the Supreme Court and some of the federal courts. It will then move on to discuss manifestation of religion at school and in the workplace following the themes of the previous two chapters.

7.2 Religious freedom within the American Constitution

Like France and England, the United States' system for the protection of religious freedom and the relationship between the state and religion rest on historical roots that have shaped the political landscape and legal framework. Religious freedom has played an important role in the history of the US and Christian ideals have influenced the American commitment to democratic values such as liberty and human dignity.[4] The First Amendment of the American Constitution of 1787 reflects a desire from America's founding fathers to establish a nation where separation of church and state and freedom to practice one's faith freely would prevail. This stems from a desire of America not to repeat European history and that of its colonies (many of the colonies had an established church) by having a national establishment which would prefer one religion over the others and lead to religious persecutions.[5] The US prohibition on state sponsored religion therefore is based on constitutional values such as religious voluntarism, religious equality, respect for the religious or non-religious identity of citizens and the promotion of a religiously inclusive political community.[6] As opposed to France, the American tradition which is more liberal than republican has a commitment to religious authority as a 'competing sovereign' where the state and religion govern different but overlapping spheres of influence.[7] This historical commitment to religious authority is reflected in the demographic landscape of the US which remains a fairly religious society in comparison to Europe with over half of the American population considering religion to play an important part in their life as opposed to Europe where the importance of religion varies between 14 per cent (France) and 28 per cent (Poland) at the highest.[8] As a result, federal courts as well as the Supreme Court have upheld government use of religious references in some circumstances.

The US Constitution, unlike the UK, provides for neutrality. But the US neutrality, unlike the French *laïcité* is supportive and accommodating of religion – it can be described as a 'qualified neutrality' in favour of religion. The US therefore has features of both France and the UK.

Religious freedom in the US is enshrined within the First Amendment of the Constitution which provides:

> Congress shall make no law respecting an establishment of religion, or prohibiting the free exercise thereof; or abridging the freedom of speech, or of the press; or the right of the people peaceably to assemble, and to petition the Government for a redress of grievances.

The First Amendment therefore establishes state neutrality by prohibiting the government[9] from endorsing any religion but at the same time it protects individuals' religious freedom by prohibiting the state from interfering with the free exercise of that freedom. The First Amendment also provides for individual freedom of speech. The United States therefore is a secular state like France but it differs from France in its treatment of religion. References to God and to religion are not uncommon in states' constitutions and official speeches; the American national motto for instance is: 'In God We Trust' and US Presidents always end their speeches with 'God Bless America.' The state neutrality principle however is upheld in state schools much like in France but not to the extent of banning religious clothing. Schools however are not permitted to endorse any religious faith and therefore school-sponsored prayers are strictly prohibited.[10] The American neutrality unlike the French neutrality is not an indifference towards religion but a more 'benevolent neutrality'.[11] It requires the US government not to favour any religion over another but also not to favour religion over non-religion or non-religion over religion. On the surface, it would seem that the American government is fairly pro-religion as compared to the French government who tends to promote non-religion over religion by pushing religion to the private sphere.[12] There are three distinctive features of the American Constitution which tend to define state–religion relations, namely, the Establishment Clause of the First Amendment, the Free Speech Clause which protects private religious expression and the 'exception'[13] to the First Amendment also called 'ceremonial deism',[14] which allows the government to engage in expression which seems to endorse and promote religion. In addition, the Supreme Court has developed a number of constitutional tests in order to assess whether the Establishment Clause has been breached.

7.3 The Establishment Clause

The Establishment Clause of the First Amendment was ratified in 1791. While it was originally directed to the national government, the US SC has extended the neutrality requirement to all levels of governments; '[N]either a state nor the Federal Government ... can pass laws which aid one religion, aid all religions, or prefer one religion over another.'[15] There are five core principles of non-establishment which derive from court decisions as well as academic and historical sources, namely, neutrality, separation, equality, liberty and civil peace.[16] Legal disputes in relation to the Establishment Clause have concerned challenges to government funding programs and to government 'religious' expression and symbolic actions.

7.3.1 Neutrality

The US SC has defined the Establishment Clause as requiring 'the state to be neutral in its relations with groups of religious believers and non-believers; it does not require the state to be their adversary. State power is no more to be used so as to handicap religions, than it is to favour them.'[17]

The meaning of neutrality however can be seen as context dependent and has been interpreted differently by the courts. In some instances, neutrality is taken to mean equality between the various religious groups as well as between religion and irreligion. This is the case notably for state funding which may be used to fund religious education. For instance, the government is not precluded from providing educational vouchers or grant education programs so long as it extends to both religious and non-religious schools.[18] However, when it comes to the use of symbols by the government, the courts have interpreted neutrality more strictly and it is clear that the government cannot be seen to openly favour one religion over the others. 'The government, of course, may speak on a large number of issues. The Constitution, however, forbids it from conveying the message that it decisively endorses a particular religious position.'[19] There appear to be no limits though on the extent to which the government may promote non-religious movements such as capitalism or environmentalism.[20] The Establishment Clause therefore singles out religion from other forms of ideologies. As long as the state does not pronounce itself in favour of a particular religion, religion in general or irreligion, the Establishment Clause is not breached.

7.3.2 Church–state separation

The idea of church and state separation is enshrined in the Establishment Clause of the First Amendment. This separation between church and state in the US can be defined as 'institutional non-involvement'[21] whereby the government does not financially support religion and religion does not abuse of the functions of the government. This is very similar to the situation in France as discussed in Chapter 5. The SC in *Everson v. Board of Education* referring to a letter written by Thomas Jefferson, one of the American Founding Fathers, declared 'the clause against establishment of religion by law was intended to erect "a wall of separation between Church and State."'[22] Despite this, the court has acknowledged that total separation is not possible in an absolute sense and therefore it is appropriate to talk of moderate separation and accommodation rather than strict or rigid separation.[23] This approach has the merit of being realistic as it acknowledges the difficulty with achieving complete neutrality which is never entirely possible, as seen with the French approach where despite neutrality the state endorses Christianity within its calendar and traditions as religion inevitably remains part of the history.[24]

7.3.3 Equality

The Establishment Clause provides for equality between and amongst religious beliefs and between religious and non-religious beliefs. In the words of the SC it is 'a principle at the heart of the Establishment Clause, that government should not prefer one religion to another, or religion to irreligion.'[25] The extent to which the latter aspect of this principle is being respected in both France and the US is highly questionable. While in France, non-religion is favoured with *laïcité*, in the US, it appears to be the opposite with government expression of religion being fairly tolerated to the extent that some have questioned whether there is in effect an exception to the Establishment Clause.[26] This will be discussed further below.

7.3.4 Liberty

The ultimate goal of the First Amendment and the Establishment Clause is religious liberty. This stems from the prohibition on the coercion of religious activity or the coerced profession of religious belief by the government. In the words of the SC,

> It is beyond dispute that, at a minimum, the Constitution guarantees that government may not coerce anyone to support or participate in religion or its exercise, or otherwise act in a way which establishes a [state] religion or religious faith, or tends to do so.[27]

At institutional level, the principle of liberty is reflected in the church-autonomy doctrine which prevents the courts from adjudicating on disputes over faith, morals, church and ecclesiastical relationships. The church-autonomy doctrine was originally intended to protect faith communities from the government exercise of power. As explained by the Court, the First Amendment 'rests upon the premise that both religion and government can best work to achieve their lofty aims if each is left free from the other within its respective sphere.'[28] In the past two decades, however the doctrine has been relaxed in order to investigate cases of sex allegations by clergy against parishioners.[29]

7.3.5 Civil peace

Another principle of the First Amendment is to preserve civil peace and harmony by limiting political divisions along religious lines. According to Justice Stephen Breyer, religion clauses 'seek to avoid that divisiveness based upon religion that promotes social conflict, sapping the strength of government and religion alike.'[30] The extent to which this is successful in practice however is debatable given the strong influence of religion in American political life.

The Establishment Clause of the First Amendment therefore aims to guarantee religious liberty by providing religious autonomy to individuals and institutions and by promoting state neutrality in order to achieve religious equality. Yet the US neutrality is not a rejection of religion. On the contrary, the government acknowledges religion, albeit in a neutral form, by referring to religion in general rather than a particular confession. Over the years, the SC has developed a number of legal tests to help the lower courts decide the extent to which the establishment clause has been breached.

7.4 The Supreme Court and the Establishment Clause

There are four tests used by the courts to determine the extent to which the Establishment Clause has been breached, namely, the *Lemon* test also called neutrality test; the endorsement test; the coercion test and the ceremonial deism test.

7.4.1 Neutrality test

In *Lemon v Kurtzman*, [31] the US SC developed the neutrality test, also called the *Lemon* test. The test requires that in order to respect the Establishment Clause, government action must be supported by a secular purpose (purpose prong), must not have the primary effect of advancing or inhibiting religion (effect prong) and cannot create an excessive governmental entanglement with religion (entanglement prong).[32] The three parts test therefore asks: (1) Does the law have a secular purpose; (2) Is the primary effect of the law either to advance religion or to inhibit religion? and (3) Does the law foster an excessive governmental entanglement with religion? These must be applied as strict requirements for a law to be deemed constitutional as, if any one of the three requirements is not met, the law is deemed to violate the establishment clause. The *Lemon* test has never been overruled by the SC but it has come under criticism by judges and academics for producing incoherent results.[33] In particular, part one of the test requiring a secular purpose does not assist in reconciling the seemingly contradictory aims between the Establishment Clause on the one hand and the free exercise clause on the other. The first prong of the *Lemon* test means that any religious exemptions cannot be made to accommodate religious minorities and the courts have sometimes rejected this implication of the *Lemon* test. Justice Scalia in particular was a firm opponent of the test, which he compared to 'some ghoul in a late-night horror movie that repeatedly sits up in its grave and shuffles abroad, after being repeatedly killed and buried, Lemon stalks our Establishment Clause jurisprudence once again, frightening the little children and school attorneys.'[34] Those accusations have led the courts to look at alternative approaches.

7.4.2 Endorsement test

The SC in *Lynch v Donnelly* [35] developed the endorsement test which focuses more specifically on the symbolic character of governmental action and reinforces the first two prongs of the *Lemon* test. The test provides that the government violates the Establishment Clause if it intends to communicate a message that endorses or disapproves of religion or if its actions have the effect of communicating such a message. The second part of the test asks whether an objective observer properly informed of the relevant history and context would find in the government's action a message of endorsement or disapproval.[36] The test was refined in *Wallace v Jaffree* which concerned a challenge to Alabama legislation as acknowledging religion by authorising public school teachers to lead their students in a daily period of classroom 'for meditation or voluntary prayer.'[37] The court did not preclude teacher-led meditation altogether or moment of silence legislation but in this particular case considered the language and history of the Alabama statute and concluded that this particular statute was 'entirely motivated by a purpose to advance religion'[38] as it was 'conveying a message of state endorsement and promotion of prayers.'[39] With the endorsement test therefore government action is problematic only if it could be seen as an endorsement or disapproval of religion from the point of view of the 'reasonable observer'. It is considered to be an objective test as opposed to the secular purpose requirement of the *Lemon* test which is mainly subjective and focuses on the intention of the government representative.[40] Over the years, the courts have defined the characteristics of the reasonable observer as one that possesses reasonable familiarity with the relevant community's history, traditions and contemporary practices. The observer must not 'look upon religion with a jaundiced eye.' The observer can reasonably situate and understand a government action in proper context and must take a non-partisan approach to its religious dimension.[41]

The Establishment Clause seeks to protect religious equality and respect the religious (including non-religious) identity of citizens in order to promote a religiously inclusive political community. Justice O'Connor in *Lynch v Donnelly* declared that 'Endorsement sends a message to non-adherents that they are outsiders, not full members of the political community, and an accompanying message to adherents that they are insiders, favoured members of the political community. Disapproval sends the opposite message.'[42] The theory of the Establishment Clause is that for the outsiders, government's action may be perceived as an insult or an assault to their identity and this is likely to create resentment and divisiveness within the political community. What is required for being neutral therefore is neither approval nor disapproval of any particular faith. We could argue however that religion and non-religion should also be given the same importance. The extent to which this neutrality exists in the US is doubtful due to government expression of religion as discussed above, which the court protects via the ceremonial deism test. This test is discussed below.

7.4.3 Coercion test

Laws that are actually or effectively coercive in a religious sense are also prohibited under the Establishment Clause. The coercion test first used in *Lee v. Weisman* [43] establishes that 'at a minimum the Constitution guarantees that government may not coerce anyone to support or participate in religion or its exercise, or otherwise act in a way which "establishes a [state] religion or religious faith, or tends to do so."'[44] Lee concerned a Rabbi's invocation and benediction at a middle-school graduation and while attendance not participation was compulsory, the court invalidated the practice because it was found to create some compulsion from the students' point of view:

> the school district's supervision and control of a … graduation ceremony places public pressure, as well as peer pressure, on attending students to stand as a group or, at least, maintain respectful silence during the invocation and benediction. This pressure though subtle and indirect, can be as real as any overt compulsion.[45]

Like the previous tests, the coercion test has been criticised for not offering enough protection to religious minorities. In particular, Peterson has argued that the coercion test is not suited to 'borderline' establishment cases such as ceremonial deism (discussed in the next section) and that the concept of coercion does not assist in balancing freedom of speech with the strict neutrality requirement of the establishment clause.[46]

7.4.4 Ceremonial deism

Ceremonial deism provides governmental religious invocation with a shield from the First Amendment by acknowledging that the concept of deity is part of the tradition of a historical and cultural connection with religion and does not as such promote religion. The phrase was first used by the courts in the case of *Lynch v. Donnelly* [47] where the court upheld the constitutionality of a city-sponsored Christmas display that featured a nativity scene as well as less-religious Christmas symbols such as reindeer and candy canes. In his dissenting opinion, Justice William Brennan wrote that while he thought this particular Christmas display was unconstitutional, less controversial expressions of religion might be permissible under the Establishment Clause. Citing Dean Rostow, Brennan argued that certain official references to a deity – such as the inclusion of God in the Pledge of Allegiance – might be constitutional 'as a form [of] "ceremonial deism".' According to Brennan, these expressions might not violate the Establishment Clause 'because they have lost through rote repetition any significant religious content.'[48] This is similar to the reasoning of the Italian Government and the ECHR in the *Lautsi* case discussed above.[49]

Prior to *Lynch v Donnelly* the concept had already been recognised by the US SC in *Marsh and Chambers* [50] where the court upheld legislative prayers on the ground that the practice was part of a long tradition. The court held that:

> While historical patterns, standing alone, cannot justify contemporary viola-tions of constitutional guarantees, historical evidence in the context of this case sheds light not only on what the drafters of the First Amendment inten-ded the Establishment Clause to mean, but also on how they thought that Clause applied to the chaplaincy practice authorized by the First Congress.[51]

On this occasion the SC found the practice of legislative prayers to be 'deeply embedded' with the 'history and tradition' of the US.[52]

The ceremonial deism test therefore provides an 'exception' to the Establish-ment Clause of the First Amendment to allow the government to sponsor reli-gious expression that is non-coercive, non-sectarian and embedded with longstanding historical practice.[53] Under this exception, the Supreme Court has endorsed government practices which at face value look to be breaching the neu-trality principle. Such practices include the presidential Thanksgiving proclama-tions, the Supreme Court's own opening phrase 'God save the United States and this honourable Court' dating back to the 19th century, the national motto since 1956 'In God We Trust.' which appears on all American currency; the language of the Pledge of Allegiance 'one Nation under God' since 1954.[54] It is difficult to see how these practices can be fully reconciled with the Establishment Clause of the First Amendment but the SC has indicated that these practices while they acknowledge religion do not promote or endorse it as such. Some judges have argued that some of those expressions have lost religious meaning and are more of a symbolic nature, part of the national heritage of the US as religious nation. Justice Brennan for instance argued in Lynch that 'The practices by which the government has long acknowledged religion are therefore probably necessary to serve certain secular functions, and that necessity, coupled with their long history, gives those practices an essentially secular meaning.'[55] References to God have been common in America's history and date back to the Revolutionary War and continued to flourish during the Republic. This is reflected in the Constitution. It is evident therefore that the framers of the Constitution intended the Establishment Clause to allow govern-ment references to God and religious symbols. Thomas Jefferson, one of America's founding fathers, invoked God in the Declaration of Independence: 'We hold these truths to be self-evident, that all men are created equal, that they are endowed by their Creator with certain inalienable Rights, that among these are Life, Liberty and the pursuit of Happiness.'[56]

Government's religious expression therefore has in some instances become an established feature of the American 'social fabric'. It is clear however that religion is favoured over non-religion but the references to religion are at least nondenominational. The governmental expression of religion remains general with references to God and religious faith but it is non-partisan in the sense of not outwardly supporting one faith over the other. As argued by O'Conkle, the exception tolerates governmental practices which do not entirely respect the identity of those with no religion which may be a threat to the religious inclusiveness of the political community.[57] This may be why there is no officially recognised exception to the Establishment Clause as the SC has refused to adopt a strict position; they have refused 'to construe the Religion Clauses with a literalness that would undermine the ultimate constitutional objective as illuminated by history.'[58] Instead, the court's approach is described as a line-drawing process which queries the extent to which the challenged law or conduct has a secular purpose or on the contrary if its primary effect is to promote or suppress religion.[59]

The Supreme Court tends to avoid setting a clear precedent for the lower courts but instead looks at each case in context and in relation to the history. This approach has created uncertainty and produced contradictory judgments. Nativity scenes in the public square for instance have sometimes been allowed to stand and in other instances been declared unconstitutional. In *Lynch v. Donnelly*, [60] the Christmas display included a Santa Claus house, a Christmas tree, a banner reading 'Seasons Greetings' and a Nativity scene. The display situated in a park owned by a non-profit organisation in the heart of the district shopping centre was part of a 40 years tradition. It was allowed to stand on the basis that Christmas has secular as well as religious significance and that it did not in the circumstances amount to the government promoting Christianity.[61] Conversely, in *Allegheny v. ACLU*[62] a few years later, a nativity scene on the staircase of a Pittsburgh courthouse was not allowed to stand and was held to amount to endorsement of religion by the government. In this case the Nativity scene was displayed on its own with a banner 'Gloria in Excelsis Deo!' (Latin for 'Glory to God in the Highest') and amounted to a government endorsement of religion.[63] The Court applied the *Lemon* test and distinguished the case from *Lynch v. Donnelly* and held that 'Although the government may acknowledge Christmas as a cultural phenomenon, it may not observe it as a Christian holy day by suggesting that people praise God for the birth of Jesus.'[64] It is not the nature of the display itself therefore which indicates whether the practice is constitutional but rather the overall context taking into account the nature of the message being communicated to the public, given the location of the display and the historical background. If it can be demonstrated that the display has a secular rather than religious purpose then it is generally not considered to breach the First Amendment. In the context of schools, we observe a similar pattern and the SC has called for particular vigilance to avoid coercion of children at an age where they are particularly vulnerable.[65]

7.5 Religion and schools

State schools in the US are torn between the two conflicting requirements of the First Amendment, namely the Establishment Clause which requires schools to maintain neutrality and the Free Speech Clause which requires schools to allow for the manifestation of individual religious expression. This section will examine those two requirements.

7.5.1 Endorsement of religion and schools

State schools are subject to the neutrality principle of the First Amendment and as such cannot endorse or disapprove of religion regardless of whether the actions in question are coercive. As a result, school-sponsored prayers and religious instruction in state schools have been invalidated by the SC although state schools remain free to teach about religion in a neutral manner.[66] The SC has outlawed teacher-led prayers and devotional exercises and school-sponsored prayers at graduation ceremonies[67] as well as extra-curricular events.[68] In *Stone v. Graham* [69] it has precluded state schools from posting the Ten Commandments in their classrooms on the ground that no secular purpose could be found for displaying the Ten Commandments in a public school. Public schools cannot schedule classroom religious instruction during the school day, even when the instructors are privately employed and when the students freely participate.[70] In *Edwards v. Aguillard* [71] a statute declaring that any public school that elected to teach evolution was required to also teach creation science was declared unconstitutional by the SC. They looked at the legislative history of the statute and concluded that the law was not designed to promote balanced treatment as claimed by the school but rather to promote and endorse a particular viewpoint.

In *Santa Fe Indep. Sch. Dist. v. Doe* [72] the SC considered a Texas school policy that allowed prayers at high-school football games but the prayers would be student-led as opposed to school-sponsored and therefore the school board tried to argue that the prayers would amount to private religious expression and as such were not subject to the Establishment Clause. The SC however rejected the argument as the underlying purpose of the policy was to perpetuate a long-standing tradition of school-sponsored prayers at football games even if the prayers would not be purely religious expression. The court held that:

> The delivery of a message such as the invocation here – on school property, at school-sponsored events, over the school's public-address system, by a speaker representing the student body, under the supervision of school faculty, and pursuant to a school policy that explicitly and implicitly encourages public prayer – is not properly characterized as 'private speech.'

This case makes it clear therefore that religious expression cannot be seen as private if it is sponsored by the government or if it can be perceived to be sponsored by the government as provided by the endorsement test in *Lee v. Weisman.* [73] Religious expression per se is not prohibited by the First Amendment but government sponsorship of such expression is. In the next section we examine individual expression of religion through symbols or hairstyles.

7.5.2 *Religious manifestation and the Free Speech Clause*

While the Free Speech Clause protects manifestation of belief for individual pupils, mandatory uniform policies are not prohibited provided that they do not suppress student expression or viewpoints.[74] Uniform policies must be neutral to religion and it must further an important government interest such as for instance increasing students' achievement, focusing on learning, promoting safety or bridging socio-economic differences. School policies must also not aim to restrict free expression and any restrictions must be no more than necessary to further the aim of the policy. State schools are normally permitted to accommodate religious clothing and attire needs of students.[75] Any prohibition on religious clothing must be justified. In addition, some states have Religious Freedom Restoration Acts requiring public bodies including state schools to demonstrate a narrow and compelling interest where religious activity or practice is substantially burdened by a law, ordinance, government rule or practice.[76] We can see therefore that there is a strong commitment in the US Constitution to protecting individual religious freedom despite the state's commitment to secularism. In that sense, the US school system is very similar to the English one if not more protective towards individual expression of religion. This does not mean however that limitations have not been placed on religious expressions within school settings.

It has been argued that in recent years and particularly in the post-9/11 socio-political climate, the SC has moved to a narrower conception of religious protection which puts emphasis on the constitutional church–state separation in order to reassure those who are concerned about the power of fundamentalist movements and that this tendency is having a negative impact on those students who display their faith publicly.[77] Numerous incidents have been reported especially in relation to the hijab and other head coverings although the incidents have usually resolved in favour of the student with intervention from civil rights organisations, religious groups or government agencies.[78] Much like in England, the US government and the SC have adopted a deference approach, leaving it to the individual states to decide on the level of protection afforded to students' religious expression and the individual states have deferred to the school districts. This results in inconsistencies similar to the ones we have observed with school policies in England. Allegedly deference allows for a case by case approach which can be tailored to the school population of each individual state and school district in contrast to implementing a complete ban on all religious symbols as in France.

In order to assess the lawfulness of a specific regulation which may restrict manifestation of belief, the SC established the 'Tinker test'.[79] In *Tinker v. Des Moines*, [80] three state schools' students were suspended for wearing black armbands protesting the Vietnam War in breach of the uniform policy. The US SC reversed previous rulings from lower courts and adopted a strict scrutiny analysis holding that the First Amendment's right to free speech applies to students in public schools even if the school does not necessarily sanction the views or ideas expressed by the students. The SC adopted a test to assist schools in deciding whether a particular regulation violates a student's free speech. The test provides that a regulation is deemed constitutional if the student's expression (1) 'materially and substantially' interfered with school requirements of discipline; and (2) invaded the rights of others.[81] Justice Fortas delivering the opinion of the court pointed out that 'In the absence of a specific showing of constitutionally valid reasons to regulate their speech, students are entitled to freedom of expression of their views.'[82]

Despite this approach, there have been some limitations to religious attire and hairstyles. In *Menora v. Illinois High School Association* [83] a High School Association's dress code prohibiting the wearing of headgear including Jewish yarmulke for basketball players due to safety reasons was invalidated by a District Court on the ground that the ban interfered with the free exercise clause because students had to choose between observing their religious belief and taking part in the games.[84] On appeal however the decision was overturned by the Seventh Circuit and the court asked the Jewish students to design a headdress which was more secure and complied with Jewish Law while addressing the Association's concerns. If the students failed to find a suitable solution they would then have to choose between performing their religious requirement and taking part in the basketball game, therefore compromising the students' religious liberty. In that case *Tinker*'s strict scrutiny test did not apply because the Seventh Circuit was able to show that the rule did not prohibit religious observance as such but merely made it more onerous and that therefore there was no infringement of free speech right and the case did not have to be decided on constitutional grounds. The outcome of the case has been criticised by academics as limiting religious expression.[85]

Similarly, the Court of Appeal in *Cheema v Thompson* [86] offered a compromised policy to Sikh students who had not been allowed at school for over a year after being told that wearing a kirpan (Sikh ceremonial dagger) to school violated their school-district no-weapons policy as well as the Californian Penal Code prohibiting knives in public places. The kirpan is part of the five Ks symbols which Sikhs are required to wear if they are baptised. It is a sword and therefore understandably can be seen by the uninformed as a threat to health and safety and as compromising children's safety within the school despite the practice being allowed by state schools in Canada, England and the US without any reported incidents.[87] Lal explained the importance of the kirpan to the Sikh community in those terms:

> The attachment to the sword, or the kirpan, must be perceived as an attachment to an 'object' that becomes an inalienable part of oneself, constitutive of a life of affirmation, honor, and self-respect; and to forgo the kirpan, at least on the orthodox view, is to relinquish one's identity as a Sikh observant of the faith.[88]

The US Court of Appeal for the 9th Circuit therefore offered a compromise solution which would allow Sikh students to don their kirpan while reassuring the school community who may see the object as a potential weapon even if the idea that the kirpan could be used as a weapon is quite inconceivable to Sikhs. The kirpan had to be rendered safe by limiting its length, requiring the blade to be dulled, tightly sown to its sheath, and worn underneath the clothing. In addition, the school district had to be given the right to inspect the kirpan for compliance.[89] So in this case, a total ban was not upheld by the court as it violated the Religious Freedom Restoration Act 1993 which required the least restrictive means to be used when limiting religious freedom.[90]

Despite the US' commitment to free speech, restrictions have also been imposed in relation to long hair and we notice in some of the case law similar trends to English courts with judges arguably acting as arbiters of faith.[91] In *New Rider v Board of Education of Independent School District No 1* [92] for instance a claim by some Native Americans to be allowed to wear their long braided hair at school despite a ban on long hair for male students was dismissed as not meriting the constitutional protection. According to the court the wearing of long braided hair by Native Pawnee American students was nothing more than a desire to celebrate their cultural heritage, not a constitutionally protected right.[93] As in the *Menora* case discussed above, the case fell short of constitutional scrutiny and as such the *Tinker* standard was not applicable. By adopting a narrow definition of religion, the 10th Circuit Court forced the students to choose between manifesting their cultural identity and complying with the school rules. The racial, religious and cultural significance of long braided hair to the Native Pawnee Americans had nonetheless been established by the expert anthropologist as part of the evidence sought by the court. Dr Weltfish testified that:

> from the viewpoint of Pawnee theology the long-braided hair has religious significance in that the Pawnees believed that the universe was created in terms of the cosmos and that the cosmos dictated the nature of the whole social, human, animal, vegetal and material order.

She testified that the core of this theological belief is that everything the Pawnee does each day has religious significance. She stated that there were certain dances which required long braided hair.[94] The court however overlooked the significance of the practice for Native Pawnees' identity and held that the wearing of long hair was not akin to pure speech and as such did not merit constitutional importance. When similar issues have arisen in England, long braided hair has been allowed in schools despite allegedly breaching the school policy. In *G v St Gregory's Catholic Science College* [95] the England and Wales High Court held that 'a genuine family tradition based on cultural and social reasons' must warrant an exception to the school uniform policy. Arguably this is a better approach affording more protection to manifestation of belief which does not cause substantial disruption to the school environment despite their initial argument that braided hair could encourage gang culture. The courts were willing to acknowledge that such strict policy could amount to indirect discrimination.

In the cases discussed above, it is the failure of some courts to acknowledge that something is a form of religious expression or that a particular requirement does place restrictions on religious freedom that leads to weaker protection. If courts were more readily willing to acknowledge the interference with religious freedom then it would allow stricter scrutiny and broader protection. This approach was adopted in *Chalifoux v New Caney Indep. Sch. Dist* [96] where the use of rosary necklaces was held to constitute a form of religious expression protected by the First Amendment. The students in question wore rosaries despite a dress code banning their use as they have sometimes been used as gang symbols but the students were not themselves gang members. In this instance, the court concluded that the students demonstrated their sincere religious beliefs by wearing rosaries as a means of emphasising their Catholic faith[97] despite there being no such requirement in the Catholic faith nor being a common practice amongst devote Catholics.[98] By applying the strict scrutiny *Tinker* standard the court was able to show that the school's blanket ban on rosaries was not proportionate to the aim of controlling gang culture. The *Tinker* standard is very similar to the ECHR proportionality test used by UK courts and this is a better approach than the one adopted in some of the earlier cases as it rests on a broader interpretation of religion which acknowledges the importance of manifestation of belief as part of the wearer's identity. In addition, something does not have to be a requirement of the faith in order to be protected.

7.6 Religious manifestation in the workplace

According to the Equal Employment Opportunity Commission[99] (EEOC), religious discrimination claims have more than doubled in the US since 1997[100] and cases of religion-based discrimination against Muslims have increased by 250 percent since 2001.[101] As in England and Wales many of the claims have concerned religious dress, hair styles, time of work for religious reasons and handling of alcohol. Much of the case law on religious discrimination in employment is brought on the basis of the Civil Rights Act 1964 (as amended in 1972), Title VII. The Federal Act which is the equivalent of the UK Equality Act 2010 applies to disputes between private parties which the Constitution does not cover. It prohibits employers with at least 15 employees from discriminating in employment on the basis of race, colour, religion, sex, or national origin.[102]

Title VII of the Civil Rights Act of 1964 (CRA) prohibits disparate treatment based on religion in all aspects of employment such as hiring, training and benefits; it also prohibits denial of reasonable accommodation for sincerely held religious belief as well as job segregation, harassment and retaliation based on religion or religious claim.[103] Employers are required to make exceptions (reasonable accommodations) to their usual rules or preferences to permit applicants and employees to observe religious dress and grooming practices such as wearing religious clothing, observing a religious prohibition or following certain hair styles such as uncut hair and beards for Sikhs, dreadlocks for Rastafarians etc.[104] An employer must accommodate unless accommodation would cause 'undue hardship' on the operation of the business. Health and safety and security may justify denying accommodation but the undue hardship needs to be an actual threat not one that is assumed by the employer. Instead, the employer must take the necessary measures to reconcile the needs of the employee with the needs of the business and offer a reasonable accommodation. So, a policy requiring employees to be clean shaven while handling food will discriminate against Sikh and Muslim employees who keep a long beard unless they can be offered an alternative such as wearing a face mask. If the employee then refuses a reasonable alternative then the courts would not rule in their favour if they pursue a claim of discrimination. However, if the aim of a no-facial hair policy is such as 'to promote discipline' then the employer would be required to make an exception because there is no undue hardship as such.[105] In addition to restrictions based on health and safety, some companies have restricted religious practice on the basis of brand and image; this is not normally accepted by the courts. This is discussed below in relation to the *Abercrombie and Fitch* case.

All aspects of religious observance, practice and belief are protected by Title VII of the CRA and religion is defined broadly and as such it includes traditional religions as well as non-traditional beliefs such as new religious movements, those which are not part of a formal church and those who are subscribed to by only a small number of people. No-religion is also protected and employers cannot impose a religious dress code upon their employees unless they are a religious organisation.[106] According to the SC 'religious beliefs need not be acceptable, logical, consistent, or comprehensible to others in order to merit First Amendment protection.'[107]

As seen in the context of schools, the jurisprudence reflects tension between the courts' duty to remedy cases of religious discrimination and the constitutional separation of church and state.[108] Dobrac and Wesley observe that in employment cases as in First Amendment jurisprudence, courts struggle to verify an adherent's religious belief, what constitutes a religious belief and how firmly that belief needs to be held to attract the protection of Title VII.[109] Courts have generally been reluctant to question the existence of a given religious tradition and do not normally dispute whether something is a religion. Like in England, the courts have taken a case by case approach which is more appropriate to the broad definition of religion and allows for a more inclusive approach. While the sincerity of a belief is generally not disputed by the courts, employers may ask an applicant or employee for information reasonably needed to evaluate the request but a recently adopted practice does not mean that it is not sincerely held, nor does one that only occurs sporadically.[110] As put by the majority opinion in *Davis v Ford Bent County* [111] courts are reluctant to interfere with individual's religious beliefs:

> This court has cautioned that judicial inquiry into the sincerity of a person's religious belief must be handled with a light touch, or judicial shyness. Examining religious convictions any more deeply would stray into the realm of religious inquiry, an area into which we are forbidden to tread. Indeed, the sincerity of a plaintiff's engagement in a particular religious practice is rarely challenged, and claims of sincere religious belief in a particular practice have been accepted on little more than the plaintiff's credible assertions.[112]

In a recent SC case involving the famous clothes retailer Abercrombie and Fitch, an employee won her case when she challenged her right to wear a headscarf which her employer had argued conflicted with the store's Look Policy.[113] The Policy prohibited headwear in general. Abercrombie tried to argue that it could not have known about the need to make such accommodation because the Plaintiff did not request it at the time of the interview but the court rejected that argument and looked instead at whether the applicant's headscarf was a 'motivating factor' in not hiring her. Justice Scalia said: 'An employer who acts with the motive of avoiding accommodation may violate [the law] even if he has no more than an unsubstantiated suspicion that accommodation would be needed.'[114]

Like in England, health and safety has been used by employers to restrict uniform policy variations. In *EEOC v GEO Group, Inc.*,[115] a private prison declined some Muslim employees request to wear their headscarf on the ground that it may pose a risk for the employees as prisoners may use the headscarves to choke the female employees during riots. The Third Circuit accepted the employers' argument and ruled that 'prison is not a summer camp'. Even if the headscarves present a limited risk, the employer was entitled to take measures to prevent that risk.

Manifestation of religion in the US workplace therefore is afforded extensive legal protection and the courts' approach has allowed for a broad interpretation of the term 'religion' which is taken as covering a wide range of beliefs and practices. The case by case approach allows for compromises to be reached between the employer and the employees. Like in England, manifestation of belief can be lawfully limited on the basis of health and safety but limitations based on company image or specific preferences are not generally upheld by the courts. This contrasts with the French approach which allows for the principle of neutrality to be reflected in employers' policies.

7.7 Reflections on country approaches

While France and the US share a constitutional church–state separation, the US and England share a commitment to protecting the expression of religious manifestation. The US secularism is not anti-religious in contrast to the French *laïcité* which seeks to restrict the expression of religion in the public domain. There is an evident link between the historical church–state relation and the legal framework for the protection of religious freedom in all three jurisdictions. The US constitution allows for the acknowledgement of the historical significance of religion while France's historical antagonism between the state and religion is reflected in a more militant *laïcité*. The English Establishment on the other hand leaves room for religious exemptions within the law and does not preclude religious pluralism. Examination of the countries' approaches has highlighted the inconsistencies in the courts' approach as well as the capacity of judges to fit practices to their categories or on the contrary to reject them as not fitting into such categories. At times, there is a discord between the social function of symbols as discussed in Part I of this book and judicial approaches presented here. The next part attempts to juxtapose the two approaches in order to propose a viable solution.

Notes

1 US Supreme Court in *Zorach v. Clauson*, 343 US 306, 313 (1952).
2 *Lynch v Donnelly* 465 US 668 (1984).
3 The religion clauses comprise the Establishment clause and the Free Speech clause.
4 There is disagreement on the extent to which the US was founded on Christianity because the Founding Fathers were Christians but also Enlightenment thinkers and rationalists and were strongly committed to the separation of church and state. See further Hall 2011.
5 Ahdar and Leigh 2005. 93.
6 O'Conkle 2006.
7 Ibid. 442.
8 Theodorou 2015.
9 The prohibition extends beyond 'Congress' to include all branches of the state and public entities more generally. Bittker, Idleman and Ravitch 2015. 149.
10 See *Sch. Dist. of Abington Twp v Schempp* 374 US 203, 225 (1963) which is discussed further below.
11 *Walz v. Tax Comm'n of NY.* 397 US 644, 669 (1970).
12 See further Chapter 5 on France.
13 See O'Conkle, 2006, op. cit.; there is no legal exception as such, but it can be inferred from the case law.
14 *Marsh v. Chambers* 463 US 783 (1983).
15 *Everson v Board of Education* 330 US 1 (1947) at [15].
16 Bittker et al. 2015, op. cit. 152.
17 *Everson* (1947), op. cit. at [18].
18 *Zelman v Simmons-Harris* 536 US 639, 652 (2002).
19 *Warnock v Archer*, 380 F 3.d 1076, 1080 (8th Circ. 2004).
20 Bittker et al. 2015, op. cit. 154–155.
21 *Sherbert v Verner.* 374 US 398, 409 (1963).
22 *Everson* (1947), op. cit.
23 See *Lemon v Kurtzman* 403 US 602, 614 (1971) where the court recognised that the line of separation between Church and State was 'a blurred ... and variable barrier depending on all the circumstances of a particular relationship.'
24 See Chapter 5 on France.
25 *Board of Education of Kyrias Joel Vill. Sch. District v. Grumet.* 512 US 687, 703 (1994).
26 See O'Conkle 2006, op. cit.
27 See *Lee v. Weisman*, 505 US 577 (1992).
28 *Mc Collum v. Bd. of Educ.*, 333 US 203, 212 (1948).
29 Adams 2007.
30 *Van Orden v Perry*, 545 US 677, 698–9 (2005).
31 403 US 602 (1971).
32 Ibid. at 612–613.
33 *County of Allegheny v ACLU*, 492 US 573 (1989) Justice Kennedy; see also Choper 2002.
34 *Lamb's Chapel v. Center Moriches Union Free School District*, 508 US 384,398 (1993).
35 *Lynch* 1984, op. cit. at 687–94.
36 Justice O'Connor in *Lynch v Donnelly* op. cit.
37 *Wallace v Jaffree* 472 US 38 (1985).
38 Ibid at [56].
39 Ibid at [59].
40 *ACLU of Ohio Found. Inc. v. Bd. of Comm'rs of Lucas Cnty., Ohio*, 444 F. Supp. 2d 805, 811 (ND Ohio 2006).

41 Bittker et al., 2015, op. cit. 178–79.
42 *Lynch* 1984, op. cit.
43 505 US 577 (1992)
44 Ibid., 587.
45 Ibid., 593.
46 Peterson 2001.
47 *Lynch*, op. cit.
48 Ibid. at 716.
49 Case of *Lautsi and Others v. Italy*, Application no. 30814/06.
50 463 US 783 (1983).
51 Ibid., 786.
52 Ibid., 787.
53 O'Conkle 2006, op. cit. 435.
54 *Lynch*, op. cit. 674–78.
55 Justice Brennan dissenting in *Lynch*, op. cit. 717.
56 The Declaration of Independence para 2 (US 1776).
57 O'Conkle 2006, op. cit. 434.
58 See Justice Berger in *Walz v. Tax Comm'n of City of New York* 397 US 664 (1970) citing Justice Jackson's dissent in *Everson v Board of Education* op. cit.
59 *Lynch*, Chief Justice Burger op. cit.
60 Idem.
61 Idem.
62 *Allegheny v. ACLU* 1989 op. cit.
63 Idem.
64 Idem, 598–602.
65 This is discussed below.
66 *Sch. Dist. of Abington Twp v Schempp* (1963) op. cit. 203, 225.
67 *Lee v. Weisman* (1992) op. cit.
68 *Santa Fe Indep. Sch. Dist. v. Doe*, 530 US 290 (2000).
69 449 US 39.
70 *Illinois ex rel. McCollum v. Bd of Education*, 333 US 203 (1948).
71 482 US 578 (1987).
72 *Santa Fe School* (2000) op. cit., 308–309.
73 *Lee v Weisman* (1992) op. cit.
74 See further ADL n.d.
75 Idem.
76 Twenty states have these laws.
77 Ali 2013.
78 See for example: Becerra 2004.
79 *Tinker v. Des Moines Independent Community School District*, 393 US 503 (1969).
80 Idem.
81 *Tinker*, 1969, op. cit., 509, 513.
82 Ibid., 511.
83 683 F.2d 1030 (7th circuit 1982).
84 Ibid., 1031.
85 See for instance Renteln 2004, 1582 and Ali 2013, op. cit. 20.
86 67 F.3d 883 (9th Cir. 1995).
87 Renteln 2004, op. cit. 1578. See also in the UK, Singh 2012.
88 Lal 1996.
89 *Cheema* op. cit. 883, 893.
90 The RFRA 1993 was overturned in 1997.
91 On England see Bacquet 2008. This is discussed in Chapter 6 above.
92 414 US 1097 (1973).
93 *New Rider* op. cit. 701.

94   Ibid., 10(1).
95   [2011] EWHC 1452.
96   976 F. Supp. 659 (S.D. Tex. 1997).
97   Ibid., 668.
98   Ibid., 670–71.
99   The US EEOC is the body responsible for enforcing federal anti-discrimination laws within employment. Its powers are defined under the Civil Rights Act 1963, section 705.
100 US Equal Employment Opportunity Commission n.d.b.
101 US Equal Employment Opportunity Commission n.d.a.
102 Idem.
103 See full text available from: https://www.eeoc.gov/laws/statutes/titlevii.cfm.
104 US Equal Employment Opportunity Commission n.d.c.
105 See *EEOC v United Parcel Service*, 94 F. 3d 314 (7th Cir. 1996) and *EEOC v United Parcel Service, Civil Aviation* No. 08-5348-cv (2009).
106 See further US Equal Employment Opportunity Commission 2008, Compliance Manual on Religious Discrimination at 12-I-A-1 para 2000 e(j).
107 *Thomas v Review Board of the Indiana Employment Security Division*, 450 US 707 (1981) at 714.
108 Dobrac and Wesley in Bittker et al. 2015, op. cit. 466.
109 Ibid. 453.
110 *EEOC v Ilona of Hungary, Inc.*, 108 F.3d 1569, 1575 (7th Cir. 1997).
111 No. 13–20610 (5th Cir. Aug. 26, 2014).
112 Citing *Tagore v. United States*, 735 F.3d 324, 328 (5th Cir. 2013).
113 *EEOC v. Abercrombie and Fitch*, No. 14–86, 575 US (2015).
114 Idem.
115 No. 09–3093 (3d Cir. Aug. 2, 2010).

References

Books

Ahdar, R. and Leigh, I., 2005. *Religious Freedom in the Liberal State.* Oxford: Oxford University Press.
Bittker, B. I., Idleman, S. C. and Ravitch, F. S. 2015. *Religion and the State in American Law.* Cambridge: Cambridge University Press.

Articles, book chapters and conference papers

Ali, F., 2013. 'Students' Religious Liberty: Religious Attire and Symbols in American Public Schools', *Rutgers Journal of Law and Religion*, 15: 7.
Bacquet, S., 2008. 'School Uniforms, Religious Symbols and The Human Rights Act 1998: The "Purity Ring" Case', *Education Law Journal*, 9(1): 13–22.
Lal, V. 1996. 'Sikh Kirpans in California Schools: The Social Construction of Symbols, Legal Pluralism, and the Politics of Diversity', *Amerasia Journal*, 22(1): 57–89. Available at: https://sites.northwestern.edu/lawreligion/files/2017/10/Context_Lal_Sikh KirpansInCASchools-1in5ao0.pdf
O'Conkle, D., 2006. 'Religious Expression and Symbolism in the American Constitutional Tradition: Government Neutrality, But Not Indifference', *Indiana Journal of Global Legal Studies*, 13(2): 441.
Renteln, A. D., 2004. 'Visual Religious Symbols and the Law', *American Behavioural Scientist*, 47(12): 1573–1596.

Singh, S. J., 2012. 'Kirpans, Law and Religious Symbols in School', *Journal of Church and State*, 55(4).

Websites

Attributed author

Adams, N. A., 2007. 'Church Autonomy after the Scandal'. *NACBA Ledger*. Fall. http s://www.hklaw.com/files/Publication/fbb183a1-f28b-4d2d-9faf-2a14ffdb3bf6/Pre sentation/PublicationAttachment/3c7cb830-06f0-4bc8-828b-cd1b5842e038/ 54292.PDF [Accessed 20 August 2018]

Becerra, H., 2004. 'Women's Scarf a College Issue', *LA Times*, 27 Feb. http://articles.la times.com/2004/feb/27/local/me-scarf27 [Accessed 21 August 2018]

Choper, J. E., 2002. 'The Endorsement Test: Its Status and Desirability', Berkeley Law Scholarship Repository', 1 January. http://scholarship.law.berkeley.edu/cgi/view content.cgi?article=1295&context=facpubs [Accessed 21 August 2018]

Hall, M. D., 2011. 'Did America Have a Christian Founding?' 7 June. http://www. heritage.org/political-process/report/did-america-have-christian-founding [Accessed 20 August 2018]

Peterson, M. A., 2001. 'The Supreme Court's Coercion Test: Insufficient Constitutional Protection for America's Religious Minorities', *Cornell Journal of Law and Public Policy*, 11 (1), http://scholarship.law.cornell.edu/cjlpp/vol11/iss1/5 [Accessed 21 August 2018]

Theodorou, A. E., 2015. 'Americans are in the Middle of the Pack Globally when it Comes to Importance of Religion'. Pew Research Center, 23 Decemberhttp://www.pewresea rch.org/fact-tank/2015/12/23/americans-are-in-the-middle-of-the-pack-globally- when-it-comes-to-importance-of-religion/ [Accessed 20 August 2018]

No attributed author

ADL, n.d. 'Dress codes', https://www.adl.org/education/resources/tools-and-strategies/ religion-in-public-schools/dress-codes [Accessed 21 August 2018]

US Equal Employment Opportunity Commission, 2008. 'Compliance Manual on Religious Discrimination 2008', https://www.eeoc.gov/policy/docs/religion.html

US Equal Employment Opportunity Commission, n.d.a. 'What You Should Know about the EEOC and Religious and National Origin Discrimination Involving the Muslim, Sikh, Arab, Middle Eastern and South Asian Communities', https://www.eeoc.gov/ eeoc/newsroom/wysk/religion_national_origin_9-11.cfm [Accessed 21 August 2018]

US Equal Employment Opportunity Commission, n.d.b. 'Religion-Based Charges 1997– 2017', https://www.eeoc.gov/eeoc/statistics/enforcement/religion.cfm [Accessed 21 August 2018]

US Equal Employment Opportunity Commission, n.d.c. 'Religious Garb and Grooming in the Workplace: Rights and Responsibilities', https://www.eeoc.gov/eeoc/publications/ qa_religious_garb_grooming.cfm [Accessed 21 August 2018]

Others

Civil Rights Act 1964. https://www.eeoc.gov/laws/statutes/titlevii.cfm [Accessed 21 August 2018]

United States Declaration of Independence 1776

Part III

The Future of Religious Symbols and the Law in 21st Century Pluralist States

8 Accommodations of minorities and the limitations of pluralist states

8.1 Introduction

What Sandberg calls the 'juridification' of religion (discussed in Chapter 4) raises doubts about the extent to which liberal democracies can accommodate different religious and cultural minorities. As seen in Part II, the increasing involvement of the courts in matters of faith signals the existence of inadequacies in the relationship between the state and religion as well as the difficulties for both parties to reach a satisfactory compromise. If individuals and groups go to court to dispute their right to manifest their religion surely it is considered a great matter to them. Parts I and II have highlighted deficiencies with the existing legal approach. In addition, the historical importance of religious symbolism as well as the role of symbols in the making of modern individual and collective identities which were studied in Part I have stressed and confirmed the significance of symbols as a key part of identity. Looking to the future therefore it is difficult to envisage modern liberal democracies free from evidence of people manifesting their beliefs, and the courts are likely to have to continue dealing with disputes on accommodation of symbols, religious or otherwise.

While some level of control by the state is inevitable to address inequalities, health and safety and security issues, too much state intervention may hinder the ability of individuals to enjoy their freedom of religion and in some instances give too much importance to religion itself over non-religious beliefs. This is demonstrated by the country approaches discussed in Part II which highlight the difficulty for states to be neutral yet protective of religion. Addressing the public display of religious symbols inevitably involves the state and its citizens being prepared to let go of the majority culture and tradition to accommodate other practices. This may have to become the reality of contemporary pluralist states where diverse religious groups live together despite critics of this approach who regard religious accommodations as privileging religion over other human concerns.

In this context, this final chapter reflects on the future of religious manifestation and its interaction with the law. It uses lessons learnt from a holistic and multidisciplinary approach to religious symbols as the basis for a reflection on the intervention of the law with manifestation of religion and beliefs and religious symbols.

8.2 The limitations of current judicial approaches

As discussed in Part II, in modern liberal democracies such as England, France and the United Sates, courts and legislators are faced with the delicate task of balancing the needs of religious minorities with the demands of more secular majorities. Constitutional models of state–religion relations are being challenged by pluralist societies. Courts and legislators have to work within the confines of those constitutional frameworks which as a result are being put into question.[1] Can a secular state like France accommodate religious minorities? Is England's Established Church compatible with the demands of modern liberal democracies or is American tolerant neutrality more suited to the needs of modern society? Ultimately, the answer to these questions is dependent on one's conception of religious freedom. Legal and political theorists have advanced many justifications for religious freedom and have also questioned the validity of those theories. In the next section we examine and question some of those theories and their impact on religious symbols and manifestation of belief more generally.

8.3 Theoretical justifications for religious freedom

Accommodation of religious minorities and toleration of manifestation of belief in the public sphere is dependent on the relationship between church and state within a given jurisdiction but also on the state's conception of religion itself. The debate is generally centred on whether religion is 'special' so as to deserve a privileged treatment from the law.[2]

Attempting to find a single theoretical explanation for the human right to religious freedom is an impossible task. However, there are multiple ways of explaining the theory behind religious freedom and interpretations usually differ depending on whether one adopts a religious or secular perspective of the issue. The key point of discord is in relation to whether religion deserves special treatment by the law. While a devotional view of religious freedom would argue that religion is a common good derived from a creator and as such it merits special protection,[3] a secularist or non-religious account sees religion as one amongst many conceptions of the good life and therefore deserving no more than equal treatment with other conceptions of the good.[4]

Accommodation of religious needs by the law is dependent on whether the state adopts a privileging view of religion. The more importance a state attaches to religion the more accommodation it is prepared to make. England and the United States for instance (as seen in Part II) acknowledge and value religious differences by making accommodations and legal exemptions. In England this practice is enabled by the Established Church which means that it is generally favourable to religion per se[5] while in the United States it is the historical recognition of religion which gives it its legal recognition. France's *laïcité* on the other hand tends to be based on a negative presumption of religion which is not seen as deserving special treatment in the eyes of the law as this would be compromising the state's neutrality principle as well as individuals' autonomy (this is discussed in Chapter 5).

There are pros and cons associated with all of those approaches and none of them provides a best model of religion–state relations, but it is apparent that within the French *laïcité* model, some practising religious minorities are placed in the difficult position of having to choose between obeying the law of God or the law of the state. A French citizen in this position is restricted in his or her education and career choices. French law therefore creates an interference with one's right to religious freedom even if it is submitted by the state that this 'interference' is essential to achieving freedom of and from religion. Non-religion is favoured over religion, thus creating some obvious inequalities. In the United States, there are similar restrictions albeit to a lesser extent,[6] while in England religious manifestation in the public sphere is generally accommodated. This is discussed in Part II above.

8.3.1 Theories in support of a right to religious freedom

The religious argument

The argument that religion is superior to other forms of belief is derived from a religious view of the universe. This view sees individuals as duty bound to a transcendental being. The believer therefore is subject to external compulsion.[7] If we follow this theory, for those who believe that they must wear symbols or perform certain acts, not wearing/performing them means divine retribution or social ostracism.[8] Such a conception puts religion on a pedestal and this suffices to justify special treatment by the law. In modern liberal pluralist states however, some have argued that this sectarian conception of religious freedom is outdated and can no longer be justified in a society where religion is one amongst many things that are valued by individuals.[9] This justification for religious freedom therefore should be rejected at the outset because it assumes that religion is superior to other human values due to its dependence upon a set of beliefs which make sense only to those who adhere to those beliefs. As such, it is exclusive and does not have its place in modern secular societies.

The historical argument

The historical argument sees religion not as superior but as a vulnerable concept in need of special legal protection. Historically, religion has indeed been vulnerable to hostility, neglect and persecutions[10] and therefore by expressly protecting religious belief we seek to prevent historical horrors from recurring and we aim for equality between religious majorities and religious minorities as well as the promotion of tolerance. With this view, religion is afforded 'special treatment' by the law because it has been at the receiving end of discrimination and prejudice just as other protected characteristics such as race, gender or disability. Since religion continues to be a cause for persecution, discrimination and prejudice, as demonstrated by recent acts of violence against the Jewish and Muslim minorities in Europe[11] or the rise of white supremacist movements in the United States,[12] it is difficult to disagree with this theory even though it may be tempting to reverse the argument and argue that religion has also been and continues to be a source of conflict over claims of territory.[13] Religion is also used by fundamentalists in order to gain power and resist modernity and as such it would seem legitimate for states to want to protect themselves from the drifting of some religions. The rise of Islamic fundamentalism is an example of this. Some states have used this argument to justify banning certain symbols which are seen as the expression of a more extreme version of religion and in such cases legal intervention is justified by protecting public safety. Examples of this are burqa and niqab bans in France and other European countries.[14] Some have argued that affording this special treatment to religion has opened the door for the rise of fundamentalism. This is discussed briefly below. While the historical argument is convincing therefore, it needs to be considered in light of recent trends.

The autonomy argument

Another argument in favour of religious freedom being protected by the state is respect for individual autonomy. Those who support this theory argue that having the liberty to choose one's religion is an essential aspect of autonomy.[15] Individual autonomy, which allows people to control their own destiny is an essential aspect of liberalism which in turn promotes tolerance.[16] Legal theorists Raz and Dworkin both advocate this approach, each in their own manner, Raz by describing the autonomous person as 'authors of this life' free from coercion in spiritual matters[17] and Dworkin through his notion of 'equal concern and respect' which provides that all people are entitled to develop their own ideas of the good life.[18] According to this view therefore it is difficult to achieve liberalism without religious freedom. However, it can also be argued that some faiths deny their believers this autonomy by advocating their own version of the absolute truth and therefore religious doctrine can also get in the way of autonomy which, as discussed in Chapter 5, is the argument advanced by the French state to justify banning religious manifestation at school. Surely autonomy must include the right to choose one's religion as well as the right to choose none or to adopt a secular way of life. Autonomy as a justification for religious freedom therefore needs to be treated with caution as it only works if the freedom of religion includes the freedom from religion,[19] hence the need for a certain degree of separation between religion and the state in order to ensure that religion is not used by the state to control its citizens.

The human rights argument

Respect for freedom of religion also promotes tolerance and pluralism and is an essential aspect of liberal tradition. The struggle for religious liberty is what gave the impetus for the struggle for human rights which led to the human rights machinery.[20] As stated in the Preamble of the UN Declaration on the Elimination of All Forms of Intolerance and on Discrimination Based on Religion and Belief:

Considering that the disregard and infringement of human rights and fundamental freedoms, in particular of the right to freedom of thought, conscience, religion or whatever belief, have brought, directly or indirectly, wars and great suffering to mankind, especially where they serve as a means of foreign interference in the internal affairs of other States and amount to kindling hatred between peoples and nations ...

The development of the human rights discourse in the 1940s put an end to years of wars, persecutions and discrimination based on religion and contributed to the understanding of equality amongst individuals. The concept of religious freedom therefore is central to human rights law. As Boyle puts it, 'the struggle to achieve religious liberty has been a fundamental aspect of the emergence of the modern world'.[21]

8.3.2 Counter arguments on the right to religious freedom

Religion should not be special

Political theorists, have questioned the extent to which the legal protection given to religion gives an unfair advantage to religious believers over non-believers. They argue that the concept of religious freedom is rooted in the sectarian view that religion is a special good which deserves special protection and that this is in contradiction with liberal values of equality. Palmer and Toddington for instance argue that religion should be protected by generic rights such as thought, belief, expression and association, otherwise the liberal state becomes exclusive.[22] With this approach, religious freedom would become a derivative right rather than a special right.[23] While this approach might have the merit of being more inclusive in modern secular societies, it runs the risk of undermining the historical root of religious freedom discussed above.

It has also been argued that the legal concept of religious freedom can be seen as giving religion 'special treatment' whereby religion is singled out from other human commitments such as sports, politics, culture or science and that this is an unfair approach which interferes with equal liberty.[24] Palmer and Toddington go as far as arguing that the right to religious freedom is superfluous in a democratic, pluralist society.[25] They argue that religious beliefs should not be deemed superior to other beliefs such as political, secular or cultural ones. As such, they defend the stance of the French government which considers religion as a private affair and does not single out religion for special protection as in England or in the US. Eisgruber and Sager, writing in the context of the US Constitution, while not opposed to protecting religion from discrimination, also challenge the singling out of religion in comparison to other deeply held commitments which they see as unfair. They argue that every member of the socio-political community should be treated equally and that their status should not be dependent on their religious belief. Instead of privileging religion they advocate 'equal regard' to what they call 'deep commitment' or 'preferences'.[26] In his critique of their work however,

Koppelman rightly points out to the vagueness of the adjective 'deep' and attempts to find some possible justifications as to which values deserve a privileged treatment.[27] For our purposes, this would allow courts to establish what does and does not qualify for protection.

Koppelman examines a number of possible approaches including 'intense and valuable preferences' as well as 'strong evaluation'. He observes that intensity is both over- and under-inclusive as it might single out for protection objects that are not worthy of such protection such as for instance heroin addiction.[28] But it can also be under-inclusive as not all religious claims are intensely felt as such. Koppelman, comments that habit and adherence to custom play an important role in engaging in religious practice and as such intensity is not well suited to determine whether something should be afforded protection by the law. Valuable preference is discarded as well, as Koppelman argues that it amounts to a utilitarian approach and lacks neutrality.[29] Such an approach within the legal sphere would not be realistic as it would open the floodgates so that anything could become worthy of protection just because it is desired by someone. The third possibility considered by Koppelman is Taylor's 'strong evaluation' which is closer to neutrality and includes some level of discrimination between good and bad independently of our desires.[30] Koppelman therefore views religion as one of many objects of strong evaluation which should be afforded government protection. Eisgruber and Sager's equal regard to 'deep commitments' becomes equal regard to 'strong evaluation'. From a legal standpoint this produces a narrower legal test which is similar to the legal test currently used in the UK (discussed below) for assessing whether a particular belief deserves protection from the law. With this approach both religious and non-religious beliefs would be treated equally without opening the floodgates which a purely utilitarian approach would entail.

At the core of rejecting an approach that singles out religion for special treatment therefore is a concern for equality as giving religion special treatment inevitably leads practices which do not fall within the remits of 'religion' as such to be excluded. This is particularly relevant in the context of religious accommodations to which we now turn.

8.3.3 Equality and religious accommodations

Critics of religious freedom generally agree that singling out religion for special protection could be compromising equality, the very notion that it initially intended to promote. Exemptions to the law in order to accommodate religious practices have faced many criticisms. Critics have argued that it is unfair to accommodate religion over other concerns. If we exempt a Sikh man from wearing a crash helmet on a motorcycle why can't we also exempt those who are claustrophobic and find the helmet oppressing? If we make adjustments to school uniform policies to accommodate Jews, Muslims and Sikhs why should we not make accommodations for political slogans or items which are of special value to the wearer such as family jewellery of particular importance? In short, why would a 'religious' artefact deserve more protection than a non-religious one? In modern democratic societies where secular values are as important as religious ones, it is a legitimate claim to be making that manifestations of non-religious belief should deserve as much protection as religious ones provided the belief is serious enough and sincerely held. In a way the ECHR has recognised this by affording a broad definition to religion which protects non-religious beliefs as well as religious ones. This guarantees that non-religious beliefs receive as much protection as non-religious ones but admittedly is dependent on the definition given to religion. As discussed in Chapter 2 this has been an issue in relation to the legal approach where courts have based their reasoning on a narrow conception of manifestation of belief requiring an act to be a 'religious requirement' before it could attract the protection of the law or where courts have excluded a particular practice or belief altogether as it did not fall within the legal definition of religion. The definition of religion and belief however has expanded over time to reflect the needs of secular societies and has therefore become much more inclusive. What remains controversial however (as discussed in Chapter 2) is that ultimately judges are the last arbiters when it comes to setting the boundaries of religion and belief.

This is especially problematic since religious freedom has tended to be construed too narrowly, following a Christian majoritarian understanding of religion and therefore it is less accommodating towards practice-based beliefs which are key aspects of minority faith.[31] It is clear that the liberal law of religion protects belief more than practice or in the eyes of the court practices which are perceived as compulsory.[32] This approach therefore does not treat all religions equality and cannot be held to contribute towards equality.

While critics of religious freedom as a legal right point to some legitimate concerns in modern pluralist societies, it is important to add nuances to this argument. Religious freedom as a human right does not always put religion in a special position. Rather, whether religion is afforded a special position is dependent on state–religion relations. As seen in Chapter 4, France makes no special accommodation for manifestation of belief despite adhering to the concept of religious freedom. As a result, however, non-religious beliefs can be said to enjoy more tolerance than their religious counterparts. As put by Koppelman, 'it is not logically possible for the government both to be neutral between religion and non-religion and to give religion special protection.'[33] Whichever model a state adopts therefore the balance will always be tipped either in favour of the secular or the religious.

Moreover, in those states that provide for religious accommodations, they are usually intended to rectify inequalities affecting minorities rather than providing them with special treatment. If the law did not make exemptions for the ritual slaughter of animals, then some religious minorities would be unable to eat meat. If state schools did not make accommodations for religious attire, some religious minorities might be deprived of free education. So, it can be argued that the accommodations by way of legal exemptions serve to rectify inequalities rather than put religious practice on a pedestal. The approach is similar to the 'reasonable adjustment' or 'reasonable accommodation' approach used in disability law which consists in requiring people and organisations to make adjustments to their policies and practices in order to accommodate people with a disability if they are placed at a substantial disadvantage due to their disability.[34] The concept of reasonable accommodation is already being used for religion in the US in the context of employment where employers are required to accommodate for religious practices unless it would cause undue hardship on the business. This is discussed further in Chapter 7 above. The concept of reasonable accommodations for religion is also used in some Canadian provinces where the law requires that reasonable accommodations are made on religious grounds.[35]

Yet, some have argued that religion and beliefs are distinct from other protected characteristics such as race, colour or disability since the former cannot be changed whereas religion and belief can.[36] This is a simplistic and paternalistic argument which does not promote equality. Suggesting that someone should act against their conscience to comply with the majority imposes a secular view upon religion which undermines the importance of religious manifestation and fails to understand the nature of religious manifestation which I hope to have demonstrated in Part I by taking a socio-historical approach to the issue.

8.3.4 Reflections

We have reviewed a number of possible theoretical justifications for religious freedom as well as theories questioning the value of the right to freedom of religion in modern secular states. None of those approaches taken by themselves however offers an adequate justification to protecting religious freedom but each one raises valid concerns. Ultimately, the importance of religious freedom lies in its impact on the protection of manifestation of belief. Those who have argued that religion should not be singled out for special protection have criticised legal exemptions which single out religious practices for special protection. The key question is whether in modern pluralist, largely secular societies religion is worthy of accommodation. And whether it is possible to provide those accommodation without singling out religion over other important human concerns.

8.4 The debate on religious accommodations

Religious and cultural pluralism have become a factual reality within the three jurisdictions under review and more generally across Europe and North America, making it a necessity for states to address the issue of religious accommodations and manifestation of belief in the public sphere. As discussed in previous chapters, differences in religious and cultural practice may lead to conflicts when those practices are at odds with modern, largely secular societies or when those practices seem to be sending messages which conflict with liberal conceptions of equality. Some religious practices such as veiling are sometimes seen as conflicting with women's rights and they are seen in the West as a symbol of paternalism and the subjugation of women to men. The debate as to whether and to what extent minority religious practices should be accommodated therefore is inevitable. Accommodation of religion usually goes hand in hand with multiculturalism policies as in the UK and the US whereas the relegation of religion to the private sphere and therefore the reluctance to accommodate is normally associated with state policies of assimilation and integration as exemplified by the case of France discussed in Chapter 5 above.

Broadly speaking the debate revolves around the necessity to make accommodations for religious practices where there is a potential conflict between the secular law and the religious conscience of an individual. While some argue that religious accommodations allow religious communities to be free from interference by the state and on an equal footing with the majority,[37] others believe that it is up to religious individuals to adapt to the law of the state and that religion belongs to the private sphere.[38] In the next section we explore a number of viewpoints on the issue.

8.4.1 Religious practice as a derivative good

A more secularist approach to the issue sees religious practice, like religion itself, as a derivative good. As such, accommodation of religious practices has been justified through notions of integrity,[39] ultimate meaning[40] or self-respect[41] but as Seglow points out, there are issues of boundaries associated with these approaches which present as over-inclusive and therefore may lack efficiency and pragmatism.[42]

Political theorist Bou-Habib for instance attempts to justify religious accommodation on the basis of the integrity of religious individuals which he argues is a basic good in the sense that if someone fails to fulfil a duty that he or she considers necessary then his or her integrity is affected.[43] For example, if someone believes that it is their religious duty not to work on Saturday to adhere to Jewish law or to go to church on Sunday in order to be a good Christian, their integrity would be affected if their employment prevented them from fulfilling those moral duties. Similarly, if someone sees it as their duty to wear a form of head cover but they are prevented from doing so in order to attend school or to work for a government department then their integrity would be affected, and they would be placed in a disadvantaged position in comparison to those who do not value those principles.

So, according to this theory, the right to religious accommodations would derive from a need to have equal opportunities for well-being since it considers the ability to perform religious conduct freely as a necessary aspect of well-being. Bou-Habib's theory provides that in order for religious accommodations to be made, a person's integrity must genuinely be at stake and it must not undermine other people's opportunity for well-being.[44] While this is an appealing justification for religious accommodations, it still requires that a particular religious practice be considered a matter of duty before being accommodated. Cases which are not clear cut may still need to be subject to judicial scrutiny.

In a sense, Bou-Habib's integrity argument to justify the need for religious accommodations is similar to the argument from conscience defended by the likes of Nussbaum[45] who view religious exemptions as a protection against being forced to do something against one's conscience. With this reasoning, legal exemptions can be justified if in their absence an individual would be forced to do something unconscionable.[46] Such exemptions already exist within the medical profession, where conscientious objection on moral grounds is a recognised justification for refusing to perform an abortion,[47] as well as within the military. The refusal to take part in military service is recognised by the European Court of Human Rights as an aspect of freedom of thought, conscience and religion.[48] The argument from conscience has the advantage of offering a more neutral approach which is inclusive of both religious and non-religious views. Conversely, it has been argued that one should bear the consequences of one's beliefs and as such religious accommodations are not necessary.

8.4.2 Religious practice as an individual responsibility

Seglow identifies two levels of individual responsibility within religious accommodations which derive from our role as 'epistemic and practical agents'.[49] He argues that as epistemic agents we are responsible and accountable for our convictions and we have the ability to form other beliefs or revise currently held ones while as practical agents we are responsible for any actions deriving from those beliefs. With this theory it becomes justifiable to impose on people costs which arise from their behaviour if they can be held accountable for those costs.[50] Individuals are thus regarded as agents responsible for their religious beliefs which become akin to a matter of taste and preference. Seglow acknowledges that this theory is not without flaws and points out that it is subject to varying circumstances which individuals may have no control over, such as for instance the structure of the working week. In addition, it is difficult to establish what level of cost an individual should bear in relation to their beliefs.[51] Seglow's theory is helpful in understanding the French approach to religious accommodations but runs the risk of creating inequalities between the religious majority who is able to fit in with the wider environment and the religious minorities who will struggle to live according to their convictions. The extent to which religious minorities are accommodated in a given jurisdiction is usually dependent on whether a state embraces or rejects multiculturalism.

8.4.3 Multiculturalism as a vehicle for religious accommodations

Those who favour accommodation of religious practice normally adhere to multiculturalism policies which encourage the recognition of minorities and the need for them to be 'visible and explicitly accommodated' in the public sphere,[52] while those who are against religious accommodations raise concerns that multiculturalism may lead to segregation of minorities as opposed to integration and assimilation. Concerns mainly arise in relation to the growing influence of religious absolutism and fundamentalism. Singh and Cowden for instance are critical of what they call 'symbolic accommodation'.[53] Using the English case of *Begum* as an example they argue that the demand of Shabina for accommodation was more than a benign expression of her religious identity but rather the expression of an assertive form of Islam. According to them moderate demands of religious accommodations open the door to absolutist forms of religious discourse.

However, one can argue that fundamentalism and radicalism are rarely the results of religious accommodations alone and therefore this is not a valid argument to oppose accommodations altogether.

On balance therefore, I would argue that accommodations of religious practice are necessary for the preservation of equality and freedom of conscience. Religious beliefs are no less worthy of protection than non-religious beliefs which go to a person's conscience and integrity, while the right to religious freedom is a potent reminder of the historical struggle for the recognition and respect of pluralism as well as tolerance for differences and therefore, any attempt to remove it should be resisted. Religious accommodations should not be seen as privileging the minority population but rather as a way to correct inequalities. Knowing when to accommodate however has been a major hurdle for courts who have struggled to set clear boundaries. In the last section of this chapter we explore a number of possibilities for facilitating this task.

8.5 Protecting religious practice without religious freedom

Attempting to decide whether or not an action is performed in pursuance of a religious belief places the courts in a difficult position. Laborde's 'disaggregation strategy' goes some way towards resolving this issue by acknowledging that some religious practices are worthy of legal protection but that this legal protection must not necessarily derive from freedom of religion.[54]

The disaggregation strategy developed by political theorist Laborde allows for an inclusive theory of religious freedom which is broad, non-sectarian and fair to both religious and non-religious people.[55] Her theory builds on James Nickel's proposal that religious activities and practices can be protected through generic rights which would make religious freedom a derivative liberty.[56] This is similar to Palmer and Toddington's approach discussed above. Laborde's approach however has the advantage of retaining religious freedom as a legal right. It disaggregates religion into various dimensions such as religion as a conception of the good life, conscientious moral obligation, key feature of identity, mode of human association etc.[57] This means that any differential treatment religion receives from the law is received because of features it shares with non-religious beliefs such as 'ethical integrity'[58] rather than being considered as above all other rights.

In a similar vein, American constitutional theorist Sager has attempted to 'rescue' religious freedom by offering a conception of religious freedom that does not entail any special privilege for religion.[59] He proposes an 'equal liberty' approach to religious freedom which is based on the equality principle and the general liberty principle. Sager argues that general liberty does not require religion to be privileged in order to be protected by the law but rather that its 'distinct structural features be acknowledged and responded to.'[60] He argues that it is religion's vulnerability to hostility and neglect that justifies legal protection from unequal treatment. This vulnerability stems from the very nature of religion which, as Sager rightly argues, is arbitrary and often escapes rationality.

An equal liberty approach to religious accommodations sees them as deriving from 'the obligation of the state to treat its members fairly by extending the exemptions already enjoyed by widely recognised and well-regarded groups to those less recognised and less regarded'[61] including religious minorities. This is based on the equality principle which provides that: 'no one with comparable needs and interests should be denied the benefit of an exemption on account of the spiritual commitments that underlie their commitments.'[62] Sager however rightly points out that publicly sponsored religious rituals and displays may carry a message that celebrates certain beliefs but denigrates others which potentially violates the equality principle.[63]

The other principle 'general liberty' provides that: 'the government should extend to all its citizens robust liberties of free expression, free association and private choice over matters best understood as belonging to individuals rather than to the collectivity.'[64] This principle defends what in English law is called occupational requirements by acknowledging religion's distinct features and responding to them by providing independence from the state allowing religious groups to regulate themselves in matters such as the appointment of religious leaders. Sager maintains that this does not equate to privileging religion and recommends that this approach should extent to non-religious groups which may be organised in the same way as religious groups.[65]

The above approaches therefore demonstrate that it is possible to justify religious accommodations without considering religion as a special right which merits special protection. Such an approach to religious manifestation would require a different judicial method which puts less emphasis on religion itself and refocuses on the integrity of the claimant and their claim to be treated equally.

8.6 Towards a more holistic judicial approach to religious manifestation

The intervention of the law with symbols therefore is based on a number of factors. I would identify two types of interventions which I would call positive and negative. A positive intervention seeks to protect citizens from harm and discrimination as well as promote equality and protect autonomy. An example of this approach would be anti-discrimination legislation. A negative intervention with symbols however is based on prejudice and unverified presumptions which fail to acknowledge the historical and social meaning of religious manifestation. An example of this approach would be militant secularism which tends to view religion as a negative influence which the state needs to put up with. Majority identity and norms can only be invoked to restrict the use of religious symbols when the latter become a danger for liberal ideals and human rights such as equality and non-discrimination or when they represent a threat to national security. Those cases need to be better identified in order to be kept to a minimum. It might be that they have to be dealt with through dialogue and cooperation with religious leaders rather than via the enactment of legislation which bans them from the public domain as is the case in relation to burqa bans.

Ultimately, what the law seeks to protect are concepts of autonomy, equality and non-discrimination. The legal approach has tended to be dependent on defining religion and belief in order to ascertain boundaries. While this is necessary in a pragmatic sense and part of a rigorous legal approach, it has proven difficult for a number of reasons which have been explored in this book, namely that it leads to the exclusion of practices which are not deemed as arising from a particular religion or are not seen as a compulsory requirement of a particular faith or that are alien to Western culture and thus perceived as a threat to secular democracies. Yet those practices are often deeply held by individuals and form part of their identity. Unless those practices are dangerous or harmful to others there should be no reason in modern liberal democracies to single them out if other practices deemed 'religious' or deriving from the majority are tolerated. In the final section we explore possible alternatives to the existing judicial approach.

8.6.1 Possible alternatives

Rather than asking whether an act is in pursuance of a religious belief, a more inclusive and human approach would consist in asking whether a particular action, ritual or symbol is essential to a person's identity. A similar approach was advocated by Gereluck in relation to uniform policies at schools. Gereluck's four limbs approach recommends schools to consider the extent to which the clothing poses health and safety issues; is oppressive to oneself or others; significantly inhibits the educational aim of the school and is essential to a person's identity.[66]

I suggest that courts should approach manifestation of belief cases from a more holistic perspective. This would imply shifting their focus away from the disputed manifestation/object itself and more towards the individual. This would have the advantage of humanising the current legal test and shifting the attention away from religion itself, which would provide a more inclusive approach. So instead of asking whether a particular action is in pursuance of a belief, courts would question the impact of prohibiting a particular manifestation of belief on the applicant's life and well-being. Approaching those cases from the individual's perspective requires an assessment as to the impact that not making an accommodation would have on the individual's well-being whether the required accommodation is in pursuance of a religious or non-religious belief. The focus would be on the individual's identity rather than the nature of the belief that drives the manifestation. This approach entails a conception of religion as well as non-religious belief as an essential aspect of identity. It takes a holistic approach to religious symbols which is closer to the anthropological approach that we have studied in Chapter 2.

With such an approach, religious freedom would remain as a legal right, therefore acknowledging the centrality of the right to freedom of religion and belief within the wider human rights framework, but would avoid the need for judges to be faced with the controversial task of deciding whether something is a manifestation of religion. As we have seen in Chapter 6, a similar approach is already being used in relation to philosophical beliefs. The *Grainger* test requires that a belief be genuinely held, be more than an opinion or viewpoint, relate to a weighty and substantial aspect of human life and behaviour, attain a certain level of cogency, seriousness, cohesion and importance and be worthy of respect in a democratic society and not incompatible with human dignity or in conflict with the fundamental rights of others.[67]

Such an approach would not put religion on a pedestal and avoid judges becoming arbiters of faith and making value judgements on spiritual matters. In assessing whether a particular symbol/manifestation of belief is central to the individual wellbeing, courts would consider other factors such as private and family life, expression as well as identity. This approach views religion as a derivative good rather than a special right but does not in any way advocate the removal of the right to religious freedom which must remain a basic human right, symbolic of the continuing fight for equality and as a testimony to the historical struggle for liberty, equality and individual autonomy.

Notes

1 Bouma 2011.
2 See Evans 2001; Olsen and Toddington 2007, Dworkin 2013. In the context of the US Constitution see Eisgruber and Sager 2007.
3 See for example Ahdar and Leigh, 2005, Finnis 2008.
4 See for example Olsen and Toddington, 2007, op. cit.
5 On the Established Church's impact on religious freedom see Garcia Oliva and Hall 2018.
6 See the discussion on 'tolerant neutrality' in Chapter 7.
7 Ahdar and Leigh 2005, op. cit. 78.
8 Idem.
9 See Laborde 2015. 585. See also Olsen and Toddington 2007, op. cit.
10 Evans 2001, op. cit. See also Sager 2008. 16, 24.
11 See for instance McAuley 2018.
12 Tenold 2018.
13 See for e.g. the Israeli-Palestinian conflict, the conflict between Catholics and Protestants in Northern Ireland or the Sri Lankan civil war.
14 BBC News 2018.
15 Evans 2001, op. cit. 29.
16 Idem.
17 Raz 1986.
18 Dworkin 1977.
19 See further Ahmed 2017.
20 Boyle 1992.
21 Boyle 1992, op. cit. 61.
22 Olsen and Toddington 2007, op.cit.
23 This view is shared by Nickel (2005).
24 Eisgruber and Sager 2007, op. cit., Olsen and Toddington 2007, op. cit.
25 Olsen and Toddington 2007, op. cit.
26 See further Eisgruber and Sager 2007, op. cit.
27 Koppelman 2006. 584.
28 Ibid., 575.
29 Ibid., 583.
30 Taylor C., 1989, *Sources of the Self: The Making of the Modern Identity*, 4, cited in Koppelman 2006. 588.

31 Bacquet 2009. This is discussed in Chapter 2.
32 Laborde 2015. 584.
33 Koppelman 2006, op. cit., 590.
34 In the UK Equality Act 2010 s. 20. In the US see the Americans with Disabilities Act 1989 and subsequent amendments in 2008.
35 See for example the Human Rights Code of Manitoba province (s. 9.1.d).
36 Olsen and Toddington 2007, op. cit.
37 See for instance Modood 2013.
38 See secularists such as Alain Finkielkraut in France, Richard Dawkins in the UK and Barry Lynn in the US.
39 Bou-Habib 2006.
40 Nussbaum 2008.
41 Taylor and Maclure 2011.
42 Seglow 2010. 52
43 Bou-Habib 2006, op. cit. 117.
44 Idem.
45 Nussbaum 2008, op. cit.
46 Seglow 2010, op. cit. 57.
47 See S. 4 of the UK Abortion Act 1967.
48 *Thlimmenos v. Greece* (Application no. 34369/97).
49 Seglow 2018. 119.
50 Idem.
51 Seglow 2018, op. cit. 120–21.
52 See for instance: Modood 2015.
53 Singh and Cowden 2014. 128.
54 Laborde 2015, op. cit. 598.
55 Ibid., 581–600.
56 Nickel 2005.
57 Laborde 2015, op. cit. 594.
58 Ibid., 597.
59 Sager 2008, op. cit. 16.
60 Ibid. 23.
61 Eisgruber and Sager 2007, op, cit. 78–120.
62 Sager 2008, op. cit. 20.
63 Ibid. 21.
64 Ibid. 22.
65 Ibid. 23.
66 Gereluck 2008, 105–106.
67 See *Grainger plc and others v Nicholson* EAT/0219/09.

References

Books

Ahdar, R. and Leigh, I., 2005. *Religious Freedom in the Liberal State*. Oxford: Oxford University Press.
Bouma, G. D., 2011. *Being Faithful in Diversity: Religions and Social Policy in Multifaith Societies*. Hindmarsh, SA: ATF Press.
Dworkin, R., 1977. *Taking Rights Seriously*. London: Bloomsbury.
Dworkin, R., 2013. *Religion without God*. Cambridge, MA: Harvard University Press.
Eisgruber, C. and Sager, L. G., 2007. *Religious Freedom and the Constitution*. Cambridge, MA: Harvard University Press.

Evans, C., 2001. *Freedom of Religion under the European Convention on Human Rights.* Oxford: Oxford University Press.

Garcia Oliva, J. and Hall, H., 2018. *Religion, Law and the Constitution.* London: Routledge.

Gereluck, D., 2008. *Symbolic Clothing in Schools.* London: Continuum.

Nussbaum, M., 2008. *Liberty of Conscience.* New York: Basic Books.

Olsen, H. P. and Toddington, S., 2007. *Architecture of Justice: Legal Theory and the Idea of Institutional Design.* London: Routledge.

Raz, J., 1986. *The Morality of Freedom.* Oxford: Oxford University Press.

Taylor, C. and Maclure, J., 2011. *Secularism and Freedom of Conscience.* Cambridge, MA: Harvard University Press.

Articles, book chapters and conference papers

Ahmed, F., 2017. 'The Autonomy Rationale for Religious Freedom', *Modern Law Review,* 80(2): 238–262.

Bacquet, S., 2009. 'Manifestation of Belief and Religious Symbols at School: Setting Boundaries in English Courts', *Religion & Human Rights,* 4(2): 121.

Bou-Habib, P., 2006. 'A Theory of Religious Accommodation', *Journal of Applied Philosophy,* 23(1): 109–126.

Boyle, K., 1992. 'Religious Freedom and the Incitement of Hatred', in ColiverS., BoyleK. and D'SouzaF. eds. *Striking a Balance: Hate Speech, Freedom of Expression and Non-discrimination.* London and Colchester: Article 19 International Centre Against Censorship and Human Rights Centre, University of Essex.

Finnis, J., 2008. 'Why Religious Liberty is a Special, Important and Limited Right', *Notre Dame Legal Studies,* 30 October, Paper No. 09–11.

Koppelman, A., 2006. 'Is it Fair to Give Religion Special Treatment?' *University of Illinois Law Review,* 2006(3): 571.

Laborde, C., 2015. 'Religion in the Law: The Disaggregation Approach', *Law and Philosophy* 34(6): 581–600.

Modood, T., 2013. 'Multiculturalism and Religion: A Three-part Debate. Part one Accommodating Religions: Multiculturalism's New Fault Line'. *Critical Social Policy,* 34(1): 121–127.

Modood, T., 2015. '"We don't do God"? The Changing Nature of Public Religion', in *Religion in Britain: Challenges for Higher Education, Stimulus Paper.* London: Leadership Foundation for Higher Education.

Nickel, J. W., 2005. 'Who Needs Freedom of Religion', *University of Colorado Law Review,* 76: 909–933.

Sager, L., 2008. 'The Moral Economy of Religious Freedom', in CaneP., EvansC., and RobinsonZ., eds. *Law and Religion in Theoretical and Historical Context.* Cambridge: Cambridge University Press. 16–25.

Seglow, J., 2010. 'Theories of Religious Exemptions', in CalderG. and CevaE., eds. *Diversity in Europe: Dilemmas of Differential Treatment in Theory and Practice.* London: Routledge. 52–64.

Seglow, J., 2018. 'Religious Accommodation Law in the UK: Five Normative Gaps', *Critical Review of International Social and Political Philosophy,* 21(1): 109–128.

Singh, G. and Cowden, G., 2014. 'Response to Tariq Modood – Accommodating Religions: Who's Accommodating Whom', *Critical Social Policy,* 34(1): 128–134.

Websites

Attributed author

McAuley, J. 2018. 'The Brutal Killing of a Holocaust Survivor Raises Anti-Semitism Fears in France', *The Washington Post*, 26 March. https://www.washingtonpost.com/world/europe/frances-jewish-leaders-raise-the-alarm-over-brutal-murder-of-holocaust-survivor/2018/03/26/28cf8686-30f4-11e8-8abc-22a366b72f2d_story.html?noredirect=on&utm_term=.47b0dba595e9 [Accessed 21 August 2018]

Tenold, V., 2018. 'America's Dark Underbelly: I Watched the Rise of White Nationalism', *The Guardian*, 17 February. https://www.theguardian.com/world/2018/feb/17/americas-far-right-white-supremacists-nationalism [Accessed 21 August 2018]

No attributed author

BBC News, 2018. 'The Islamic Veil across Europe', 31 May. https://www.bbc.co.uk/news/world-europe-13038095 [Accessed 21 August 2018]

Others

Americans with Disabilities Act 1989

The Human Rights Code of Manitoba province, http://web2.gov.mb.ca/laws/statutes/ccsm/h175e.php [Accessed 22 August 2018]

UK Abortion Act 1967

UK Equality Act 2010

9 Conclusion

The purpose of the research was to investigate an aspect of religious symbols which has so far been neglected by legal scholars, namely the nature of the relationship between individuals and religious symbols or other forms of religious manifestations such as rituals. Instead of focusing on whether manifestation of belief should be accommodated by the law which has been at the core of the legal debate, the book took a step back in order to gain a deeper understanding of the role of symbols in contemporary, mostly secular societies as it was felt that this understanding is key to assessing the current legal approach.

The book began by highlighting the changing nature of the geopolitical landscape resulting in a *de facto* pluralist society where ethnic, religious and cultural minorities are forced to negotiate their share of the public domain. As modern liberal democracies adapt to those demographic changes we witness new types of conflicts between the secular majority and minority faith and cultures who claim a right to publicly display their faith even if some of their practices are at odds with modern secularised societies. Majority identity and norms at times are used by states to restrict the display of religious symbols. The law has had to mitigate those conflicts and as a result judges have been caught in legal battles involving manifestation of belief in the public sphere and the extent to which it should be accommodated. As the book demonstrates in Part II, while religion as belief is relatively easy for the adjudicator to grasp, religion as identity and religion as a way of life have been more problematic as they are concepts mostly alien to the Christian majority in Europe and North America. Yet, these are often at the origin of religious persecution and discrimination.

The book therefore was premised on the idea that there is a need for a deeper understanding of religious manifestation and the significance of religious symbols and that this understanding could inform and enhance the legal approach. The book started with exploring how symbols are used by human beings to create meanings and manifest deeply held religious or cultural beliefs. Such an analysis required an understanding of the relationship between law and religion. It was felt that an interdisciplinary approach would be better suited to gaining such understanding. History, anthropology and sociology, due to the nature of their disciplines, take a more contextual approach than law and as such are more attuned to the social function of religion and symbolic manifestation. The anthropological approach in Chapter 2 highlighted the significance of symbols and religion for society as well as the notion that symbols can have multiple meanings. This is in contrast with the legal approach which has tended to reduce symbols to a single 'official' definition in order to establish boundaries. While this is part and parcel of a rigorous legal approach, in the context of religious symbols it has proven difficult for a number of reasons, which the book explored.

The historical approach in Chapter 3 highlighted the perennial aspect of symbols as well as their original function and as such enhanced our understanding of how religious manifestation through symbols and rituals became worthy of legal protection. We have seen that symbols and rituals emerged as a means of making sense of the then seemingly inexplicable forces of nature and conferred power, status and reassurance on humans by acting as a bridge to the sacred. It is through symbols and rituals that humans became aware of their individual and collective identities. The empirical evidence in Chapter 4 showed that in contemporary pluralist societies, human beings continue to use symbols to articulate their interconnection with divine forces. Religious dress for instance provides wearers with a sense of identity and belonging while also bringing them closer to the history of their community and fulfilling religious obligations. Rituals and sacred spaces contribute to community building and reinforcing group identity while providing a spiritual sanctuary for believers. The empirical data also demonstrated that the relationship between individuals and their religious symbols is a deeply intimate one driven by religious and cultural emotions. For some, religious symbols are a religious requirement, for others it is a link to their community or a way of life. In all cases, for those who display them, symbols are charged with emotional and spiritual meaning and are part of one's identity. This has reinforced the need for courts to approach manifestation of religion and belief from the perspective of identity as well as the necessity to broaden the traditional definition of religion and provide protection to non-religious markers of identity which may fulfil a similar function to religious symbols.

The book showed that with modernisation and the secularisation of society the role of religion in society transformed but individuals' need for spirituality remained and, in some instances, became even stronger in modern, globalised societies where identities can easily be absorbed and even lost. Religious symbols and rituals can fill this identity void by providing a sense of belonging, comfort and reassurance while maintaining a connection with the divine.

Part II of the book provided a case study of religious manifestation and the law across three jurisdictions with different constitutional set ups and varying models of state–religion relations. While France and the US share a constitutional church–state separation, the US and the UK share a commitment to protecting the expression of religious manifestation. The US secularism however is not anti-religious, in contrast to the French *laïcité* which seeks to restrict the expression of religion in the public domain. In all three jurisdictions the link between the historical church–state relation and the legal framework for the protection of religious freedom became apparent. The comparative approach illustrated the difficulties faced by liberal democracies in accommodating religious and cultural minorities and the inherent tension between catering for the secular majority without discriminating the religious minorities or being seen as privileging one religion over the other or religion over non-religion. The comparative analysis is evidence for the ever-increasing amount of litigation on religious matters, placing judges in the difficult position of arbiters of faith. The case law discussed across all three jurisdictions as well as case law of the ECHR and HRC evidenced the inconsistencies in courts' decisions involving manifestation of belief.

Part III linked theory and practice and began a discussion on the future of religious manifestation in modern pluralist states. Chapter 8 examined different theoretical justifications for religious freedom and religious accommodations and suggested a modified legal test which would look at symbols in a holistic manner rather than in isolation. The examination of theoretical justifications for religious accommodations demonstrated that it is possible to accommodate religious manifestation without putting religion on a pedestal and giving it special protection but that such a theory requires a modification of the current judicial approach which places less emphasis on religion itself and more focus on the individual. At the same time, the historical approach taken in Chapter 3 highlighted the importance of religious freedom as a human right and the need to protect this right as a symbol for the historical struggle for religious freedom which in 21st century modern pluralist states is not over, as demonstrated by continuous acts of discrimination against religious minorities such as anti-Semitism or Islamophobia.

The book therefore drew the following conclusions:

The 'juridification' of religion points to the difficulties that modern pluralist states face in accommodating religious manifestation. They are caught between on the one hand guaranteeing religious freedom and on the other hand preserving the neutrality of states while protecting others from any discrimination arising from religious beliefs. Yet, pluralism has become a reality of modern, mostly secular liberal states and as a result manifestation of belief is a fact that states have to grapple with. Symbols which are part of religious manifestation for minority faith have a historical significance and play a key role in shaping modern collective and individual identities. Different models of church–state relations are more or less accepting of religious manifestation. In general, courts have struggled to remain neutral arbiters of faith due to the nature of religious symbols and their limited capacities to be moulded to a strict legal approach.

A multidisciplinary approach to religious symbols is key to understanding the function of manifestation of belief in modern pluralist states. Disciplines such as history, anthropology and sociology are more attuned to the fluctuating nature of religious manifestation. Those disciplines take a more holistic approach than law and look at symbols as part of society rather than in isolation, as the law tends to do. Understanding the nature of the relationship between individuals and symbols through the lens of history, anthropology and sociology therefore helps us to highlight the relevance of manifestation of belief.

When judges grapple with manifestation of belief they are limited by legal definitions which are necessary to create boundaries. While those definitions are necessary for the law they sometimes result in under-protecting some symbols and over-protecting others if they are deemed to be a religious requirement. As the book has shown, the notion of something being a requirement of a particular faith is an abstract notion and one which is biased towards a textual interpretation of religion.

In light of this and in keeping with theories of religion which are non-sectarian and which view religious freedom as a derivative good, the book suggested that in the courtroom the focus should shift away from religion itself and religious symbols/manifestation of belief towards individuals and the impact that doing away with a particular symbol would have on their overall wellbeing. In arriving at those conclusions and in order to retain boundaries, courts would need to have regard to identity, way of life, livelihood, coherence and cogency. With such an approach however, it may be tempting to argue that the right to religious freedom becomes redundant as judges can rely on the right to freedom of expression, non-discrimination or the right to family life. But the book argues against doing away with a right which is a potent reminder of the struggle for religious freedom. The right to religious freedom embodied within the international legal framework indeed serves as a symbol of the historical struggle for the recognition of pluralism and is a fundamental aspect of democracy.

In modern pluralist states, individuals should be free to manifest their belief either religious or secular, in public or private, provided they do not cause harm or present a risk to the rest of the population. Accepting differences and being prepared to let go of a majoritarian mostly Christian culture is inevitable in modern pluralist societies. Surely there will be practices which are alien to the majority culture, but this is an unavoidable aspect of living in modern liberal societies based on acceptance and the recognition of differences. Majority norms should only restrict religious symbols when they interfere with the rights of others.

The intervention of the law with religious symbols therefore must be kept to the minimum needed to protect individuals and groups from discrimination. Banning a religious symbol on the grounds that it is religious is an unfair approach which is biased towards non-religion. Over-protecting religion at the expense of secular beliefs can also result in exclusions and is biased towards religion. Looking forward, a more contextual approach which focuses on individual and collective identities is needed.

Index